Creative
Ethnicity

Creative Ethnicity

Symbols and Strategies of Contemporary Ethnic Life

STEPHEN STERN

AND

JOHN ALLAN CICALA, EDITORS

Utah State University Press
Logan, Utah
1991

Second Printing, January 1992
Third Printing, December 1992
Fourth Printing, November 1993

Library of Congress Cataloging-in-Publication Data

Creative ethnicity : symbols and strategies of contemporary ethnic life /
edited by Stephen Stern and John Allan Cicala.
    p. cm.
Includes bibliographical references.
ISBN 0-87421-150-6
1. Folklore—United States. 2. Ethnicity—United States 3. United
States—Social life and customs—20th century. I. Stern, Stephen. II.
Cicala,
John Allan.
GR105.C74 1991
398'.0973—dc20   90-19205
                                                          CIP

The paper used in this publication meets the minimum requirements
of the American National Standard for Performance of
Paper for Printed Library Materials, Z39.48-1984. ∞

Book and jacket design by Joanna V. Hill.

Dedication

This book is dedicated to Linda Dégh, who greatly influenced both editors in their thinking on ethnic folklore while they were students at Indiana University and through her many publications on ethnic folklore which paved the way for contemporary discussions of creative ethnicity.

Contents

Preface ix

Introduction
STEPHEN STERN xi

I. Untangling Complexities of Ethnic Sources,
Representations, and Meanings

1. Pasties in Michigan's Upper Peninsula: Foodways,
Interethnic Relations, and Regionalism
YVONNE R. LOCKWOOD AND WILLIAM G. LOCKWOOD 3

2. Dutchman Bands: Genre, Ethnicity, and Pluralism
in the Upper Midwest
JAMES P. LEARY AND RICHARD MARCH 21

3. "I Gave Him a Cake": An Interpretation of
Two Italian-American Weddings
JANET S. THEOPHANO 44

4. On the Tail of the Lion: Approaches to Cross-Cultural
Fieldwork with Chinese-Americans in New York
MADELINE SLOVENZ-LOW 55

II. Symbolic Responses to Ethnic Tensions

5. The Atlanta Child Murders: A Case Study of
   Folklore in the Black Community
   PATRICIA A. TURNER   75

6. *Corridos* and *Canciones* of *Mica, Migra,* and *Coyotes*:
   A Commentary on Undocumented Immigration
   MARIA HERRERA-SOBEK   87

III. Realigning Ethnic Boundaries: Strategies of Adaptation

7. Strategies of Ethnic Adaptation: The Case of Gypsies
   in the United States
   CAROL SILVERMAN   107

8. Iranian Immigrant Name Changes in Los Angeles
   BETTY A. BLAIR   122

9. Ethnic Selection and Intensification in the
   Native American Powwow
   BARRE TOELKEN   137

IV. Contracting and Expanding Networks and Communities

10. The Celebration of Passover among Jewish Radicals
    DAVID SHULDINER   159

11. Weddings among Jews in the Post-World-War-II
    American South
    CAROLYN LIPSON-WALKER   171

V. Showcasing Ethnicity: Transformations from Private to Public Arenas

12. St. Lucia in Lindsborg, Kansas
    LARRY DANIELSON   187

13. Making a Place Home: The Latino Festival
    OLIVIA CADAVAL   204

14. The Brokering of Ethnic Folklore: Issues of Selection
    and Presentation at a Multicultural Festival
    SUSAN AUERBACH   223

Notes on the Contributors   239

Preface

This volume explores how ethnic group members living in the United States adapt and modify their folklore in response to living in a pluralistic society. The idea for this book was generated by our dissatisfaction with prevailing academic models of ethnicity, both those which characterize ethnicity as abstract group processes and those which view ethnicity as emerging in small networks of interaction.

These foci have restricted folklorists to thinking about ethnicity in terms of specific stereotypes, identity complexes, values, and bodies of tradition. For most ethnic Americans, however, ethnicity is more dynamic and personal, reflecting the richness and diversity of the ethnic experience.

Contributors to this volume develop a model of ethnic folklore that assumes that ethnicity is a creative response to personal and social problems. In their essays, written especially for this book, folklorists provide examples of this creativity derived from such traditional forms of expression as ceremony, festival, song, rumor, narrative, celebration, and naming practices arising among a cross-section of ethnic groups in American society.

We are both ethnic ourselves, Steve coming from Los Angeles Jewish, and John from Detroit Sicilian, backgrounds, and are sensitive to complex issues pertaining to ethnic persistence, identification, and values. We share with other Americans a fascination with the rise of race and nationality consciousness that began in the 1960s and allowed disenfranchised groups to assert their right to be heard and to become major forces in the cultural, social, and public arenas of the Republic.

In the early eighties, we discussed publishing an anthology considering the broader representational issues involved in the study of ethnic folklore, especially in the ways in which folklore may be used to reflect imaginatively notions of community, identity, and worldview. We solicited essays that would investigate the complexity of ethnicity and how it lends itself to multiple meanings.

The publication of this book is due in no small part to the many people who supported its birth and development. We would like to acknowledge the encouragement of Simon Bronner, Professor of American Studies at the Pennsylvania State University at Harrisburg, who assured us that there would be continuing interest in the theme of creative ethnicity. Without Simon's positive reinforcement, this project would never have been completed. We owe a special debt of gratitude to Shalom Staub, Executive Director of the Governor's Heritage Affairs Commission of Pennsylvania, who foresaw the importance of a work that would be useful to public sector, as well as to academic, folklorists.

We would also like to acknowledge the assistance of Robert A. Georges and Sharon Sherman who read drafts of the introduction at various stages and made helpful comments. A special thanks goes to the reviewers at Utah State University Press who really pushed the editors to obtain as wide as possible a representation of ethnic groups and expressive forms. Although the role of reviewers often goes unmentioned, their comments were essential in contributing to this volume in its present form. Finally, we would like to thank the contributors whose work, interest, and continuing patience made this book possible, and for offering us a novel perspective on the study of ethnic folklore.

Stephen Stern
John Allan Cicala

Introduction

STEPHEN STERN

The subject of *Creative Ethnicity* is the process by which members of American ethnic groups absorb, invigorate, modify, and transmit folk expressions in a multicultural, pluralistic society. Interaction with members of one's own ethnic group, and response to the cultural values of other groups, lead to the evolution of symbols and strategies that in turn draw on vast and varied cultural resources. Ethnic folklore therefore reflects an entire range of ethnic issues, from the preservation of ethnic communities to the formulation of ethnic identities to the development of ethnic values.

Ethnicity in American society has always been problematic. The uncertainties of life in a multicultural society have been reflected in the folklore of ethnic groups, and these groups have found power and promise in folklore's ability to represent ethnicity imaginatively and to offer new ways of thinking about ethnicity itself. The essays in this volume frequently describe cultural scenes in which ethnics adapt traditional folklore genres to new settings or invent new forms for strategic incorporation into traditional culture. This creative flexibility in many forms of cultural expression suggests that ethnicity is a dynamic and evolving force in American life rather than a conservative grouping of old and outmoded ways.

This is not to say, as Werner Sollors has recently remarked, that ethnicity is a concept invented merely to give the appearance of traditionality.[1] Ethnic cultural resources are often as ingrained in the history and experiences of ethnic groups even as they are made relevant to contemporary situations. Stability and change exist in dynamic interplay. Each performance of ethnic folklore is a product of this creative interaction. The consequence is that folklore expressions are continually added to the pool of a groups' cultural resources, which, in turn, are used to examine new problems and concerns. It is as common for traditional ethnic sentiments to be modified, to take on new meanings, to be communicated through newly created folklore, as it is for recently introduced practices to be labeled as traditional.

This constant need to balance available resources with demands for relevance arises because ethnicity is precarious. Being in a minority position requires constant reflection on one's position and place in the ethnic scheme. Expressing one's ethnic pride or hiding, temporarily, one's ethnicity require the individual to be highly creative in understanding how and why to demonstrate ethnic allegiance. Choosing an ethnic expression, applying it to diverse situations, and transmitting it through time and space are based on decision-making and community interplay that require a great deal of creativity and inspiration.

Folklorists are no strangers to examining how creativity affects the need for stability and the impulse for change. Indeed, definitions of folklore have made continuity and variability defining characteristics; together they maintain the feeling of an abiding familiarity while at the same time generating surprise and novelty.[2] Similarly, ethnic folklore has been viewed as maintaining a balance between stability and change, between the enduring and the novel. For example, the pioneering studies of Beatrice Weinreich and Elizabeth Mathias have demonstrated that Passover practices and Italian funeral rituals, respectively, persist but in highly modified form to reflect American influences.[3]

Investigators writing in the 1970s and '80s extended the analysis of these forces of stability and change from macro to micro levels.[4] Creativity, they concluded, should not be considered as a by-product of the clash of abstract forces, as Weinreich and Mathias had, but as emerging in concrete social relationships. Ethnic meaning, they argued, arises only out of the social interaction of individuals whose expressions of ethnicity can be confirmed by other participants. Ethnicity is constantly negotiated, and outside of such encounters has little relevance. Such was the conclusion drawn by Shalom Staub in his analysis of the behavior of Yemenite restaurateurs. Ethnicity, Staub declared, is "therefore an identity which resides not within the individual person, or even the particular group, but *between* individuals and *between* groups engaged in social interaction."[5]

Unsatisfied with both these extreme views, that ethnicity is the product of abstract external forces, on the one hand, and the minute negotiations between social interactants, on the other, folklorists are searching for ways in which ethnic folklore may be viewed as representing both the broader historical conditions that influence ethnicity as well as the manner in which ethnicity shapes peoples' quests for meaning.

The contributors to this volume believe the answer lies in observing how folklore offers solutions to problems caused by living in a modern world. Every ethnic expression — whether in verbal or material form, according to Kenneth Burke — reflects and artistically treats a problematic situation.[6] These texts examine both significant symbols and a variety of strategies to endow them with meaning. The continual need to wed ethnic resources with attributions of relevance guarantees both a fund of symbols to draw from and a host of strategies by which to apply them. It is the choice of those symbols and the selection of strategies used to relate symbols to current contexts with which this book is concerned.

Through the process of symbol creating and maintenance, folklore supplies the language of ordinary ethnic discourse. Legends, songs, ceremonies, rituals, and foodways permeate every facet of ethnic life, from dislocation to rites of passage to the maintenance of ethnic enclaves and institutions. A literature documenting the presence of these traditions demonstrates how extensive such symbols are in American society.[7]

Symbols of ethnicity are not merely static products of ethnic culture but are solutions to problematic situations that characterize, project, and parody everyday life. The contributors to this volume perceive ethnic symbols as ways of bringing real and ideal worlds more closely into alignment. Through these symbols, ethnic men and women define their place and position in regard to their ethnic past and present. Janet Theophano's essay in this collection, for example, describes how an Italian-American woman arranged weddings for two daughters, serving different styles of food for each. Symbols, then, are not fixed points of tradition, but rather frames of reference and meaning within which ethnics respond to social, political, religious, or economic pressures.

Ethnic folklore consists not only of recognizable forms and symbols, but also of techniques and strategies used to present them in novel ways. Strategies of ethnic adaptation influence how ethnic symbols are applied to concrete situations and how they are modified to changing contexts and times. Strategies bring symbols to life, set the stage for their consideration, and highlight their significance.

This sense of strategy is less calculated than the one widely used by social scientists, who characterize it as the conscious control of impressions people desire others to have of them or the deliberate manipulation of traditional ideologies to promote political ends.[8] As used in this volume, strategy is the appropriate rendering of symbols in order to dramatize solutions to ethnic problems. Following Kenneth Burke, strategies "size up the situations, name their structure and outstanding ingredients and name them in a way that contains an attitude toward them."[9]

The strategies explored by contributors to this volume demonstrate the variety of stylistic resources used in ethnic communities. Silverman, for example, points out how masking value conflicts affords Gypsies opportunities to blend into American society while remaining inwardly ethnic. Danielson illustrates how hyperbole used in speaking of Swedish festivals exaggerates the beneficial qualities of Swedish culture. Others show how various modes of blending—regional merging (Lipson-Walker), fusion of artistic styles (Lockwoods, Leary and March), homogenization of customs (Toelken), and layering of contexts (Cadaval) encourage the juxtaposition of cultural elements and the diversification of ethnic ties.

By emphasizing some traditions while downplaying others, and by combining various traditions, styles, and interpretations of ethnicity, ethnic men and women take greater control of their lives. They come to play active roles in determining what cultural features are relevant to their understandings of ethnicity. In turn, the proliferation of these flexible and "hybrid" traditions makes it easier for ethnics to choose how and why they relate to their ethnicity. Viewed in dynamic interrelationship, symbols and strategies constitute the expressive vocabulary of ethnicity, the "social poetics" of ethnic discourse that reveals how folklore creatively expresses these combinations and recombinations.[10]

The enormous possibilities for expressing "styles" of ethnicity create formidable challenges for the would-be symbolic analyst. The essays contained in this volume are organized to reflect these challenges and consider a variety of ways of dealing with (1) ethnic complexity and multiple levels of representation, (2) daily tensions, (3) shifting ethnic boundaries, (4) the contraction and expansion of ethnic networks and communities, and (5) the expression of ethnicity in the public arena.

The Lockwoods and Leary and March capture the complexity of the myriad transformations undertaken by the Cornish pasty in the Upper Peninsula of Michigan and the Dutchman style of music in the Upper Midwest. In both cases, ethnic traditions may be shared by several groups simultaneously. Pasties, for example, are claimed by the Cornish, Finns, Italians, and Slavs, yet have become varied and distinctive enough to accommodate all these groups. What grounds each modification in some overall pasty tradition is its status as a regional dish that represents the entire Upper Peninsula. This transformation of the pasty as a symbol of multiple groups has resulted in its undergoing several changes, from diversification among several groups to regional standardization to rediversification by new groups and commercial eateries. Leary and March demonstrate this process of appropriation in the many cultural styles that contribute to the development of the Dutchman music of the Upper Midwest. Although there is a recognizable central style of Dutchman music, variations have developed organically since the 1920s as a result of influences from the music of Germans, Bohemians, Czechs, and Scandinavians, and from the musical styles of country, bluegrass, and jazz. It is this composite of cultural influences, according to Leary and March, that is meant by the Dutchman musical tradition.

Janet Theophano studies the complexity and flexibility of ethnic involvement of the Italian-American mother who orchestrates the weddings of her two daughters in order to send distinctive messages to her new sons-in-law, and to her family and community. Theophano's analysis shows that foods mirror the purposes of their users, the nature of the relationships generated by such intentions, and the resulting consequences. Food choices, Theophano demonstrates, can reflect an individual's desire to communicate something about her heritage, her identity, and her own conflicts.

This variability in an individual's role is paralleled by the experiences of folklorists who are often called upon to represent the views of the members of ethnic groups whom they study as well as the academic community of which they are a part. Madeline Slovenz-Low discusses the constant need for fieldworkers to reassess their status in a personal account of her involvement with Chinese kung-fu groups organizing a New Year festival. Beginning as an outsider, she eventually became a spokesperson for the group. Her definition of community, identity, and worldview expanded to fit her new circumstances and had to be renegotiated. The very definition and identity of the term "ethnographer" became a metaphor for the exchange of worldviews.

The second challenge of responding to contemporary ethnicity is cataloging the variety of daily tensions confronting ethnic people. In the face of personal frustration, public ostracism, and the conflicting demands made by insiders and outsiders, ethnics make enormous sacrifices to retain their identities. Because ethnic participation varies greatly and ethnic commitment is a matter of degree, scholars need to be sensitive to the fine shades of ethnic attachment, to the processes of tuning in and out, to the converts and the disenfranchised, and to the numerous budding cults and "counter" groups from which possible friction may arise.

Perhaps most compelling and most ominous is the antiethnic hostility expressed by outsiders. Patricia A. Turner's essay shows how African-Americans interpreted the murders of black children in Atlanta as symbolic attacks on African-Americans generally. Rumors circulated throughout the United States that the killing of these black children was a conspiracy perpetrated by the racist Ku Klux Klan or a conspiracy with the FBI, the CIA, and the Centers for Disease Control. Blacks told these urban legends, Turner suggests, as a way of taking control of the information being communicated about the murders and as a way of demonstrating solidarity among African-Americans nationwide.

María Herrera-Sobek illustrates how Mexican-American immigrants deal with the anxieties of crossing illegally into the United States. Faced with almost insurmountable odds, immigrants have created a body of *corridos* to describe their yearnings for a "green card" and their negative attitudes toward the border patrol and *coyotes* (smugglers). These songs speak ironically of the immigrant's negative expectations for permanent residence in the United States and for fair treatment from government agents and smugglers alike.

The third challenge is to develop methods to deal with how ethnics learn to maneuver in a nonethnic world, a process often fraught with friction. Such maneuvering has usually been viewed as a sign of assimilation, in which changes are made in the direction of less ethnic identification. The essays included in this section eschew such a model and document how a greater intensification of ethnicity is just as likely to occur from sustained contact with the general population. What is important is how ethnics assess competitive forces and how they incorporate segments of several identities in trying to make the best of all possible worlds. Students of ethnicity must be willing to follow members of ethnic groups as they align and realign their ethnic boundaries in relationship to others and as they foreground folklore to assess the significance of those relationships in multiple settings.

The construction of boundaries between insiders and outsiders is discussed by Carol Silverman in her study of American Gypsies. Contrary to the popular view that Gypsies have been assimilated into American society, she argues that beneath the appearance of compliance with mainstream culture, Gypsies have developed strategies for participating fully in the economy while remaining ethnically distinct. Their mobility, desire for independent occupations, and residence in urban areas—often regarded as barriers to maintaining an ethnic commitment—in fact allow Gypsies to move within American society without compromising their ethnicity. Indeed, the more adept they are at being American, the better they are able to deflect others' awareness that they are Gypsy and the more opportunities they have to practice their ethnicity without interference.

Similarly, Betty Blair demonstrates that when Iranians change their names to adapt to American society, they are not expressing a wish to assimilate. Rather, they are attempting to size up the host society, to take control of their lives, and to communicate to non-Iranians how adaptable they really are. In their own homes, they continue to speak Persian, to teach Persian to their children, and to give their children Persian names.

A comparable problem exists for American Indians, as discussed by Barre Toelken, who are attempting to maintain individual tribal affiliations while empathizing with the difficulties common to all Indians. The powwow addresses this issue by allowing for the simultaneous expression of tribal and pan-ethnic identity. In the powwow, each group has the opportunity to dance a tribal dance, by virtue of serving as either host or guest, while participating in the dances common to all. The powwow also addresses relationships to the general society through dance, in which external pressures of competition and integration are balanced with American Indian values of cooperation and ethnic identification.

The fourth challenge is to deal with small pockets of ethnicity which may seem to have little chance of survival. There is a tendency to overlook those groups which, by virtue of their size and low profile, do not exhibit their ethnicity readily. Within these groups, folklore becomes a way of rethinking their relationship to the broader traditions of which they are a part, both historically and in the immediate present.

David Shuldiner explores how a small antireligious Jewish faction of socialists maintains its belief in universal brotherhood while retaining cultural ties to its Jewish past. Shuldiner shows how the Passover *haggadah* (a book narrating the exodus from Egypt) is a paradigmatic text for working though the dual allegiances of members. Accepted and used by all Jews on Passover, the *haggadah* is stripped of its religious connotations and turned into a labor manifesto. The suffering of Jews becomes a metaphor for the suffering of working-class people everywhere, and the hope for a messiah is transformed into a vision for the establishment of a classless society. Far from being a survival from the past, the sacred text of the *haggadah* speaks to the present by incorporating concerns of Jews reacting to new historical developments and ongoing interpersonal relationships with non-Jews.

Carolyn Lipson-Walker shows how southern Jews create a sense of community. Unable to rely on the religious and communal resources of the large Jewish communities found in northern cities, they expand their notion of community to include the south in its entirety. Public celebrations—such as weddings, picnics, retreats, reunions, and jubilees—serve as rallying points for southern Jews to celebrate their regional Jewishness. The wedding, in particular, is a telescoped representation of the extensive symbolic links forged by Jews in the South. Marked by ostentation, hospitality, festivity, and the reuniting of family, friends, and acquaintances from far and wide, the wedding expresses the desire of southern Jews to create a closed set of social arrangements that would guarantee in-marriages. A new tradition of celebration is thus born out of the confluence of region and religion.

The fifth and final challenge undertaken by contributors to this volume is to describe the transformations taking place in the increasingly visible public arena. Richard M. Dorson has noted that folklore passes through various levels of society, from the esoteric lore of private individuals, through communal celebrations designed exclusively for members of ethnic groups, to the public festivals that bring together several different ethnic groups and generations.[11]

The three essays included in this section concern the public festival, which is becoming the celebration par excellence of cultural pluralism in the United States. Although folk festivals were organized as early as the 1920s to introduce immigrant cultures to the American people, today's festivals have expanded as an important vehicle for promoting multiculturalism.[12] Richard M. Dorson, who originally coined the word "fakelore" and who had once been skeptical of the role of public-sector folklore, came to view these festivals as having the potential to "substantially enlarge the audience for the genuine values of folklore."[13] But folklore in the public arena faces a most demanding test, because it is the subject of much controversy. Since so much is expected of festivals in terms of promoting cross-cultural understanding, failure to adequately demonstrate success in this style of public education threatens to undercut its future.[14] The three essays which follow discuss these issues from the vantage point of three types of festivals ranging from one organized for members of a single group to one encompassing several interacting Hispanic subgroups to one involving multiple ethnic groups of widely divergent cultural backgrounds.

Larry Danielson explores the role of public festival among Swedish residents of Lindsborg, Kansas, who celebrate St. Lucia on December 13. St. Lucia is an example of ethnic regeneration; in response to declining economic resources, residents have turned to their ethnic traditions to bolster pride in the community. The challenge for festival promoters was to decide which traditions should be revived and how they should be integrated. As the St. Lucia celebration has developed from private expression to community-wide festivity, it has incorporated increasing layers of civic participation, several ethnic generations, and expanding forms of expressive behavior. In turn, public festivities have been reincorporated into home celebrations.

Olivia Cadaval provides an example of a community festival midway between the small town and the large metropolis. The Latino festival brings together several groups to celebrate the *barrio* in which they live. Cadaval shows how a single festival may relate simultaneously to three levels of commercialization: tourist exhibits catering to nonethnics, street vendors selling traditional foods to Latinos, and family-organized centers of food distribution that bring kin together. She argues that none should be regarded as any more authentic than the other because all three are considered by festival participants as important ways of introducing Latino culture to others.

Even more intricate are multiethnic festivals held under the auspices of local and national arts and culture commissions. Susan Auerbach, the former city folklorist of Los Angeles, suggests that multicultural festivals are creating a model of a "mediated" culture, one which falls between the private and public arenas of ethnic contact and communication. In dealing with the problems of what groups to invite, which persons best symbolize a culture, and what forms of folklore should be performed, the multicultural festival proposes a means of institutionalizing cultural pluralism. As such festivals increase in number and popularity, they may offer a way to increase mutual understanding and cooperation among ethnic groups and to counter stereotypical views held by one group about the other.

In exploring ethnic problems and solutions, contributors to this volume are adding their voices to those who wish to consider the implications of cultural diversity in American society. The symbols and strategies employed in displays of public festivals, formations of community, reconstructions of the past, personal quests for ethnic identification, and the dispelling of ethnic rumors and stereotypes are just some of the many creative solutions which ethnic men and women have developed in realizing a culturally pluralistic society. In its broadest role, folklore thus helps to envision a society based on intercultural understanding and exchange.

Notes to Introduction

1. Werner Sollors, ed. *The Invention of Ethnicity* (New York: Oxford University Press, 1989).

2. Barre Toelken, in his textbook *The Dynamics of Folklore* (Boston: Houghton Mifflin, 1979), 34, states that "balancing the dynamism of change in performance is the essentially conservative force of tradition."

3. Beatrice Weinreich, "The Americanization of Passover," in *Studies in Biblical and Jewish Folklore*, ed. Raphael Patai, Francis Utley, and Dov Noy (Bloomington, Ind.: Indiana University Press, 1960), 329–66; Elizabeth Mathias, "The Italian-American Funeral: Perspectives Through Change," *Western Folklore* 33 (1974): 35–50.

4. See, for example, Stanford M. Lyman and William A. Douglass, "Ethnicity: Strategies of Collective and Individual Impression Management," *Social Research* 40 (1973): 344–65.

5. Shalom Staub, "The Near East Restaurant: A Study of the Spatial Manifestation of the Folklore of Ethnicity," *New York Folklore* (Summer 1981): 115.

6. Kenneth Burke, *The Philosophy of Literary Form* (Baton Rouge: Louisiana State University Press, 1947), 296.

7. See the bibliography compiled by Robert A. Georges and Stephen Stern, *American and Canadian Immigrant and Ethnic Folklore: An Annotated Bibliography* (New York: Garland, 1982).

8. Lyman and Douglass, "Ethnicity"; Abner Cohen, *The Two-Dimensional Man* (Berkeley and Los Angeles: University of California Press), 1974.

9. Burke, *The Philosophy of Literary Form*, 1.

10. The term "social poetics" is developed by Michael Herzfeld in *The Poetics of Manhood: Contest and Identity in a Cretan Mountain Village* (Princeton: Princeton University Press, 1985).

11. Richard M. Dorson, "The State of Folkloristics from an American Perspective," *Journal of the Folklore Institute* 19 (1982): 71–105.

12. I am grateful to Barbara Kirshenblatt-Gimblett for bringing the early history of festivals to my attention.

13. Dorson, "The State of Folkloristics from an American Perspective," 103.

14. Barbara Kirshenblatt-Gimblett discusses the perils of public sector folklore in "Mistaken Dichotomies," *Journal of American Folklore* 101 (1988): 140–55.

I.

Untangling Complexities of Ethnic
Sources, Representations, and Meanings

1. Pasties in Michigan's Upper Peninsula:

Foodways, Interethnic Relations, and Regionalism

YVONNE R. LOCKWOOD AND WILLIAM G. LOCKWOOD

The transformation of an immigrant culture to an ethnic culture is a complex process. Immigrant communities are not (as they were so often treated in the past) detached pieces of the Old Country. Even in the period immediately after arrival, the culture of immigrants has already been changed due to selective processes on emigration and the immediate effects of the journey and the new environment. Acculturation—the focus of attention of most existing studies—is only one aspect of the cultural transformation that takes place. The new cultural configuration of immigrants draws not only from "mainstream" American culture, but from that of other immigrant groups as well. Groups previously arrived from other countries are emulated. Cultural traits of the majority population are imposed and sometimes eagerly accepted. Old customs acquire new functions and meanings. The cultures of a variety of regional and social groups from the same country of origin are amalgamated and standardized. Eventually the culture of the ethnic group diverges significantly from that of the homeland, which, of course, has continued to evolve along its own path. Elsewhere we have discussed this process of ethnogenesis in greater detail.[1]

Ethnogenesis can be demonstrated in virtually any aspect of culture, but nowhere is it more graphically illustrated than in American foodways. In this essay, we will trace the natural history of a single item of prepared food — the pasty (pronounced pass-tee) — in the Upper Peninsula of Michigan to demonstrate the complex development of ethnic cultures. By observing how the pasty, introduced by one ethnic group, was claimed by many ethnic groups and the region as a whole, we will illustrate the complex relationships existing between immigrant, ethnic, and regional identity and culture.

The U.P. (as it is called by Michiganders) is a peninsula separated from the remainder of Michigan by the Straits of Mackinac, Lake Michigan, and Lake Huron. Not until 1957, when the Mackinac Bridge was completed, was direct connection made between the two parts of the state. Previously, one could get to the lower peninsula only by ferry or by traveling the length of Wisconsin and circling back through Chicago. Consequently, the U.P. is a region much more closely related culturally, historically, and demographically to northern Wisconsin and northeastern Minnesota than to the lower peninsula of Michigan. Yoopers (from U.P.ers) have a highly developed regional consciousness. Because the lower peninsula of the state includes the large population centers, the important industries, the major cultural institutions, and the state capital, Yoopers feel neglected by state government and looked down upon by the rest of the population. This situation has given rise to a separatist movement, only half in jest, to establish the U.P. as the fifty-first state of Superior.

Soon after Michigan became a state in 1837, some residents traveled north to investigate the upper peninsula that Congress had included in the state's territory. The reports they brought back triggered the first major mining boom in the United States.[2] From the beginning of the iron and copper industry, Cornish immigrants played a major role.[3] By 1844, two copper mining companies with some twenty Cornish employees were already in operation. Since they had experience with the deep-mining techniques and machinery used in the tin mines of Cornwall, these Cornishmen were valuable to the developing mining industry and set the pattern of mine work in the U.P.[4] By the late nineteenth century, when the origin of European immigration to the United States shifted eastward and southward, the Cornish were already well established in the mines as skilled workers, foremen, bosses, and mining captains. Sons of Cornish immigrants were among the first graduates of the new Michigan College of Mines (now Michigan Technological University) in the 1880s, and many of them took professional positions in the local mining industry. More recently arrived Finns, Italians, Poles, Croats, and Serbs provided the unskilled labor. As mining technology developed, the need for skilled workers lessened. Consequently, the unskilled were promoted very slowly, if at all, which encouraged the entrenchment of the earlier immigrants in a hierarchical position over more recent arrivals.

Just as Cornish influence was felt in methods of mining, the Cornish also established much of the cultural life of the mining communities. The new immigrants looked upon the Cornish as representatives of American culture.[5] They had status and their lifestyle was taken as a model of American life. This situation was typical of cultural relations between members of the New and Old Immigration.[6] Elsewhere the Irish—as the most numerous of the "Old Immigrants"—were often emulated by newly arrived eastern and southern Europeans. In Detroit, for example, some new immigrants "Americanized" their Serbian family names Obradović and Dragić by changing them to O'Bradovich and O'Dragich.[7]

Thus, the earlier immigrants from northwestern Europe often influenced the cultural patterns of later-arriving immigrants from southern and eastern Europe. From the perspective of these "greenhorns" from the other side of Europe, the practices of earlier arrivals, whose immigrant cultures had already been transformed to ethnic cultures, were accepted as the "American Way." These earlier arrivals, after all, were the Americans with whom new immigrants were most apt to have contact. It was likely to be their neighborhoods in which new immigrants settled, and they who were most likely to be the foremen and supervisors in the mills and mines where the immigrants went to work. It is not surprising, then, that the ethnic culture that took shape was profoundly influenced by that of earlier immigrants. Ethnic foodways provide particularly good examples of this process.

The pasty is a turnover with a pie-like crust filled with a variety of food combinations. It is the national dish of Cornwall, and it played an important role in the diet of Cornish-Americans wherever they settled.[8] The pasty was quickly adopted by newer immigrants who worked by their sides and under their direction in the mines of the U.P. It was not just a recipe that was passed from one ethnic group to another, but an entire cultural complex including the occasions for which pasties are prepared, the ways they are prepared and eaten, and some of the folklore associated with them. At the same time, significant alterations and innovations in the pasty took place during the process of diffusion and adoption by non-Cornish.

A principal reason that the Cornish pasty was readily adopted by members of other ethnic groups in the U.P. was its close association with work. Philip Harben, writing on the traditional dishes of Britain, observes:

The Cornish pasty [is] one of the best examples in the world of what one might call *functional food*. For the Cornish pasty . . . is not merely delicious food, it was designed for a certain quite definite purpose; it was designed to be carried to work and eaten in the hand, to be taken down the mine, to sea, to the fields. You will see a Cornishman munching his tasty pasty squatting in the narrow tin-mine workings, sitting on the nets in his leaping fishing boat, leaning against a grassy bank whilst the patient plough-horses wait.[9]

In Cornwall, the pasty was particularly associated with mining.[10] It is very well suited to this context: it is easily carried in pails or specially made sacks, it retains its heat for a long time, it can be eaten with the hands, and it is a hearty meal-in-one. Little wonder that the Finns, Italians, and Slavs who saw their Cornish foremen eating pasty soon were demanding the same of their own wives.

Today, the Cornish are a relatively small component of the U.P.'s population. The largest ethnic group is the Finns. The first Finnish immigrants to the U.P. began to arrive in 1864, well after Cornish immigration but thirty years prior to the massive Finnish immigration to the United States that began around the turn of the century.[11] By 1880, foreign-born Finns numbered over one thousand. The first arrivals tended to be skilled workers who were given employment as carpenters, blacksmiths, and skilled yardmen at the mines. Thus, they were well established and somewhat acculturated by the time of the mass immigration. It was probably from these earlier Finnish arrivals, rather than from the Cornish themselves, that later Finnish immigrants adopted the pasty.[12] Some Finns were receptive to pasty because they had similar regional dishes—such as *piiraat* and *kukko*—which resemble pasty. These are dough-enveloped specialties of meat, fish, vegetables, rice, and so on, varying in size from individual turnovers to large loafs.[13] How was a Finn newly arrived in America, seeing a pasty in the lunch pail of a fellow countryman arrived some twenty years before, to know that this was not merely a regional variant of food with which he was already familiar? Thus, we would argue, many Finns came to believe the pasty was a Finnish food. In a similar way, some Italians in the U.P. also regard the pasty as Italian.

The development of a U.P. regional culture was thereby shaped not only by mainstream "American" culture, but also by the cultural traditions of ethnic groups in contact with one another. The adoption and finally the standardization of pasty is the result of its appropriation by many ethnic groups. The development of a "polka subculture" in the United States, drawing upon and amalgamating Polish, German, Bohemian, Slovenian, and Croatian traditions, is an example of the same kind of process occurring nationwide.

Despite the regionalization of the pasty, it is still claimed as the ethnic heritage of several groups. By and large, Yoopers know the Cornish origin of pasty because of attention to it by mass media. Some even refer to it as a "Cousin Jack mouth organ," Cousin Jack being a popular synonym for Cornishman. On the other hand, its association with Finns cannot be ignored. For example, Raymond Sokolov, former Michigander and free-lance ethnoculinary journalist, writes of the "Finnish flavor" of pasties.[14] Some U.P. Finns themselves regard pasty as a Finnish food. This belief is perpetuated by family tradition, Finnish "ethnic" church suppers, and annual Finnish traditional celebrations, where pasty is a featured Finnish specialty. This Finnish association can be explained historically by the role of Finns in the diffusion of the pasty and by the predominance of Finns in the U.P. Many pasty shops, for example, seem to be owned and staffed by Finns. On the other hand, the family is an important factor in the issue of ethnic attribution: pasty is first and foremost a family tradition. Yoopers make and eat pasties according to the recipes and traditions of their mothers and grandmothers. The authors know Michigan Finns who were unaware that other ethnic groups also make and eat pasties. This is also true of in-laws not from the U.P. who assume pasty is Finnish because the spouse's Finnish family serves it.

In the course of its transformation from monoethnic to multiethnic, the pasty has been diversified, then standardized, and, finally, rediversified. In Cornwall today, as in the U.P. at the turn of the century, pasty can be made from a variety of ingredients: rice and leeks, egg and bacon, meat and potatoes, lamb and parsley or venison, fish, apple, and so on. The possible variants are endless, so much so that it is said "the devil never dared cross the Tamar River from Devonshire to Cornwall for fear of the Cornish women's habit of putting anything and everything into a pasty."[15] The content of the pasty, as it developed in the U.P., is a standardization of but one of the many Cornwall variants: a basic mixture of meat, potatoes, onion, rutabagas, and/or carrots. Although some variation still occurs, it cannot deviate far from this particular combination of ingredients and still qualify as pasty. Meat may consist of beef, a beef and pork combination, or even venison when available. Some may add parsley; others omit both carrots and rutabagas. But for U.P. residents today, the U.P. pasty is this meat and root vegetable specialty.

One area of particular controversy is the crust. Crust recipes are usually guarded secrets. In Cornwall, pasty is made with either a puff pastry or a crust similar to that used for American pie. It is the latter that was adopted for the U.P. pasty. The dough, according to Yoopers, should be light and short and hold together, yet not be quite as flaky as pie crust. The secret lies in the proportion of shortening and water to flour and in the type of shortening used. Traditionalists, both Cornish and non-Cornish, claim that suet is the original and best shortening. Others use lard because it is more convenient and, they state, just as good as suet. With the contemporary emphasis on lighter foods, vegetable shortening is now being used which, claim purists, produces an inferior, tough, and tasteless crust.

Sealing the pasty is another area for variation. According to older Cousin Jacks and Cousin Jennies, a "real" Cornish pasty is sealed by "making a rope," a particular method of tightly closing the dough, usually across the top of the pasty.[16] Today few Yoopers—including those of Cornish background—know this technique. Instead, most make a seal by pinching, folding, or crimping the edge as they would for pie. Those few Yoopers who do use "the Cornish rope" are invariably Cornish-Americans.

Another distinctively Cornish feature is the addition of initials indicating for whom the pasty is intended. These are formed from dough and baked on top of one end, serving to identify pasties made to suit individual likes and dislikes, through the omission or increase of certain ingredients, and to mark uneaten parts of pasties for later consumption. This tradition is observed in some Cornish Yooper families with toothpicks: one, two, or three toothpicks stuck into the crust designate to whom it belongs.

Although pasty ingredients have been standardized, adaptation to the U.P. context has produced variation in pasty construction and consumption and in attitudes and values about pasty. Most Yoopers agree that ingredients should be chopped with a knife, though for convenience many will use ground meat—usually hamburger, ground chuck, or "pasty meat" (a coarsely ground beef, with or without pork, sold in local markets). Some maintain that all ingredients should be mixed so that the flavors blend during baking. Others, especially Cornish, argue that ingredients should be layered (potatoes topped by rutabagas and/or carrots, followed by onions and, finally, meat, salt, pepper, and butter or suet—either of which are optional) so that the meat juices and seasonings percolate down through the vegetables. This latter view is probably the older, and we assume that mixing was first done, again, for the sake of convenience.

Accompaniments and condiments with pasty have become highly variable, with patterns strongly linked to family tradition. Some Yoopers would not enjoy pasty without catsup. Other accompaniments are equally essential for different individuals or families: chowchow pickles, crisp vegetables, tea, buttermilk, beer, tomato juice. These accompaniments are not casual choices. One or several of them is absolutely necessary to complete a satisfactory pasty meal.

Originally pasty was hand food. Its traditional shape, size, and substantial crust attest to its function as a working person's meal intended to be carried in a pocket or lunch pail. Rolled into a circle and folded into the shape of a half-moon approximately seven to nine inches long, the crust enfolds its ingredients and is sealed across the top or along the lower edge. The traditional way to eat pasty is to begin at the end, holding it parallel with the body so the juices keep the filling moist. However, more and more Yoopers now eat pasty on plates with forks, a manner which opens the door to still more variation. Once pasty rests on a plate, it lends itself to innovations that some regard as abuse: its crust is broken in the center, releasing its moisture and heat, and it is smothered with butter, gravy, or other substances. Change has also occurred in structure. Although the half-moon shape remains standard, a common family version has evolved known as "pasty pie": pasty ingredients baked in a pie pan with a bottom and top crust and served in wedges on plates. Since the interwar period, pasties have not only been made in this form but also oversized in the traditional shape and cut in half to serve. Both forms are acknowledged as quick innovations, and are reserved for family.

The U.P. pasty remained relatively stable in form and content for many decades; the narrow range of variance that exists usually is associated with particular ethnic groups. For example, rutabagas in pasty are said to be Cornish and carrots Finnish. Pasty accompanied by buttermilk is regarded as a Finnish ("bad") habit, especially by the Cornish. "Chipping" rather than chopping the meat and rutabagas, closing with a "rope," and layering ingredients, are known as Cornish. Although these examples are not exclusive to one ethnic group, they are stereotyped as such, even to the extent that "carrot pasty" is a derisive term for Finnish-style pasty. Acknowledgment of an Italian variation is communicated in the expression "the Cornish originated it; the Finns disseminated it; the Italians improved it." This was heard in the university communities of Houghton and Marquette, but we were not able to discover there or elsewhere what is considered distinctive about an Italian-style pasty.[17]

Only one Yooper, in the western end, recognized his Italian mother-in-law's pasty as different: she adds "a little bit of hot banana pepper."

Marked changes are now occurring in pasty; it is rediversifying. One used to hear about individuals who put peas, for example, into pasty secretly, knowing neighbors would not approve. Now similar "violations" of U.P. tradition are openly admitted: pasty with kidneys, pasty with condensed onion or mushroom soup, pasty with gravy. These variants are still repugnant to many Yoopers and often are attributed to specific groups or to other areas, i.e., "it's those other guys." Dousing pasty with gravy, for example, is said to be Cornish (by Finns), French Canadian (by others), Mennonite (by a pasty shop owner who learned to make pasty from Finns), eaten only in the eastern U.P. (by those in the western end) or eaten only by non-Yoopers. These views, however, are exoteric beliefs about "them" and attempt to explain a drastic change in tradition.[18]

Further signs of rediversification are appearing as a consequence of commercialization. Both health food stores and a few standard pasty shops now offer a vegetarian version, often with whole wheat crust. Other less-than-traditional versions are found in establishments that cater largely to tourists. For example, some restaurants offer pasty with cheese, bacon, or chili topping. Some pizza parlors offer "pizza pasty"—pasty ingredients enfolded by pizza dough, much like calzone. Thus, the pasty, which became standardized within relatively narrow limits, is again appearing in greater variation.[19]

The first pasties available outside the home were sold at church pasty sales. In addition to raising funds, the church pasty preparation and sale is a popular social event. Despite long hours of work, participants speak of these activities both as enjoyable and as an effective way to initiate newcomers into church functions and U.P. tradition. In this context, knowledge about pasties is exchanged between individuals, thus reinforcing pasty tradition. Even women who bake their own pasties will buy at church sales. The product is regarded as homemade and "the real thing," because older women usually dominate at these affairs. Either they are deferred to because of their experience and age, or they take an active supervisory and authoritative role and monitor the work of younger women. As a consequence, in one town young women are intimidated and hesitate to volunteer because of possible criticism from the older women. One of these guardians of tradition, a ninety-year-old Cousin Jenny, stated emphatically that she could not eat any pasties but her own and those from her church because the others are only poor imitations.

The first commercial pasty shops began to appear just before World War II. Yoopers recall that in Hurley, Wisconsin, located at the Michigan state line and then known as "sin city," an Italian-American entrepreneur baked pasties in his kitchen and peddled them from bar to bar in the early-morning hours. About 1938, he opened a pasty shop. After the war other shops appeared across the border in Ironwood. Today pasties are made and sold in at least one outlet in nearly every U.P. community: pasty shops, bakeries, restaurants, bars, fast food counters, Dairy Queens, and grocery stores. Often they can be purchased hot, cold, partially baked, frozen, and day-old.

Yoopers regard homemade pasties as better, but on occasion even people who regularly make their own pasties buy commercial ones when they are too tired to cook; when they need a large number, as for a wedding supper; when they go fishing or hunting; or when they are feeling lazy—like sending out for a pizza elsewhere in the United States.

During its decades of industrial development, the U.P. experienced an economic boom. But because the economy was based on extractive industries—the primary production of iron, copper, and lumber—the area was directly and immediately affected when production fell off and large corporations were pulled out by their absentee owners. The U.P. had been exploited and then abandoned. The economy began a gradual but steady decline about 1920 and, despite occasional spurts of activity, never recovered.[20] The subsequent secondary status felt by U.P. residents has contributed negatively to their self-image and has resulted in an inferiority complex.[21] Since completion of the Mackinac Bridge in 1957, access to the U.P. has been easier, and tourism has become increasingly important in the local economy. One result is that pasty shops have proliferated. Along a seven-mile stretch of highway leading west from the bridge, some thirteen pasty shops, advertising in three-foot-high, glow-in-the-dark letters, exist to the virtual exclusion of other eateries. The personal names of the establishments, such as Granny's, Lehto's, and Suzy's, assure strangers of a homemade treat. Thus, the pasty has come to symbolize the Upper Peninsula. This consciousness of the regionalization of pasty is used, in effect, as a rhetorical strategy to enhance U.P. self-image.[22] According to Kenneth Burke, rhetoric serves to imbue individuals with heightened awareness and to persuade them by manipulating materials and ideas in an aesthetically pleasing manner.[23]

Traditional forms of culture are especially effective as persuasive devices because they bear the test of time and elicit a sympathetic response.

Members of the media, restaurateurs, and other U.P. residents have used the power of traditional expression to their advantage in creating a strategy for regional identification. The strategy includes editorializing on the use, meaning, and significance of the pasty for regional inhabitants.

Narratives about pasty emphasize ties with occupation and environment, as well as with specific groups. Legends tell of hardworking miners who warmed pasties on shovels held over the candles of mining lamps. Others recall that miners carried hot pasties wrapped in cloth sacks or newspaper in their shirts and were kept warm on cold U.P. mornings and in damp, chilly mines. As they worked, miners, in turn, kept their pasties warm. Undoubtedly a warm pasty is comforting carried next to the body in severe temperatures; hunters and fishermen, possibly influenced by this workers' tradition, carry pasties in this way today. But one might assume that the physical exertion of mine work would transform any pasty so carried into a crumbled mess. One explanation is, of course, that pasty crust of fifty years ago was tougher and not as flaky as that of today. Also, it is possible that over time pasties have become larger. Both features would explain why pasty is not as durable today as folklore describes it.

Much of the folklore about pasty concerns the crust. The description above is of quite a different pasty than what meets present ideal standards of the perfect crust—not so flaky that it falls apart in the hand or so tough that it can survive a fall. Consider a narrative that explains the origin of pasty:[24]

> In Cornwall, the women searched for a good meal for the miners other than sandwiches; the men were tired of sandwiches. They experimented with potatoes, meat, and onions wrapped in dough and were pleased with the result. It was a whole meal in one. At meal time, the women brought their pasties to the mine and dropped them down the shaft to the men below. They didn't even break.

When Richard Dorson collected a variant in 1946, it was told in jest.[25] The above example was told to our informant by his Cornish neighbor as historical information.

Pasty as a missile is a recurring motif in popular expression. For example, a former resident of the U.P. expressed disbelief about the authenticity of this legend of the pasty's origin, but later recalled that his mother could toss her pasties into the air and catch them without breakage.[26] A cartoonist very familiar with the U.P. plays with this same image.[27]

Ritualizing events has been another strategy in the regionalization of pasty. The ultimate example of use of the missile motif occurred at the First Annual Pasty Throwing Contest in April 1983. Encouraged by the widespread saying that a "good pasty can be dropped to the bottom of a mine shaft without splitting open," the Finlandia Cafe and Bakery of Marquette sponsored the contest and also donated a batch of burned, unsalable, and inedible pasties.[28] The winner threw his pasty 155 feet, acquiring a trophy crowned with a gilded pasty and possible mention in the *Guinness Book of World Records*.

In addition to symbolic representation of the region, pasty lore is also manipulated to express group boundaries to distinguish Yoopers from outsiders. The folk terms "gut buster" and "ulcer bun," for example, communicate a shared knowledge about pasty that expresses social solidarity. These metaphors for pasty, although seemingly negative, are rather a good-natured, even affectionate, reference to pasty's substantial nature. It is a heavy food, one that goes a long way to satisfying hunger. But unless one is a Yooper, one might construe these terms as slurs. Shared knowledge also allows for in-group jokes. Based on awareness of the Catholic custom of meatless Fridays, the pasties of one Italian shop are known as "Catholic," because "they are skimpy on meat."

Lack of this knowledge by outsiders further reinforces pasty's link to the region. Enticed by the deluge of pasty advertisements, curious tourists identify themselves when they inquire about "pay-stee," thereby providing more grist for the folklore mill. U.P. residents never cease to be amazed by this pronunciation and its confusion with the accouterment for striptease dancers. Nor do they tire of recounting such incidents and ridiculing the outsider, who otherwise contributes to the Yooper's negative self-image. A prize-winning limerick by a U.P. resident focuses on this widely shared regional joke:

> A Casper widow named Patsy,
> Earned her living by selling of pasties,

> When a fudgy hasty demanded a pastey,
> Her response was rather nasty.[29]

The media and state government have played no small role in the rhetoric of regionalizing pasty. In 1968, Governor George Romney designated May 24 as Michigan Pasty Day. Local newspapers often feature articles about pasty. One such story sparked a long debate about what constitutes a real pasty.[30] In 1979, WLUC Television in Marquette aired a short Michigan promotional film, "Stay for It," featuring local folk historian Frank Matthews. Looking for all the world like a stereotypic miner, this senior Yooper informs viewers about pasty's Cornish origin and function. The film was an attempt to build regional pride by stressing pasty's aesthetic qualities and its historical and occupational tie to the U.P. As Mr. Matthews bites down on a tempting pasty, he urges viewers that "pasties are part of the Upper Peninsula heritage and that's why you should stay for it and try one!" Like Caucasian muses singing the praises of Dannon yogurt, this wizened regional authority promises a treat with a long and proud U.P. tradition.[31]

The use of pasties in cartoons attests to the food's ability to act as a commentary (see below). At the time Cliff Wirth printed his cartoons in 1982, Michigan had suffered plant shutdowns that led to thirty percent unemployment in some regions, mass migration out of the area, and generalized psychological depression. Tradition, as reflected in the last cartoon, may be antidotal to such problems. Drawing on the Holland, Michigan, Tulip Festival and the U.P. pasty, the cartoonist suggests we turn to these pleasurable, fulfilling regional cultural traits for comfort and to assist in revitalizing statewide pride.

The idea that pasty is unique to the U.P. is widely shared. Residents' esoteric beliefs about pasty's enigmatic qualities reinforce its symbolic regional meaning. For example, during and after World War II, many residents left the U.P. for industrial centers in the Midwest and West. With them went the pasty. Numerous stories are told about individuals who tried to start shops as close to the U.P. as Green Bay, Appleton, and Ashland, Wisconsin, but were unsuccessful, because, according to folk belief, people elsewhere were ignorant of pasty and would not eat it. A notable exception is a person who sold his pasties at factory gates at mealtime, thereby recalling pasty's working-class origin. In another case, a pasty shop owner in Ironwood enjoys telling about the problems he encounters when he orders matches printed with the name and address

of the shop. Invariably, printers who are not local print "pastry" instead of "pasty."

The case of Yoopers moving to Detroit, however, suggests a more successful transplantation of U.P. culture. During and after World War II, large numbers of Yoopers moved to Detroit to work in various industries. In the new urban context, they became more aware of their U.P. identity. Knowledge of regional esoteric folklife, such as that of the pasty, played no small part in the self-conscious awareness of membership in a regional folk group. Thus, Detroit became home to a U.P. social club, a U.P.-dominated Finnish social club, and an Episcopalian church, whose congregation consists almost entirely of Cornish Yoopers. Like their friends and relatives in the U.P., these groups continue the U.P. custom of sponsoring fund-raising pasty dinners and bake sales.

"If I were governor I would decree that everyone wear a Holland tulip on their lapels and eat at least one genuine Cornish pasty from the Upper Peninsula every day. Then I'd sit back and watch Michigan's problems vanish!"

Pasty shops owned by former Yoopers have been part of the Detroit scene for decades. According to one of these owners, about ninety percent of his customers are from the U.P. or have spent considerable time there:

> That's where the pasty came from. It didn't come to Detroit from Cornwall, but from the U.P. Pasty is the tie to the U.P. Invariably, a customer will tell me he is from the U.P., as if that's any surprise. I certainly didn't think he was from Alabama![32]

The ability of pasties to link the U.P. with other areas has contributed to the creation of a new self-consciousness in the Upper Peninsula. The same informants who remember business failures forty years ago are now predicting that pasty shops will soon exist all over the United States.

Yoopers are witnessing the increasing fame of pasty among tourists; skiers, hunters, anglers, and campers take as many as fifty pasties home to freeze. Some residents now refer to pasty as "U.P.'s contribution to American culture."

Pasty always seems to have been a link between generations and among different groups. But, since the mid-1960s, it has emerged with new meaning as a public, regional symbol that recalls the past, speaks of the present, and implies the future. The Bicentennial was a significant catalyst in this process. References to the history of the pasty, to its multiple ethnic associations, to its occupational and regional functions—as well as descriptions of its aesthetic effects—have bestowed new status on the pasty. Serving pasty to outside visitors is a conscious, predictable act intended to impress and thereby persuade them about the good quality of U.P. life. The tantalizing aroma, pleasing form and color, and delicious ingredients of pasty are often the focus of praise. The acceptance of pasties by outsiders is symbolically a validation of U.P. culture in general. While participation in pasty foodways reinforces cultural tradition, it also is a statement of regional identity.

Identity, however, is complex and always contextual. Pasty is symbolic of the U.P., but it also is deeply rooted in ethnic and family traditions. While it is available to anyone seeking to reinforce his or her ethnic roots, pasty's ethnic associations are secondary to region. Thus, a certain ambiguity exists regarding ethnic versus regional culture. But these two categories of cultural expression need not be mutually exclusive; rather, the separate identities, existing as they do at different levels of organization, are seldom in conflict. The adoption and transformation of the Cornish pasty by other immigrant groups was an essential part of its regionalization. As each group made the pasty its own, pasty became both an ethnic specialty of each and, ultimately—first implicitly, then explicitly—a specialty of the region.

Notes to Chapter 1

1. William G. Lockwood and Yvonne R. Lockwood, "Ethnic Roots of American Regional Foods," in *Current Research in Culinary History: Sources, Topics, and Methods*, proceedings of a conference sponsored by the Schlesinger Library of Radcliffe College and the Culinary Historians of Boston, Radcliffe College, June 14–16, 1985, edited by Jillian Strang, Bonnie Brown, and Patricia Kelley (Cambridge: Culinary Historians of Boston, 1985), 130–37.

2. Doris B. Mclaughlin, *Michigan Labor. A Brief History from 1818 to the Present* (Ann Arbor: Institute of Labor and Industrial Relations, 1970), 77;

Willis F. Dunbar, *Michigan: A History of the Wolverine State* (Grand Rapids: Willam B. Eerdmans Publishing Co., 1970), 498. Iron ore and copper mines became primary industrial employers in the U.P.

3. Jane Fisher, "Michigan's Cornish People," *Michigan History* 29 (1945): 379. See also John Rowe, *The Hard-Rock Men: Cornish Immigrants and the North American Mining Frontier* (Liverpool: Liverpool University Press, 1974), especially 62–95.

4. A. L. Rowse, *The Cousin Jacks: The Cornish in America* (New York: Charles Scribner's Sons, 1969), 168.

5. Fisher, "Michigan's Cornish People," 380.

6. Leonard Dinnerstein and David M. Reimers, *Ethnic Americans*, 2d ed. (New York: Harper & Row, 1982), 10–48.

7. Cultural geographers have argued that in the United States the first European population that established the economy and society of an area usually had decisive influence on later patterns that defined it as a cultural region, e.g., Wilbur Zelinsky, *The Cultural Geography of the United States* (Englewood Cliffs, N.J.: Prentice Hall, 1973), 5–35, and Raymond D. Gastil, *Cultural Regions of the United States* (Seattle: University of Washington Press, 1975), 26–27. Cf. George Foster's explanation in *Culture and Conquest* (Chicago: Quadrangle Books, 1960) of why the cultural patterns established in Mexico were nearly all Andalusian in origin even though immigrants from throughout Spain contributed to the colonial population of Mexico. Foster calls this phenomenon *cultural crystallization*. Since Andalusians were the first to arrive in Mexico, it was they who established the cultural patterns for later arrivals.

8. See, for example, Philip Harben, *Traditional Dishes of Britain* (London: The Bodley Head, 1953), 9–13; R. R. Roberts, *Cornish Recipes* (St. Ives, Cornwall, England: James Pike, Ltd., 1977), 3, 16; Marika Hanbury Tenison, *West Country Cooking* (London: Mayflower Granada Publishing, 1978), 77–105; Kathleen Thomas, *West Country Cookery* (London: B. T. Batsford Ltd., 1979), 57–58; Adrian Bailey, *The Cooking of the British Isles* (New York: Time-Life Books, 1971), 20–21.

9. Harben, *Traditional Dishes of Britain*, 9–10.

10. Roberts, *Cornish Recipes*, 3; Tenison, *West Country Cooking*, 78; Bailey, *Cooking*, 20. Also see Richard M. Dorson, *Bloodstoppers and Bearwalkers* (Cambridge: Harvard University Press, 1952), 117–18, for folk narrative associating the pasty with mining.

11. Arthur E. Puotinen, "Early Labor Organizations in the Copper Country," in *For the Common Good*, edited by Michael G. Karni and Douglas J. Ollila (Superior, Wis.: Tyomies Society, 1977), 123; Matti E. Kaups, "The Finns in the Copper and Iron Ore Mines of the Western Great Lakes Region, 1864–1905: Some Preliminary Observations," in *The Finnish Experience in the Western Great Lakes Region: New Perspectives*, edited by M. G. Karni, M. E. Kaups, and D. J. Ollila, Jr. (Turku, Finland: Institute of Migration, 1975), 59.

12. There is no way to document this claim except possibly through oral tradition, examples of which we did not find. No doubt the recipes were passed on orally. The Finnish cookbooks from that period were not published in the region and, therefore, do not contain pasty recipes. See, for example, Toinen Painos, *Keittokirja* (Fitchburg, Mass.: Suomalainen Sosialistinen Kustannusyhtiö, n.d.); Mina Wallin, *Suomalais-Amerikalainen Keittokirja* (New York: By the author,

1914); Recent Finnish-American community cookbooks published in Michigan inevitably include pasty recipes, e.g., *We Thank Thee, Lord* (Hancock, Mich.: Franklin Street Church, 1973) and *Ethnic Flavors* (Farmington Hills, Mich.: Finnish Center Association, n.d. [1990]).

13. Kirsti Tolvanen, *Finnish Food* (Helsinki: Kustannusosakeythiö Otava, 1959), 81–85.

14. "Tasty Pasty in Michigan, a Cornish Delicacy Is Given a Finnish Flavor," *Natural History*, 89, no. 1 (January 1980): 101–3.

15. Tenison, 78; Bailey, 20.

16. Cookbooks published in Great Britain refer to this process as "the Cornish crimp."

17. The origin of this saying might be attributed to a few popular pasty shops with Italian bakers at the time of this study. However, recalling Catholic church pasty sales, U.P. residents of different ethnic groups did not regard Italian-made pasties as different from others.

18. People who do put gravy over pasty—individuals belonging to different ethnic groups in the central U.P.—reason that pasty would otherwise be dry. No one seems to know exactly where the idea came from. Some suggested possibly an influence from meat pies or restaurants.

19. The former Madelyne's Original Foods of the U.P. had provided commercial pasties in the region for decades. According to the *Green Bay Press Gazette* (September 11, 1983), Madelyne's began to market pasty in California as a convenience food. Encouraged by orders ranging from 4,000 to 7,000 pasties a day from food distributors in Los Angeles and San Francisco, Madelyne's decided to vary its "original" recipe (meat, potatoes, rutabagas, and parsley) and offer chicken with cheese, Italian sausage with mozzarella cheese and potatoes, vegetable and cheese, and apple.

20. Jess Gilbert and Craig Harris, "Unemployment, Primary Production, and Population in the Upper Peninsula of Michigan in the Great Depression," in *A Half Century Ago: Michigan in the Great Depression*, edited by Frederick Honhart and Victor Howard (East Lansing: Michigan State University Archives and Historical Collections and the American Studies Program, 1980), 23–24.

21. For a folk perspective on this economic and social decline, see William Ivey, "The 1913 Disaster: Michigan Local Legend," *Folklore Forum*, 3 (1970): 100–114.

22. See Roger Abrahams, "Introductory Remarks to a Rhetorical Theory of Folklore," *Journal of American Folklore* 81 (1968): 143–58.

23. *A Rhetoric of Motives* (New York: 1950), 46.

24. Middle-aged Italian-American pasty shop owner in the western U.P., 1980.

25. See Dorson, *Bloodstoppers*, 107, 109, 117–18, for folklore collected about pasty. He also presents the folk explanation of the origin of pasty on 117.

26. Cornish, middle-aged male residing in the Detroit area, 1981.

27. All cartoons are reprinted with the permission of the artist, Cliff Wirth.

28. *Ann Arbor News*, April 10, 1983.

29. This limerick appeared in an Upper Peninsula paper, *The Pick and Axe*, 1976. "Fudgy" is a pejorative term for tourists who, while on vacation, purchase large quantities of Mackinac Island fudge.

30. "U.P. 'Adopts' Miners' Meal," *Upbeat*, the Sunday magazine section of the *U.P. Times*, April 16, 1978.

31. Mr. and Mrs. Matthews also served as informants for *American Cooking: The Eastern Heartland* (New York: Time-Life, 1971), 25–29.

32. Wayne State University Folklore Archive, 1970 (No. 119). This shop, however, like those in Colorado, California, northern Minnesota, and Florida, where Cornish and Yoopers have moved, serves pasty as a specialty; i.e., pasties have not been regionalized in these areas.

2. Dutchman Bands:

*Genre, Ethnicity, and Pluralism in the Upper Midwest**

JAMES P. LEARY AND RICHARD MARCH

Leary: How do you see yourself in ethnic terms?

Brueggen: German. Bohemian. [Pause.] There's where we need Dad. Hey, Dad! Come here! I ain't sure what I am. I think I'm part mutt.

March: Well, what kind of music do you play? German music? Wisconsin music?

Brueggen: Dutchman music. Dutchman kind of means an old-time flavor with a lot of drive to it. That's Dutchman music.[1] *April 30, 1988.*

Twenty-two-year-old concertina player Brian Brueggen had just finished a set with his band, Brian and the Mississippi Valley Dutchmen, at the Red Barn Polka Festival in Evansville, Wisconsin (figure 1). Clad in stage attire (blue jeans, a red satin shirt with billowy sleeves, and a plumed but rumpled alpine jaeger's hat), surrounded by musical products

* Fieldwork was carried out by James P. Leary in connection with the Wisconsin Folklife Center's German Music Project with funding from the National Endowment for the Arts, and by Leary and Richard March in connection with "Down Home Dairyland," a series produced by the Wisconsin Arts Board for Wisconsin Public Radio with funding from the National Endowment for the Arts. Interview materials have been deposited in the Wisconsin Music Archives of the Mills Music Library at the University of Wisconsin. Earlier versions of this essay were presented as papers to the American Folklore Society: Leary, "The Cultural Meanings of Dutchman Music" (Cincinnati, 1985), and Leary and March, "Polkas and Public Images in the Upper Midwest" (Albuquerque, 1987). Special thanks to LaVern Rippley and Christy Hengel for making historical photographs available.

Figure 1. Brian Brueggen and the Mississippi Valley Dutchman, 1989. Photo by James P. Leary.

and promotional materials (his latest record album, fliers listing upcoming gigs, stickers imprinted with the band's name and Brian's grinning face), he settled back in the seat of his family's van to answer questions for our radio series, "Down Home Dairyland."

Brueggen confounds the models scholars conventionally apply to ethnic expression in the United States. He is no immigrant nurturing old-world survivals, nor is he a thoroughgoing ethnic preoccupied with the revival and preservation of an authentic heritage, nor is he a neat synthesizer of foreign and mainstream American life. Instead he reckons tentatively that he, and by extension his audience, is German and Bohemian, but he is more certain he is "part mutt." His music is at once archaic or "old-time" and distinguished by its presumably modern "drive." His band's title combines its leader's first name with a nearby river valley, with, perhaps, an allusion to the Netherlands. His jeans connote rustic youth; the loose red shirt is an American version of a generalized Central European look favored by polka bands; the hat is alpine (possibly Austrian, or Bavarian, or Bohemian, or Slovenian, or Swiss) and its worn condition signals carefree use, not haughty show. Like any successful musical group, whatever the genre, Brian and the Mississippi Valley Dutchmen travel in a customized van, dispense commercial products, and are accustomed to media attention.[2]

On the surface, Brueggen's presentation of self is an amalgam offering no obvious unified image. Nonetheless, he typifies participants in scores of self-described Dutchman bands, practitioners of a musical genre that has dominated the hinterlands of central Wisconsin, southern Minnesota, the eastern Dakotas, northeastern Iowa, and northwestern Illinois for more than fifty years. The increasing commodification of twentieth-century American entertainment has effected the transformation of Upper Midwestern immigrant and ethnic ensembles from town bands and informal local combos to professional touring polka bands. The ballroom, radio, television, and recording studio have become standard venues for such bands as they claim a regional corner of a national entertainment industry. Bands like Brian Brueggen's have accordingly adopted a kind of strategic planning in selecting their instrumentation, repertoire, and style of play; their name and promotional rhetoric; and the look of their clothing, publicity photographs, LP covers, and other graphic materials.

These choices are intended to create an image which will at once retain a narrow in-group following and attract a broad segment of the region's public. Dutchman bands in the Upper Midwest typically strike a precarious balance between exclusivity and inclusion, between the marginal and the mainstream, by manipulating appropriate symbols. The symbols are invariably musical, verbal, and visual; each draws upon lineal, temporal, and spatial domains; and each indicates some musical, verbal, or visual stance along an axis between polar oppositions. Lineal affiliation is emphasized, expanded, obscured, feigned, or denied as bands variously stress a single, or dual, or generic, or would-be, or absent ethnicity. Temporally, bands present themselves as archaic or contemporary, as old-time or modern, as rooted in the nineteenth century or spawned by the twentieth. Spatially, they appear as rural or urban, local or regional, regional or national. Social space is no less important than geographical as the bands declare themselves uncouth or sophisticated, rowdy or respectable, familiar or distant. Since several musical, verbal, and visual symbols from each domain are expressed simultaneously, it is not surprising that the images bands project are not only complex but also more often fluid and ambiguous than consistent. Indeed Dutchman bands exemplify a sometimes bewildering interplay of ethnicity and pluralism shaped by regional and national forces across five generations.

Dutchman bands trace their musical lineage to the Upper Midwest's nineteenth-century German-speaking immigrants, with considerable debts to Czech- or Bohemian-American neighbors and to the ferment of pluralistic regional life. At the genre's center is a rhythm section anchored by an "oompahing" tuba and martial drums over which a concertina push-pulls dance melodies. Dutchman bands often build around this basic concertina-tuba sound, dubbed "concertina oompah," with combinations of harmonizing brass and reeds.[3]

The tuba (or "brass bass" or "bass horn") and assorted trumpets, saxophones, and clarinets stem from larger town and church bands which practiced regularly throughout the year for performances at summer picnics and concerts. Paralleling this public community tradition was that of private neighborhood house parties where smaller, quieter ensembles held forth. The button accordion and, especially, the concertina were often at the center of house-party music, since a capable concertina player could produce rhythmic chording with the left hand while articulating a reedy melody reminiscent of clarinets and saxophones with the right. Concertinas were often supported by some informal combination of violins, guitars, trumpets, saxophones, or clarinets.

The synthesis of concert-band and house-party traditions into a musical style was an evolutionary process that happened throughout the rural Upper Midwest in the early decades of this century, but its most influential practitioners were "Whoopee John" Wilfahrt and Harold Loeffelmacher, both based in New Ulm, Minnesota.[4] Wilfahrt (1893–1961) began playing concertina in 1912 for weddings and house dances with a brother on clarinet and a neighbor on trumpet. A few years later he had a ten-piece band; by the mid-1920s, with regular radio shows emanating from Minnesota's Twin Cities and 78s issued by Okeh, Columbia, and Brunswick, Wilfahrt was playing in regional dance halls nearly every night of the year. A consummate showman, Whoopee John was noted for spectacularly stretching and twisting the concertina overhead, while his deft playing established it as *the* solo voice in Dutchman bands. Meanwhile, thanks to the forceful, imaginative playing of Harold Loeffelmacher (1905–1987), the tuba abandoned the staid metric background role it occupied in town bands to achieve a romping, improvisatory, occasional lead status.

The dance tunes favored by Dutchman bands, like the genre's instrumentation, owe their lineage to Germany and Central Europe where polkas, waltzes, schottisches, marches, and laendlers emerged as the nineteenth century's vernacular dances. Such tunes must also be rendered in a way that musicians—like concertinist Dan Gruetzmacher of Wausau,

Wisconsin—regard as essentially German, with a touch of Czech. His comments typify Dutchman partisans who have little use for differing but related styles.

> Germans have the real old way of playing, with an old-time repertoire you can sing German to. Germans set the standard. They emphasize the melody, they accent the basses more, their notes are clearer. A real concertina player goes for the Dutchman or the German style. The poorer concertina players, they go for the Polish style. The Polish drag notes and blur melodies. Slovenians drag the first bass; they make the first note long and the rest short. Bohemian music emphasizes a constant, heavy melody. Dutchman and Bohemian music get along because of a love of melody.[5]

In short, the Dutchman instrumental style is exemplified by a "German" emphasis on melody, straightforward square rhythms, and round true notes.

Conforming to this old-world aesthetic, singers articulate a clear melody through measured phrasing. Vocals in German and a "stage Dutch" Germanized English were common in the 1920s and 1930s, and after a hiatus in the 1940s have been heard once again over the past thirty-five years. In either parlance, subjects range from exuberant and sentimental tributes regarding wanderings through an old country "heimat" to goofy bibulous paeans of festivity.

Not surprisingly, however, World War II and its immediate aftermath curtailed German and dialect vocals, although musicians like Whoopee John continued to punctuate tunes with yodelesque falsetto whoops and a guttural "Ach Ja!" Wisconsin bandleader Syl Groeschl of Calumetville, a fourth-generation German-American who grew up speaking German, recalled a near-beating in the 1940s when using his mother tongue in a restaurant.[6] English singing assumed primacy thereafter, although presently most have reasserted the genre's linguistic heritage with at least an occasional song in German.

The influence of World War II on the Dutchman genre indicates that its practitioners were hardly hermetically sealed in ethnic enclaves. Indeed, the German and—to a lesser extent—the Bohemian and the more generalized alpine elements of Dutchman music have been incorporating musical features of varying lineage ever since the genre's emergence in the 1920s. Dutchman bands and their audiences might be rooted in rural communities settled by central Europeans, but those communities also included numerous Anglo-Celts and Scandinavians. Many a young Irishman or Norwegian was inspired by the music of his Dutchman neighbors, and more than a few joined Dutchman bands. The surnames of

Whoopee John's 1920 sidemen, for example, were Bauer, Domier, Stueber, and Wilfahrt, but players named Anderson, Boyle, Bundy, Greggory, Rice, and Stephenson sat in over the next thirty-five years. The audiences of Dutchman bands were likewise mixed. Meanwhile, both musicians and audiences listened to extra-regional bands via radio, recordings, and concerts at Upper Midwestern ballrooms and county fairs. Such regional and national forces compelled many Dutchman bands to broaden their instrumentation and repertoire. Innovations, however, were incremental rather than radical, and were congruent with continuing forces of cultural interchange in the Upper Midwest.

The four-string or tenor banjo appeared in Dutchman ensembles as early as 1930, and is prominent in the recordings of both Wilfahrt and Loeffelmacher. In the hands of some players, it interjected a "Dixieland" feeling into Dutchman rhythms. African-American in origin, it contributed rhythm to the nationally popular hot jazz of black bands in the 1920s and early 1930s. But the banjo had also been appropriated nearly a century earlier by white minstrel show performers whose northern tours helped establish the banjo in the Upper Midwest. Though commonly regarded since the nineteenth century as an American instrument, the banjo was widely adopted in the region by Norwegians who typically combined it with fiddle and piano. Dutchman bands favoring the banjo have chiefly been located in southern Minnesota and western Wisconsin, areas settled by a mixture of German and Norwegian immigrants.

In similar fashion, an array of Scandinavian dance tunes entered the Dutchman playlist by the late 1930s, and there they have remained ever since. While an occasional Nordic hambo might require esoteric steps, the bulk of Norwegian and Swedish tunes in Dutchman repertoires were polkas, waltzes, and schottisches ("Hasselby Steppen Polka," "Lordagsvalsen," "Lingonberry Schottische")—dance forms familiar to all central and northern European ethnics.[7] Nor were Dutchman bands unaffected by the round- and square-dance forms of Yankee and Anglo-Canadian Upper Midwesterners. The twin-tempoed "Rye Waltz," a couple dance derived from the Scottish "Coming Through the Rye," has long been as popular as the "zweifacher" piece "Herr Schmidt." And few Dutchman bands play a job without calling a set of circle two-steps and other "mixers" with elements of contra and square dances. New Ulm, Minnesota's Fezz Fritsche, for example, placed German specialty dance tunes like "Lott Ist Tot" and "The Finger Dance" alongside Anglo-Celtic favorites of the square dance crowd on *An Album of Waltz Quadrilles and Other Old Tyme Folk Dances*.[8]

Country (or "county and western") music has likewise had a sustained effect on Upper Midwestern ethnics since the late 1920s when many were moved by its powerful sound and working-class themes, chiefly disseminated through radio and recordings, and they formed stringbands combining "hillbilly" music with their own "foreign" repertoires.[9] Dutchmen have performed country tunes since at least the 1940s, some interjecting a guitar. Standard Dutchman instrumentation, however, has lent itself more easily to another form promulgated through the popular media, big-band jazz. Young players in the 1930s, like New Ulm trombonist Babe Wagner, were schooled in the Dutchman tradition but captivated by African-American approaches to the same instruments. Wagner toured with jazz drummer Gene Krupa in the 1940s before returning home to form Babe Wagner's Dutchmen. Dutchman bands for nearly half a century have included an occasional big-band or "modern" set amidst their "old-time" offerings.

Their approach to jazz tunes, as with tunes borrowed from other genres, is typified by underlying Dutchman stylistic preferences, though some bands change instrumentation slightly to accommodate the bigband sound. The Jolly Lumberjacks and the Sota Band of Minnesota and Wisconsin's Shamrock Band all featured a bass horn player who could shift to string bass on the "modern" set. Since many Dutchman sidemen are adept on both brass and reeds, a typical wind section of two trumpets and two clarinets can be transformed into three saxes and a muted trumpet, while the drummer exchanges sticks for brushes, to deliver slow foxtrots ("Stardust," "Careless," "My Funny Valentine") in an approximation of the 1940s dance-band sound.

Despite these shifts in instrumentation, there is no difficulty distinguishing a Dutchman rendition of this material from the original item. Retaining their basic adherence to melody, Dutchman improvisation is restricted to grace notes and runs; extended improvised solos are quite rare. Dutchmen seldom play the jazzier "swing" repertoire, but concentrate on the so-called "Mickey Mouse" popular tunes of the 1930s and '40s: tunes with "modern" chord progressions and fluid melodies that allow Dutchman bands to play in an "old-time" German manner emphasizing the melody.[10]

"Old-time" and "modern" are important designations in the Dutchman world. Bands like that of Erwin Suess play "strictly old-time," while others like that of John Check offer "old-time and modern" in roughly equal measures. Declarations of musical lineage, the terms fundamentally refer to time. Indeed, the musical flexibility of the Dutchman genre has an obvious temporal dimension that is mirrored in the dialectic between ethnicity and pluralism, between region and nation, between conservatism and innovation.

But not all change has come from without. Ever since Whoopee John and Harold Loeffelmacher established the genre, Dutchman music has had numerous innovators whose chief inspiration has come from within the tradition and whose genius has been to create, in Brian Brueggen's deft phrase, "an old-time flavor with a lot of drive." To mention only a few: in the 1950s, Elmer Scheid of New Ulm seized upon the Bohemian technique of antiphony between brass and reeds to distinguish his "hoolerie" sound; in the 1970s, Ray Dorschner of Menasha, Wisconsin, energized standard Dutchman arrangements with accents, dynamics, and subtle interplay by a front line that switched instruments constantly; in the 1980s, young virtuoso concertina players like Karl Hartwich, Brian Brueggen, and Kevin Liss have brought that instrument to the fore.

Meanwhile the button accordion, paradoxically, has come into fashion by virtue of its antiquity. Edged out by the more versatile concertina as the Dutchman genre's chosen squeezebox, the button accordion had largely disappeared from public performance by the 1920s. During the 1970s—a period of ethnic revivalism throughout the United States—it had been rediscovered by many bands, often to fulfill the audience's demands. Wisconsin bandleader Jerry Schneider:

> We run into this many times at dance jobs we play. A fellow will bring one to the job. And he'll say, "My grandpa, this was my grandpa's button accordion. Why don't you play a tune on it? I just want to hear how it sounds." So we do it, you know. And the guy just smiles. It brings a lot of smiles to his face because he heard his grandpa play it years ago, but then it sat there for probably thirty years or so.[11]

New songs and tunes have also entered the Dutchman repertoire from Germany and Austria as bands and their followers travel on packaged tours to the Munich Oktoberfest, the Black Forest, or the Austrian Tyrol. Acquisitions like "Das Kufstein Lied" or "Schneewalzer" simultaneously reinvoke lineal connections to Europe *and* align the past with the present.

They also condense space. The old-time musical features of the Dutchman genre superimpose central Europe over the Upper Midwest on participants' cognitive maps. Country and modern elements in combination with old-time do likewise with the national and the regional. Social space is no less important than geographical. While instrumentation and repertoire assert place, musical style articulates both distance and familiarity.

Town bandsmen in the past sat in chairs and scanned sheet music on raised stages and bandstands for formal concerts with a predetermined program, while house-party musicians jostled with revelers and figured out in their heads what music to play as they went along. The former stressed the elevated, ceremonial, professional status of the musician as possessor of secret knowledge; the latter emphasized the egalitarian musical capacities of Everyman. Some contemporary Dutchman heirs like Ivan Kahle seem most comfortable astride chairs atop a stage with eyes fixed on books of arrangements. In contrast, Ray Dorschner's band is compelled to stand, move around, even stride into the audience; Ernie Coopman frets about tumbling off stages and would rather play on ground level; Karl Hartwich plays chiefly by ear and invariably challenges his sidemen, in jam-session fashion, to recognize a given tune from its initial notes.

The names of bands reveal that the lineal, temporal, and spatial aspects of Dutchman music are as complex as their musical counterparts. The central word "Dutchman" was bestowed on the genre almost accidentally by Harold Loeffelmacher, well after its musical emergence as a distinctive style. The group he formed in the early 1930s was called variously the Broadway Band and the Continental Band, but such urban, cosmopolitan tags didn't move his rural, regional audiences and it wasn't until Loeffelmacher tried Six Fat Dutchmen that his career accelerated. It apparently mattered little that the band generally numbered more than six musicians, that few of them were fat, and that not all of them were even Dutchmen—Six Fat Dutchmen somehow caught the roly-poly old-time ethnic contours of the region's most popular dance music. And while the immediate appearance of bands calling themselves the Eight Dutchboys, the Jolly Dutchboys, and the Skinny Dutchmen might have suggested mere opportunism, scores of self-labeled Dutchman bands persisted. Some used the word in their band's official name, still more used it to supercede less precise descriptive terms like the "Minnesota style," "Whoopee John Music," and "Oompah." Like bluegrass, jazz, and rock and roll, a genre had found its name. And like that nominal triad, the genre's verbal designation not only lagged well behind its musical emergence, but also carried with it a rich and sometimes independent connotative legacy.

The "Dutch" in Dutchman derives from "Deutsch" (i.e., German) and since the colonial era has been applied sloppily by Anglo-Celtic Americans to neighboring New Yorkers from Holland and to the "Pennsylvania Germans" (be they Palatines, Swabians, Alsatians, Hessians, or Swiss).[12] Certainly Dutchman has been in use in the Upper Midwest since the mid-nineteenth century as a blanket term for German speakers from any old-world principality, irrespective of dialect. The chief exception involves the use of "Hollander" or "Holland Dutch" in communities where Netherlanders are numerous. Farther west, nineteenth- and twentieth-century sources reveal that immigrant miners to Colorado from the Austrian and Italian Tyrol were dubbed Dutchmen, while in west-central Texas, Dutchman served as "a contemptuous name applied to any foreigner or even to a disliked native."[13]

Such alien and pejorative connotations are paralleled in an array of compound words in use throughout the United States. The *Dictionary of American Regional English* offers sixty-three entries for Dutch or Dutchman, very few of which are neutral in denotation.[14] Culinary references abound. "Dutch Boiled Dinner" with its dumplings contrasts with "New England Boiled Dinner." A "Dutch Brown" loaf is dark bread, baked longer than in Yankee ovens. "Dutch Loaves" are unusually large, while "Dutch Cakes" are unpalatable unless dunked. The preference of German speakers for supposedly outlandish foods include "Dutch Goose" (stuffed pig stomach), "Dutch Pike" (not the sportsman's pike but the bottom-feeding bullhead), and "Dutch Quail" (a bird "inferior as food"). Similarly distasteful elements may constitute a "Dutch Mess" (any strange concoction of food mixed together), washed down with "Dutch Milk" (beer).

Beer provides "Dutch Courage" (bravery from a bottle) to get the "Dutch" (dander) up, perhaps causing one to speak incomprehensibly in "High Dutch," "Double Dutch," or just plain "Dutch"; or to apply a "Dutch Rub" ("the act of rubbing someone's scalp vigorously, usually with the knuckle as a trick or punishment"); or to administer a "Dutch Kiss" wherein the kisser pinches the ears or butts the head of the kissee. The lexical Dutchman is also "Dutchy" (sloppy, slovenly, dowdy), likely to sleep in a (disarranged) "Dutch Bed," or to cut his foot on a "Dutchman's Razor" (to step in cow manure).

While such terms are artificially combined here, they nonetheless indicate that, from an Anglo-Celtic perspective, America's "Dutch," have long and widely been viewed as foreigners whose food ranges from different to disgusting, whose only beverage is beer, whose personality is volatile, whose speech is unintelligible, and whose appearance and manners are rude. Yet despite its chiefly negative use by outsiders, Dutchman became self-applied by insiders for positive ends. In the nineteenth-century Upper Midwest, for example, Dutchman became a unifying term, an indication of German-Americanism or "Deutschtum" that drew together Pomeranian and Bavarian, Westphalian and Sudetenlander, Lutheran, and Catholic, in a region where Yankees and Dutch often contended in the socio-political realm.[15] A catchall expression of identity for first and succeeding generations of German-Americans, Dutchman was also a safer public appellation than German in view of the two world wars. At least one bandleader, Syl Liebl, changed the name of his band from the Jolly Germans to the neutral Jolly Swiss Boys in the late 1930s.[16] The ambiguous Dutchman served as well for others.

Nowadays this blurred pan-German word from English parlance is often used in equally fuzzy fashion by some third-, fourth-, and fifth-generation musicians to explain their lineage as performers.

> [T]he Dutchman style is pretty much on the Minnesota style, maybe hankering toward the German part of, the edge between Germany and Bavaria. But the music originally came from Holland—really. But it was rewritten over in western Germany and part of it in Bavaria. And that's where you get your Dutchman style out of. But it got very popular here in Minnesota.[17]

This erroneous cartographic pogo-sticking throughout German-speaking Europe and even beyond is paralleled in an article in the polka fanzine, *Music and Dance News*. "Whoopee John" Wilfahrt—whose family actually came from the Sudetenland in present-day southwestern Czechoslovakia near the German and Austrian borders—is said to be descended from grandparents who "migrated from the Austrian Black Forest near Switzerland."[18] In other words, "Dutchman" has come to signify a music to which any Upper Midwesterner of vaguely German heritage might lay a blood claim.

To complicate matters further, the presence of bands led by Scandinavians and Poles—Paulsen's Dutchmen, Don Koloski and the Champion Valley Dutchmen—suggest that musicians irrespective of ethnicity can not only play in Dutchman bands, but can also present themselves to the public as full-fledged Dutchmen without any possibility of contradiction. As the Upper Midwest's dominant indigenous music, the Dutchman sound has attracted all comers in the same way that African-American blues gripped southern whites like Elvis Presley or that country and western attracted black performer Charley Pride. Indeed there currently exist entire bands of Poles (like the Jolly Chaps, the Ray Konkol band, and the Polka Stars, all from Stevens Point, Wisconsin) who work largely in the Dutchman mode. As self-styled Milwaukee Dutchman Ken Megal put it, "The Germans invented the concertina, but it took us Polacks to play it."[19]

Like the Preservation Hall Jazz Band, Johnny Burnette and the Rock and Roll Trio, and the Bluegrass Cardinals, many Dutchman-style bands have incorporated that key term into their official name: Babe Wagner's Dutchmen, Paulsen's Dutchmen, the Ridgeland Dutchmen, Cliff Hermel and the Valley Dutchmen, Brian and the Mississippi Valley Dutchmen, Don Koloski and the Champion Valley Dutchmen, Ray Dorschner and the Rainbow Valley Dutchmen, Harvey Becker and the Riverside Dutchmen; Karl and the Country Dutchmen, Les Schuft and the Country Dutchmen, The Town and Country Dutchmen, Doug Young's River City Dutchmen, The Watertown Dutchmen, the Badger Dutchmen, Bobby Art's Wisconsin Dutchmen, John Check and the Wisconsin Dutchmen, Whoopee Norm Edlebeck and the Dairyland Dutchmen, Erwin Suess and the Hoolerie Dutchmen, Ivan's Jolly Dutchmen, Elmer's Jolly Dutchmen, Roger's Jolly Dutchmen, the Big Fat Dutchman Band, and Harold Loeffelmacher and the Six Fat Dutchmen. Not all Dutchman bands adopt such obvious names, however. Beyond stressing lineage, band names can also situate the genre in time and space.

The profusion of bandleaders' names above, for example, is an extension of nineteenth-century custom for the formation and naming of house-party and town bands. The personnel of house-party bands was fluid and aggregations usually had no set names, although references might be made to prominent and recurrent players ("the Korgers," "Johnny and the boys"). Town bands were primarily associated with a municipality (Ashland, Friestadt, Kiel), but they might be secondarily dubbed the Rott Band or the Eske Band if a particular family or band leader was dominant. Typically, Dutchman bands have a similar core, often several members of an extended family, as well as a roster of sidemen that may shift from one job to another. Bands with compound names are often reduced by their audiences to a leader's or family's name: Brian, John Check, Ray Dorschner, Erwin Suess. Indeed, compound names for Dutchman bands have been rivaled over the past fifty years by groups named solely after a leader or family. To mention just a few: Emil Domier, Melvin Grewe, Christy Hengel, Ivan Kahle, Slim Kalz, Ray Konkol, Glen Moldenhauer, Marv Nissel, the Schroepfers, the Wendingers, Eddie Wilfahrt, Whoopee John, Orville Wog.

Many Dutchman bands evoke their nineteenth-century roots more directly by mentioning their "old-time" repertoire, sometimes pseudo-archaically spelled "tyme," on business cards and fliers. While folklorists commonly associate the term "old-time" with pre-bluegrass Southern string-band music, it probably was applied to music independently in the Upper Midwest where various ethnics had similar designations in their native tongues: "gammaldans" (old-time dance) for Scandinavians, "starogradske pjesme" (old town songs) for Serbs and Croatians. Dutchman bands do strike a balance between past and present, however, by stressing on printed paraphernalia that their "old-time" repertoire is spiced with "modern," "country," "rock," or "variety" selections, but none have followed the new wave titular tactics of neighboring Polish polka bands. Minnesota's Mrozinski Brothers Aleatoric Ensemble has a decided "new age" ring, while Wisconsin's TJB (The Julida Boys) responds to the contemporary vogue for acronyms in the names of rock bands like the DBs, INXS, REM, and XTC.

The conservative chronological stance of Dutchman bands has spatial parallels, for most have situated themselves, at least nominally, in rural, local, and regional milieus ever since Harold Loeffelmacher abandoned his geographical associations with Broadway and the Continent. Their compound names describe a familiar Upper Midwestern landscape of ridges, rivers, valleys, dairying, the country, an occasional town, and the state of Wisconsin. Indeed, practitioners of Dutchman music present as much of a "country" image as their Anglo-Celtic counterparts on the Grand Ole Opry.

Nonetheless, some Dutchman bands, like their "countrypolitan" Nashville brethren, have found secondary ways to stress their cosmopolitan nature. John Check's promotional language emphasizes institutional recognition (he has been inducted into the Concertina Hall of Fame), media success (his Wisconsin Dutchmen are "TV Recording Artists"), and advanced education (his band is comprised mostly of "music teachers"). Sophistication, gentility, and urbanity are underscored by other groups through trademark references to "Bernie Roberts, with Blondie and Her Golden Trumpet"; "the smooth old-time sounds of Ivan Kahle"; "Ray Konkol, with his velvet touch on concertina."

But elevated social status is more often exchanged for, or at least mitigated by, down-home familiarity. Most bands are fronted by fellows whose preference for diminutives, abbreviations, and nicknames suggest that they want to be pals: Bobby, Christy, Eddie; Doug, Marv, Ray; Babe, Slim, and Whoopee. The music stands of Emil (Dumpfy) Domier's 1930s New Ulm band were even emblazoned with the sidemen's nicknames: Shorty, Stuff, Swede, and Lefty. And those maintaining such proper names as Harold (Loeffelmacher) are paired with sobriquets that reveal they are also Fat, Jolly, or plain Big.

Once named, a band must develop a trademark stage presence to assert a visual dimension. Dutchman groups combine musical and verbal imagery with visual strategies of self-presentation. Band leaders give a good deal of thought to their choice of costume; to the use, design, and decoration of music stands and bass drumheads adorned with initials, logos, drawings, or painted pictures; and to the stylized gestures and body language affected while playing. Beyond the visual elements integrally connected to actual performance, such trappings of the bands' commercial operations as business cards, letterheads, schedules, record jackets, buses, and trailers often use graphics designed to evoke the desired Dutchman image.

Refinements of visual self-presentation, like their musical and verbal counterparts, developed gradually. A chronology of publicity photographs of the Whoopee John Orchestra is instructive. In the early, less formal house-party ensembles, band members tended to wear ordinary "dress up" clothes, as seen in a 1914 photo of the Hans Wilfahrt Trio—before Hans had become the famous "Whoopee John" (figure 2). The flat floral backdrop situates the musicians in a photographer's studio, their rural origins betrayed by the frumpiness of their Sunday-go-to-meeting clothes and their solid footwear—suitable for the barnyard.[20]

By 1920 (figure 3), Wilfahrt had abandoned house-party attire for an alternative regional musical identity appropriate to a six-piece town band. The Wilfahrt group appears in band uniforms—caps with narrow visors and floppy bow ties. Their dress, vaguely evocative of military garb, also presents an ethnic, although not a peasant, image: that of the sophisticated but merry burghers of a central European town.

By 1926 (figure 4), the band had assumed still more of the accoutrements of professionalism with an image further emphasizing the sophisticated and urbane European. Garbed in formal wear emblazoned on the chest pocket with a "W," presumably for Wilfahrt, they stand before a painted backdrop depicting a manicured European park, while a similar scene adorns the bass drumhead. The entire tableau might have been conceived for *Koenig und Kaiser* (king and emperor) in Vienna.

Another metamorphosis is evident in the Wilfahrt image of 1935 (figure 5). The popular appeal of the classy European orchestra has apparently waned, while the concertina-playing bandleader's persona has become emblematic of the entire orchestra. No longer the sophisticated Hans Wilfahrt, he is the ridiculous "Whoopee John," a nickname attributed to his exhilarated rhythmic whooping at strategic musical moments. Clad in the lederhosen and jaeger's hat of the stock Bavarian villager (despite his own family's Sudetenland origins), the portly Whoopee John performed lively antics on stage: spinning his concertina by the neck strap in a swooping arc above his head, or parading without an instrument, stomach protruding, in front of the band.

Figure 2. Hans ("Whoopee John") Wilfahrt Trio, 1914. Courtesy Christy Hengel and LaVern Rippley.

Figure 3. Wilfahrt Band, 1920. Courtesy Christy Hengel and LaVern Rippley.

Figure 4. Wilfahrt Band, 1926. Courtesy Christy Hengel and LaVern Rippley.

Figure 5. "Whoopee John" Band, 1935. Courtesy Christy Hengel and LaVern Rippley.

Visually Wilfahrt came to epitomize the humorous stereotype of a German or German-American rube, a classic "Dutchman," an Upper Midwestern old-timer analogous to his comic contemporary, the Grand Ole Opry's banjo-banging Kentuckian, Grandpa Jones. The stereotypical image was paralleled and emulated by others. Harold Loeffelmacher's bus sported a cartoon "Fat Dutchman" whose striped pants barely contained sumptuous rolls of fat and whose flat, wide-brimmed peasant hat doubtless concealed a hairless pate. Meanwhile Ray Dorschner's business cards, band schedules, and recordings have variously featured a diminutive, rotund Dutchman saxophonist clad in too-small formal clothing and a stingy-brimmed derby (figure 6).

Yet such comic presentations have invariably been tempered with mainstream urbanity. Music stands might be painted with a caricature of Whoopee John Wilfahrt's comic persona, but they also suggested the musical literacy of popular jazz dance bands. The sidemen's business suits lent additional sophistication. By the 1940s, the Whoopee John persona had become so well known that Wilfahrt could appear in ordinary dress, relying on his jaeger's hat and a goofy conductor's gesture to convey the Whoopee alter ego (figure 7).

Figure 6. "Dutchman" logo of Ray Dorschner and the Rainbow Valley Dutchmen. Courtesy Ray Dorschner.

Indeed, ever since the evolution of Hans Wilfahrt into Whoopee John, many Dutchman bands have carefully maintained a visual balance between the ethnic clown and the American sophisticate. In 1930 (figure 8), the John Fritsche Band donned the striped jackets and bow ties of a collegiate "Dixieland" band. Yet Harold Tastel, flourishing his concertina "about a mile," evoked Whoopee John. Nearly six decades later, Erwin Suess's Hoolerie Dutchmen (figure 9, lower right), perched behind music stands and surrounded by squeezeboxes, incongruously top off formal attire with alpine hats.

While still vital to the immediate heirs of Whoopee John, the visual dialectic between big-band urbanity and German-American rubishness has not been as relevant to musical Dutchmen born in the 1950s and 1960s. By then, the big-band sound had been dislodged on the national scene by rock and country. Favoring the latter, the young Dutchman "stars" of today—Karl Hartwich, Kevin Liss, Brian Brueggen—sport blue jeans in simultaneous reference to their rural origins and their

Figure 7. Whoopee John Wilfahrt in the 1940s. Courtesy Christy Hengel and LaVern Rippley.

generation's preference for comfortable dress. Hartwich, the leader of the Country Dutchmen, titled his first pair of LPs *Down on the Farm*, with covers decorated with cartoon pigs lolling in corn. Hartwich, Liss, and Brueggen likewise play by ear, eschewing the formalities of painted music stands and books of arrangements for a casual look. In tune with their times, Hartwich, Liss, and Brueggen nonetheless hearken back to Whoopee John and Dutchmen of old through concertina-stretching antics and the omnipresent plumed jaeger's hat.

Ethnic and country images are further synthesized in the vests favored by many Dutchman bands. Solid red, white, black, or blue vests may also be decorated with embroidery to suggest an unidentifiable ethnic background. Vests may also be cut in cowboy style, with darts and synthetic fringe, and combined with western bolo ties. These uniforms closely resemble the vests of organized dancing groups like the Polka Lovers Klub of America (figure 10), thus linking musicians and dancers within a larger polka subculture. At the same time, such costumes also approach

Figure 8. John Fritsche Band, 1930. Courtesy Christy Hengel and LaVern Rippley.

square-dance attire. Indeed, both polka and square-dance regalia is commonly sold by mail-order houses that set up shop at larger polka festivals.

While these visual permutations of the Dutchman image are the most common, more are possible. In April 1989 we witnessed Ernie Coopman, former leader of the Jolly Brewers, with his current band, the Stagemen. Encircled by concertinas, Coopman wore a two-toned snap-brim cap of the sort favored on golf courses, and a blue satiny vest with white fringe. Perplexed, we asked Ernie if he was trying to look like a golfing German cowboy. He thought for a few seconds, grinned, and reckoned "That's us. Just like our music, there's something for everybody."[21]

That the musical, verbal, and visual images projected by practitioners of the Dutchman genre have stressed present-oriented pluralism as often as they have backwards-looking ethnicity should come as no surprise to those familiar with the Upper Midwest. Upper Midwestern culture has

Figure 9. An array of Dutchman record jackets. Photo by James P. Leary.

not been dominated historically by an Anglo-Celtic majority; it has been and remains more of an amalgam of the particular Northern and Central Europeans who settled the region in the nineteenth century. Like the youthful "part mutt" Brian Brueggen, Upper Midwesterners, even to the fifth and sixth generation, are intensely conscious of ethnicity—their own and others'. And, like Brueggen, whose Dutchman sensibilities combine "an old-time flavor with a lot of drive," they are active participants in shaping the cultural life of their rural region.

Although a few Upper Midwesterners seek to rediscover, revive, preserve, and promote "pure" ethnic culture from a re-created old-world region, most are content with overlapping boundaries, with evolutions and combinations that have emerged in their pluralistic region. Like Cornish pasties, Norwegian pickled herring, Bohemian kolaches, Swiss cheese, Polish sausage, Ojibwa wild rice, and Italian spaghetti, the Dutchman genre (the musical equivalent of sauerkraut, bratwurst, and beer) is recognized and appreciated by Upper Midwesterners for its intrinsic

Figure 10. Members of the Polka Lovers Klub of America (P.O.L.K.A.), 1985. Photo by James P. Leary.

German qualities. Yet it can also be made and consumed by everyone, on diverse occasions, for a myriad of reasons, and its "recipe" is not fixed.

Notes to Chapter 2

1. Brian Brueggen, tape-recorded interview by James P. Leary and Richard March, Evansville, Wisconsin, April 30, 1988.

2. For an introduction to the European-American musical mix in the region, see James P. Leary, "Old Time Music in Northern Wisconsin," *American Music* 2:1 (1984): 71–87.

3. The Dutchman genre is sketched alongside Slovenian, Polish, and Bohemian polka styles by Richard March, "Music of Midwest Polka Bands Comes in Four Ethnic Flavors," *The Folklife of the Upper Midwest* 4:2 (1988): 4–7; *Ach Ya! Traditional German-American Music from Wisconsin*, volume 3 in the Wisconsin Folklife Center's ethnic series, provides an aural introduction.

4. These pioneers are finally receiving their due from scholars. Although La Vern Rippley's survey of German bands in New Ulm, Minnesota, with special

attention to Wilfahrt and Loeffelmacher, remains unpublished, Kip Lornell's "The Early Career of Whoopee John Wilfart" appears in the *JEMF Quarterly* 21:75–76 (1989): 51–58.,

5. Dan Gruetzmacher, tape-recorded interview by Philip V. Bohlman for the Wisconsin Folklife Center, Wausau, Wisconsin, February 28, 1985.

6. Syl Groeschl, tape-recorded interview by James P. Leary, Calumetville, Wisconsin, August 13, 1985.

7. The Scandinavian standards mentioned were all recorded by the Whoopee John Band in a session for Decca at Chicago, September 19, 1939; see Richard K. Spottswood, *Ethnic Music on Records: A Discography of Commercial Ethnic Recordings Produced in the United States, 1894 to 1942* (Urbana: University of Illinois Press, 1990) vol. I, 275.

8. *Fezz Fritsche's Oom-Pah Style*, FM Record Co. 333–336, ca. 1950.

9. For an overlapping treatment, see James P. Leary, "Ethnic Country Music on Superior's South Shore," *JEMF Quarterly* 19:72 (1983): 219–30.

10. Francis McMahon, tape-recorded interview by Richard March and James P. Leary, Madison, Wisconsin, May 9, 1988.

11. Jerry Schneider, tape-recorded interview by James P. Leary, Appleton, Wisconsin, May 4, 1988.

12. Don Yoder, "Pennsylvania Germans," in *Harvard Encyclopedia of American Ethnic Groups*, edited by Stephan Thernstrom (Cambridge: Harvard University Press, 1980), 770.

13. Carolyn Bancroft, "Folklore of the Central City District, Colorado," *California Folklore Quarterly* 4 (1945): 317; H. L. Mencken, *The American Language*, Supplement Two (New York: Alfred Knopf, 1948), 219.

14. Chief Editor Frederick G. Cassidy of the University of Wisconsin kindly allowed us access to materials compiled for volume 2 of the *Dictionary of American Regional English* (Cambridge: Harvard University Press, forthcoming).

15. Contention between Germans and Yankees in Wisconsin is a common theme throughout LaVern J. Rippley's *The Immigrant Experience in Wisconsin* (Boston: Twayne Publishers, 1985); Chapter Four, "The Post-Civil War Period," treats particularly heated disputes over parochial schools and liquor laws. For an earlier study, see Joseph Schafer's four-part series, "The Yankee and the Teuton in Wisconsin," *Wisconsin Magazine of History* 6 (1922–1923).

16. Regarding musical exchanges between Wisconsin's Swiss Germans and Germans, see James P. Leary, *Yodeling in Dairyland* (Mount Horeb: Wisconsin Folk Museum, 1991).

17. Mel Knaack, tape-recorded interview by James P. Leary, Watertown, Wisconsin, March 27, 1985.

18. Pat Watters, "Whoopee John Wilfahrt," *Music and Dance News* 14:49 (1977): 6–7.

19. Ken Megal, tape-recorded interview by James P. Leary, Milwaukee, Wisconsin, April 11, 1985.

20. Historical photographs of Wilfahrt and other Minnesota German bands were originally published in the *Old Timers Picture Album* (Mankato, Minnesota: Katolight Corporation, ca. 1972).

21. Ernie Coopman, field notes of informal interview by James P. Leary and Richard March, Hollandale, Wisconsin, April 15, 1989.

3. "I Gave Him a Cake":
An Interpretation of Two
Italian-American Weddings*

JANET S. THEOPHANO

In the study of American ethnic groups, food has been viewed, like language, as an indicator of the degree to which the group has retained or shed its culture of origin.[1] In fact, it has been argued that food is one of the last aspects of culture to be discarded, that food is particularly resistant to change.[2] In this view, the presence or absence of a food item, dish, or recipe on a particular occasion may indicate the continuity of culture or its breach. Conversely, the presence of an item of food from the so-called dominant culture seems an intrusion.[3]

This account of two Italian-American weddings departs from these perspectives in several ways. The study sought to discover not only patterns of food use, but the principles by which meals and events are constructed in the organization of one family. This view therefore moves away from *food items* as the focus of study to the system of beliefs, values, and ideas about food and social life that organize any event.[4]

These life-cycle events were not studied in isolation; rather, I observed the whole fabric of everyday life in which these rituals were embedded.

*I would like to thank Karen Curtis for the historical data in the paper, which is the result of her thorough and meticulous documentation of the history and development of the community. I am deeply grateful to Jeffrey Shultz for his careful, lucid, critical comments; without him the paper would not have this form. Michael Owen Jones also read and commented on the paper. His wise suggestions have been incorporated and gratefully so.

Together, both ritual and mundane enter into the family's food system, and it is only through knowledge of both that either can be understood. I could not have interpreted the significance of the two occasions I describe had I not participated in the everyday life of the family.[5]

The interpretations I provide are my own. I derive them from stories and conversations that occurred before and after the events I portray. Wherever possible, I use the words of the women and their families or, at the least, paraphrases of statements and conversations about their activities. Because of the continuity of my relationship with members of the community, my analyses have been read and sometimes changed by corrections they have made. But in the final analysis, this interpretation is based on delicately balancing conscious statements and beliefs with the additional desires, fears, or concerns that I infer motivated family members' actions. In the words of Janice Radway, who has constructed an analysis of women's reading of romance novels, I moved back and forth "between the readers' perceptions of themselves and their activities and a more distant view of them that makes an effort to include the unseen cultural ground or set of assumptions upon which they stand."[6]

Though the food patterns of a wider network were observed and recorded, this account focuses on one woman, Marcella Fiore. It is, after all, *individuals* who create, change, and continue a culture. A woman in her fifties now, Marcella has thick, wavy, silver-colored hair framing large brown eyes. Her brows have never been thinned and are dark, setting off her expressive, lively face. Her features are generous in proportion, her smile wide. She had dieted on and off for years, but is, by her own account, still somewhat overweight.

Marcella is a prominent member of the Italian-American community of Maryton, a small suburban town in the northeastern United States. At the turn of the century, residents of Maida, Calabria, in southern Italy were imported to the town, which was then inhabited primarily by people of English and Welsh background. The Italians' task was to work the stone quarry and do construction for one man who owned a large asbestos plant. The industrialist so controlled the town that the Italians were not permitted to live near the original residents. Instead, they were segregated by the railroad tracks, forced to live in poor housing, often without indoor plumbing. For two generations they were required to remain apart.

Finally the industrialist lost power, and the Italians who had previously lived on the margins of the town were able to move to other, more desirable locations—yet they chose to live, again, close to other Italian families. At the time of their arrival, their propinquity to one another had been imposed, yet there is little doubt that much of their interaction was voluntary, for it afforded companionship in a strange world. Later, when mobility might have encouraged separation, they chose, once again, to remain close to one another spatially and socially.

This community is the center of Marcella's world. It is no coincidence that Marcella herself stands at the center of a large network of family and friends. These range from the mayor to the sisters at the convent and include local merchants, fellow choir members, and bingo and "girls' club" friends. She is also one of six siblings, each of whom is married with children and grandchildren. In addition, many cousins, aunts, and uncles live nearby.

Marcella has a widespread reputation as a traditional cook. Many people in the Italian community rely on Marcella's expertise and knowledge of traditional cooking, and she uses food as gifts and as payment in an unending bond of reciprocity. Over the years the Italian residents of Maryton have developed, among other cultural forms, a shared food system, which though changing is still perpetuated. Basically there are two components to the system: an Italian meal called "gravy" composed of macaroni and tomato sauce combined in many forms, and an American "platter" or serving of meat, starch, and vegetable. This dual meal system has been elaborated into several festive formats which are considered appropriate celebratory meals for calendrical and life-cycle events.[7]

Life-cycle events are usually celebrated with a "buffet" consisting of multiple dishes from the American and the Italian repertoires. A typical buffet might present meatballs in "gravy" (red sauce), American and Italian cold cuts, Italian bread, potato salad, coleslaw, Jello molds, and an assortment of desserts.

An exception to this pairing of buffet format and life-cycle event is the wedding. Since it is the most formal of the occasions, the wedding requires a "sit-down dinner" for all of the guests. The content of the celebratory meals may vary from occasion to occasion and from family to family, but the expectation of the appropriate mode of celebration remains.

Because of these shared expectations, even the most subtle changes in the presentation of the food are statements about what is going on. As I reviewed the circumstances of each of the weddings of Marcella's daughters, which had at first seemed unusual, I began to see the significance of the food choices and the meaning of these events for Marcella and her family, the messages she conveyed to them through food.

Like other cultural idioms, food is multivalent; only in particular contexts does meaning emerge.[8] Though it may carry the symbolic load of ethnicity, food may also be a vehicle for expressing other issues and concerns, such as the nature of relationships within the ethnic group. In these cases, food was used by Marcella to signify her changing roles, her relationships to her family and community, and her identity as a woman in an Italian-American family.

Marcella and Pat Fiore have three daughters. Within a three-year period, the middle child, Jeanette, and the eldest, Roxanne, both married. But during this period, the family underwent several dramatic changes. Marcella expressed the nature of these social transformations in the mode for which she is noted — food.

Jeanette, the first to marry, had an Italian wedding. Only Italian foods prepared by Marcella and her sisters appeared at the wedding meal. Sandwiches made with provolone and pepperoni, baccala (dried cod) salad, and Italian salads were served with Italian bread and rolls. Three years later Roxanne was married. Her formal dinner featured "English" foods:[9] veal cordon bleu, green beans with almonds, and baked potatoes. As with the first wedding, Marcella's choices were deliberate and meaningful. Why did Marcella want an all-Italian meal for her middle daughter's wedding but an "English" meal for the eldest's marriage? I was especially puzzled when I remembered Marcella's comment that Roxanne's husband wanted to marry, in his words, "an old-fashioned Italian girl," and they had been introduced on that basis. Knowing Marcella's life situation provided me with some clues. I felt the answers could be found in the interpersonal dynamics of the family and Marcella's relationships with her daughters and her husband, who in the years between the two marriages had asked for a divorce.

On a Saturday in November 1976, Jeanette Fiore married John Peterson. She was then eighteen years old. She chose a young man, a non-Italian, who was regarded as irresponsible. Marcella said: "He won't be any kind of husband to Jeanette, or a father to her children." Many in the Italian community were skeptical about the match, but Jeanette was adamant. She said, "We love each other and we want to marry." Since the marriage was not sanctioned by Pat or Marcella, the wedding itself became a matter of controversy. Despite this, the family and community wished to demonstrate their support and provide a joyous celebration for the couple. They hoped for the best.

They decided to have the wedding reception at home. It would be small: about a hundred people were invited. The ceremony would take place in the chapel at church with only family members present.

Further, Marcella was adamant about the wedding meal. She decided that she would serve nothing but Italian foods. "I wanted to have all Italian, no American or English food." She prepared the wedding meal herself with the help of her sisters and presented it in the old-fashioned way.

The reception took place in the Fiore home in the late afternoon. Marcella served provolone and pepperoni sandwiches, without mayonnaise,[10] presented in clothes baskets in the traditional way. Accompanying the sandwiches were baccala salad, antipasto, tossed Italian salad, and Italian bread and rolls. No potato, macaroni salad, or coleslaw was served. There was a "bar" with wine, beer, and mixed drinks. A tray of cookies bought from a well-known Italian bakery in Philadelphia provided dessert. Such trays include pizzelles,[11] pepper cookies, fruit-filled cookies, and macaroons, among others, and are served at all significant life-cycle and calendrical events.

The wedding thus featured traditional foods, but the format was a marked departure from that of most wedding celebrations in the community. The wedding meal was pointedly not a sit-down dinner, which is requisite to this life-cycle event and indicates its importance.

In contrast to Jeanette's wedding, the marriage of Roxanne to Robert D'Amico provides an illuminating comparison. In May of 1979, Roxanne married a young Italian policeman whose home is in Philadelphia. Their courtship began when Robert asked a friend if he knew any "old-fashioned Italian girls." He was introduced to Roxanne. The two soon became engaged and plans were made for their wedding during the engagement period, which lasted a full year. By this time Jeanette's marriage had ended, and she was struggling to earn a livelihood and care for her young son. Marcella's twenty-five-year marriage to Pat had also ended. She had been stunned by his abandonment of her and their family.

The full financial responsibility for the family fell to Marcella. The economic stress was complicated by Jeanette's situation. Nonetheless, Marcella decided that her eldest daughter would have an elegant wedding; every aspect of it would be the best it could be. The groom's father, with whom the newly married couple would live, offered financial assistance to Marcella. She refused. Though she had no idea how she would pay for the wedding, she felt it her responsibility to assume the financial burden. Often she said, "I'm doing this wedding the American way, where the bride's family pays for it. The Italian way is to have each family pay for half."

Eventually Marcella accepted Mr. D'Amico's offer to help with some of the costs of invitations and other paraphernalia. The rest of the wedding expense was hers.

Formal invitations were mailed to almost two hundred people. The marriage ceremony was a High Mass followed by a reception at an elegant, expensive, nearby country club. The bride and bridesmaids were dressed in fashionable and elaborate gowns and carried bouquets of silk flowers. Nearly everyone who was invited attended.

For weeks before the wedding, friends and family prepared dozens and dozens of cookies. Marcella had decided that the customary "two large trays of cookies on either side of the wedding cake" was not a good idea. The reason she offered was that in such situations not everyone had a choice of the best cookies. Especially if the cookies were bought at a bakery, the finest cookies were only a single layer on top of the inexpensive variety. People had a habit of selecting the best and leaving the remains for those who followed. She wanted everyone to have a choice of all the cookies, and so decided that a tray of cookies would be placed at each table. Family and friends worked for three days to assemble the cookie trays, which were decorated with sugar-coated almonds and silver thread.

The wedding cake was an elaborate confectionery. A local bakery prepared the alternating layers of Italian cream cake and chocolate-chip pound cake. The groom had wanted the first, the bride the latter. The cake consisted of three pedestals, each with three tiers. The three sections were joined by a plastic ramp which held miniature figures of the wedding party. Underneath the central section was a fountain which splashed pink liquid.

The cake was reminiscent of the elaborateness of the ice sculptures of the formal dinners of another era. Importantly, the cake was decorated by Jeanette, who had learned the art of cake decorating at the local bakery. It took five hours to decorate and assemble it the night before the wedding.

The banquet room of the country club was the site of the wedding meal. The dining tables were arranged in a large circle to leave the center of the room free for dancing. The head table was placed in front of a large window overlooking the grounds. In front of the head table was the cake. The groom's family was seated to the right; the bride's family to the left. The menu, chosen by Marcella, included veal cordon bleu, accompanied by green beans with almonds and "scooped baked potatoes with cheese." A fruit cup would begin the meal, followed by a Caesar salad. Dessert was a strawberry parfait. The meal was not atypical of that offered and served by many catering establishments.

Marcella's reasoning was that veal was expensive and elegant and that the dish itself was unusual. One of the tacit rules of eating behavior in this community is that "eating out" is something special, and choices made on those occasions are of dishes that are not served in the home.

The groom would have preferred an Italian meal. Marcella was resolute that if she were paying for the meal then she would select an exotic menu.

While the bride and groom received the guests, there was an "open bar" and cheese and crackers were served. Following the wedding dinner, the guests were able to select drinks of any variety. Once again the emphasis was on extravagance. Marcella was careful about her decisions; the primary criterion was quality; cost was disregarded. Pat Fiore was involved only in that he "walked his daughter down the aisle." He was not invited to the wedding dinner. Members of his family were invited, although many of them did not attend.

At the wedding, people said, "This is Marcella's wedding." And it was. In many senses, this was the beginning of a new life for Marcella. She was no longer married. For her, this was a disillusionment and a personal tragedy but simultaneously what she considered freedom from the tyranny of marriage. In her efforts to provide the finest wedding she could, she was also acknowledging her new status. Further, Marcella was communicating something to her husband and the community. The wedding was a matter of pride. As she put it, "I can make it on my own. I don't need help from Pat. God has always taken care of me and He will provide now." After mourning the loss of her husband and their marriage, her bitterness now emerged as hope. She submerged her own disappointments with marriage and glorified the occasion in order to show that she had not lost her faith, her hope, or her belief in the cultural values with which she had been raised.

One of the central themes of both weddings had to do with the threat to traditional values that each situation engendered. Though the weddings stand in marked contrast to one another, they share a common concern with the stability of the community and the continuity of a way of life.

Superficially, the weddings seem to have different meanings. One might even interpret the variation between the two events as signifying the loss of ethnic identity. One might assume that Marcella and her family had somehow relinquished the values of their parents in favor of "American culture." At the first wedding, the meal and the presentation of the food were "traditional." Three years later the Italian fare seemed rejected for an American menu and a standardized caterer's format.

Viewing the two weddings as members of a single class of events might engender such an interpretation, but a closer look suggests otherwise. Only in contrasting the two weddings do Marcella's food choices become meaningful.

In the first case, Jeanette married a non-Italian. By itself, this choice—in today's world—was not significant. However, her choice of a mate was not approved. Family and friends were concerned that the marriage would not last. John's behavior was perceived as that of a child. He was not responsible. And he would not be responsible in the ways which Marcella felt were important. He would not be a good husband or father. To Marcella, marriage signifies the acceptance of responsibility of adult life. Her daughter's happiness was important, her well-being a concern. Marcella expressed those concerns through her choice of foods and the structure of the occasion.

Not only was her family threatened by the intrusion of a "stranger," but her family's relationship to the group and the group's values were threatened as well. By selecting Italian foods in a situation of potential embarrassment and vulnerability, she was affirming the very values which were threatened. Her refusal to permit anything "English" to be used in the celebration of her daughter's wedding was an attempt to shun and reject not only the male who violated her family's honor and boundaries, but the culture with which he was identified. By drawing her family into an intimate and bounded group at this time, she protected the sanctity of the family domain. Only the family would witness the marriage itself; only close friends would be invited to celebrate the occasion.

The format which Marcella chose, the buffet—"the old way"—was both an affirmation of a way of life and, simultaneously, a marker of the lower status accorded to this event, given the format usually reserved for the wedding meal: "the sit-down dinner."

A "sit-down dinner" for a large number of guests is a prestigious and expensive occasion. In some ways it is an American ideal, both the creation of caterers' institutions and an ideal conception of the American way of life. It signifies wealth, success, and achievement as well as communion. Without a meal of such prestige, Jeanette's wedding was glossed as hurried, unplanned, and lacking the joyousness of this event, which theoretically should be the pinnacle of a young man's and woman's life.

Jeanette's wedding took on added importance at another level; it was a celebration of traditional values and an affirmation of continuity for the celebrants. Marcella protected her world by circumscribing the boundaries clearly, marking them with the food that represented her world, the culture of her parents' generation.

Roxanne's marriage responded to a violation of another sort, one from within. It was the dissolution of her own marriage that Marcella confronted in the wedding of her eldest daughter.

Roxanne married an Italian, who had himself articulated in his search for a woman his respect for "traditional" values. Their lives were to be guided by Robert's father. The bride and groom were an approved match.

Roxanne's and Robert's wedding celebration marked the beginning of that union and the end of another, that of Pat and Marcella. Marcella's choice of the prestigious and normative "sit-down dinner" at an elegant location outside of the home was an acknowledgment that her eldest daughter had married with her approval and married well. Her choice of the expensive and elaborate meal, though "English," was not an expression of distance from Italian culture, but a statement of her independence and pride. In conforming to the standard format of such occasions, and in choosing the finest meal available, she showed the community that she could and would continue to care for herself and her family without the support of a husband. No breach would occur in their lives because of his leaving. She would give him no satisfaction watching her struggle.

For the rest, the marriage was as it should be. With no threat to the community or its values, there was no need to mark the boundaries of the group. Adherence to the shared community pattern affirmed the appropriateness of this occasion and the choices Marcella had made.

The weddings of both Jeanette and Roxanne Fiore dealt with the issues of male abrogation of responsibility and the threat to the values and membership of the culture group. In the first case, the violation was perpetrated by an "outsider"; in the second case the dishonor came from within. In both instances Marcella expressed her concerns and those voiced by the community through her manipulation of the food system. She used common understandings of the meanings of foods and the structure of events to underscore and amplify the community's knowledge of these events and her feelings about them.

The use of food in these two contrastive but similar occasions suggests that food contributes to the creation of meaningful social discourse. Clifford Geertz has said that "cultural forms can be treated as texts, as imaginative works built out of social materials."[12] Food is one of culture's most redundant and pervasive materials. It has the capacity to communicate, in any one event, many layers of meaning. The particular interpretations given to such cultural texts are dependent upon the "readers," in this case the participants in these ritual events.

What was being expressed in these weddings had not only to do with weddings and the institution of marriage, or even with Italian weddings and marriages, but with the affirmation and acceptance of one woman's changing relationship to her family and society. There is an expression in the Italian community which means that someone got his dues, his comeuppance. Marcella felt that both Pat Fiore and John Peterson got what they deserved: she "gave them a cake."

Notes to Chapter 3

1. This perspective assumes that immigrant or ethnic groups are stable, bounded, and homogeneous enclaves living in relation to a dominant society. It also presumes that culture change is unidirectional and irrevocable; that groups of people will eventually merge with the cultural mainstream. See, for instance, Milton M. Gordon, *Assimilation in American Life* (New York: Oxford University Press, 1964). The influence of these ideas is apparent in Nathan Glazer and Daniel P. Moynihan's *Ethnicity: Theory and Experience* (Cambridge: Harvard University Press, 1975).

2. Melford Spiro, "The Acculturation of American Ethnic Groups," *American Anthropologist* 57 (1955): 1240–52.

3. Concurrent with these foci has been the assumption that the meaning of the food inheres within the item itself. For example, spaghetti with tomato sauce is accepted as part of the Italian diet. According to this perspective, then, the serving and eating of this dish by Italians signifies an identification with Italian culture. This view assumes not only that food carries meaning intrinsically, but that it carries one primary meaning, that of continuity for the culture group.

4. McKim Marriott, "Caste Ranking and Food Transactions" in *Structure and Change in Indian Society*, edited by Milton Singer and Abner Cohen (Chicago: Aldine-Atherton, 1968).

5. Fieldwork was carried out jointly with Karen Curtis, Department of Anthropology, Temple University. The principal investigator was Dr. Judith G. Goode, Chairman, Department of Urban Studies and Associate Professor, Anthropology Department, Temple University. Funding was provided by the Russell Sage Foundation, New York, under the directorship of Dr. Mary Douglas. The research was conducted from December until June 1979. Four families were observed, each for a period of one or two months. We spent from morning until bedtime, each day, observing and recording the food and eating behavior of the families. This involved participating in shopping, visiting, mealtimes, and special occasions. The fieldwork experience gave us the opportunity to observe domestic life in all its facets; we asked questions and were asked many in return. We observed, recorded, and talked about daily occurrences and, in particular, the role that food played in the lives of the people with whom we stayed. Pseudonyms have been used for the name of the town and for the names of family members.

6. Janice A. Radway, *Reading the Romance: Women, Patriarchy, and Popular Literature* (Chapel Hill: University of North Carolina Press, 1984), 10.

7. Janet S. Theophano, "It's Really Tomato Sauce, but We Call It Gravy," unpublished doctoral dissertation, Department of Folklore and Folklife, University of Pennsylvania, 1982, contains a more detailed account of these issues.

8. Arjun Appadurai, "Gastro-Politics in Hindu South Asia," *American Ethnologist* 8 (1981), 494–511.

9. Although the food served at Roxanne's wedding could best be described as "continental" or "French," it is referred to here as "English" or "American," the terms used interchangeably by Marcella and others in the community to refer to non-Italian foods.

10. Mayonnaise is considered American or English food. Newly immigrated Italians reportedly refuse to eat it.

11. A pizzelle is a type of Italian cookie. In Italian, the word is pluralized as "pizzelli" or "pisselli," but in this community the plural is Anglicized and pronounced "pizzelles."

12. Clifford Geertz, *The Interpretation of Cultures* (New York: Basic Books, 1973).

4. On the Tail of the Lion:
Approaches to Cross-Cultural Fieldwork with Chinese-Americans in New York

MADELINE SLOVENZ-LOW

The relationship between ethnographers and the subjects they study has become of considerable interest among folklorists. Questioning the ideal of remaining objective and distant from the persons with whom they interact, folklorists have begun to examine how their own identities and roles shape the fieldwork process. In ethnic studies, for example, it has been commonplace to argue that mutual understanding could occur only when the ethnic identities of researcher and subject matched. African-American scholars, it was asserted, would be best at interpreting the complex histories and cultures of their own communities, as would Mexican-American researchers, Native American scholars, and so on. In the 1960s and 1970s, Ukrainian Robert Klymasz studied Ukrainian ethnicity in Canada; Herminia Menzez, a Filipino, studied the folklore of her people; Robert Georges studied Greeks; Stephen Stern conducted fieldwork among his fellow Jews. Other folklorists married into ethnic families and became "honorary" ethnics: Barre Toelken studied the Navajo; Kenneth Thigpen wrote on Romanian-Americans; and Elizabeth Mathias observed Italian-American customs in the United States.

The ambiguous status of "adopted" ethnic researcher, which has resulted from my marrying a Chinese-American, is only one of many roles I have had to accommodate to during my fieldwork. In the span of my research on Chinese lion dancing in New York (1986 through 1989), I went from curious observer to culture broker to adopted daughter and martial arts student to sympathetic partner. Through most of this period I was acutely aware of the differences in our cultures and especially concerned about how those whom I studied would perceive my work. I would continue to live and work as a folklorist in the same city as the people I studied, and it was important to me that they recognize themselves in my writing. However, my delicate position, situated precariously between folklorist and adopted ethnic, has created controversy over my authority to represent the Chinese I have studied and threatened both my status within the Chinese community and my husband's.

Entering the Field as an Outsider Looking In

My first experience at fieldwork among Chinese-Americans was in New York City in 1986 studying the Lunar New Year lion dance street processions. Chinese lion dancing is a vigorous cultural performance that virtually fills the streets of New York City's Chinatown each Lunar New Year; more than a dozen different organizations conduct concurrent processions that travel from door to door throughout the Chinese business community. To the accompaniment of drum, gong, and cymbals, each group follows its own route bringing good luck blessings in the form of lion dances (as well as dragon and *ka-lun* dances[1]). As the processions progress, the event becomes completely enshrouded in smoke as firecrackers explode continuously to scare away evil spirits that may be lingering from the old year. The firecrackers are also effective in keeping tourists and casual curiosity seekers at bay. In previous years I had never been a fan of this event because the firecrackers seemed dangerous and the lion dance performances appeared inarticulate and reckless, but something changed my attitude.

On February 9, 1986, the first day of the New Year, a group of about fifteen students, led by New York University's Professor Barbara Kirshenblatt-Gimblett, trekked down to Chinatown to observe the street celebrations. This was one of several scheduled field visits required in a course titled "The Aesthetics of Everyday Life." We arrived at the Wai Jow Association[2] on East Broadway at 11 o'clock in the morning to note how this group celebrated the New Year. Professor Kirshenblatt-Gimblett had arranged for two Chinese-American high school students to be our guides, and they suggested that ten students go inside Wai Jow to the second floor to watch the preparations in the small, crowded meeting room. I was thrilled to be among those allowed to go inside. It is rare for non-Chinese to be invited into the private rooms of Chinese benevolent associations.

Once inside I had mixed feelings: pleased to have the privilege of being on the "inside" and embarrassed to be part of a group of intruders who did not blend in. This was far from my first encounter with cross-cultural fieldwork, but it was the first time I had made initial contact as a member of a large group. There were no formal introductions, no welcoming gestures, in fact, as far as we could tell, we were ignored. More than a year later, I learned that the room was buzzing with questions about who we were and who had invited us, but since no one seemed interested in us, and because everyone was speaking Hakka and Cantonese, we did not know about their concerns.

The room was a combination meeting hall and game room adorned for the occasion with glittering Christmas decorations. The mah-jongg tables were pushed back to clear the space. The room was filled with Chinese men, a few with families. The atmosphere was casual. People mingled, drank coffee, ate pastries, and smoked cigarettes. A small group of musicians played loud percussive music on drum, gong, and huge cymbals. It was deafening. There was no way to communicate easily. We stood around not sure what we might observe.

A large ornately painted beast with papier-mâché head and multicolored silk body was laid out in the middle of the floor. We learned later it was a *ka-lun*, not a lion as we had originally thought. Once the *ka-lun* was stretched out and placed in the middle of the floor, the mood shifted to a state of attentiveness and anticipation as people jockeyed for a good viewing position on each side of it. Someone broke out a box of cotton and started to pass it around to those who wanted to plug their ears for protection from the firecrackers. A member of the association passed the cotton to our group. At last we were acknowledged and included in the action. A few of the men started to pass long flagpoles out the window to the street below. This must have signaled the police, because two uniformed officers came up to the meeting room to inquire if the group was ready to leave. They were assured the time was near.

The musicians shifted to a different rhythm and two young men, one taking the tail and another taking the head, swung the *ka-lun* three times around like a jump rope. On the third rotation they deftly maneuvered it up and over, and in one broad gesture covered their bodies. After a short interlude of energetic character dancing in which the *ka-lun* consumed a head of lettuce and a red envelope, the *ka-lun* dancers gushed forward, sweeping the beast's head from side to side. Suddenly, they turned and disappeared around a corner. I attempted to follow; but one of the men gestured for me to stop.

Most of the observers went downstairs and out onto the street. Eventually, the *ka-lun* descended the main staircase and exited the building. By the time the beast was on the street, there was such a huge display of firecrackers outside that those of us who had followed were trapped inside the doorway. Through the glass door we tried to see the dancing on the street, but the smoke was too dense. Each time we opened the door we quickly shut it. Firecrackers were hanging in a long string from the fire escape above and someone was lowering them as they exploded. It was frustrating not to be able to see, but exhilarating to be frightened by the firecrackers. I was unprepared for the impact of that day's events. I felt like a child again—terrified, but loving every minute of it.

By the time the firecrackers stopped, the *ka-lun* was heading down the street. The creature, tattered and burned by all the firecrackers, looked small and insignificant.

As the *ka-lun* traveled from door to door performing a simple blessing in exchange for a red envelope containing money, each shopkeeper gave it a send-off with a generous display of firecrackers. When one landed on my foot, rather than shake it off, I left it there to see what it felt like. It felt good. The music, the explosions, the smoke dominated my consciousness. The dancers became "my" dancers. There was magic in the air. I felt as if I had gone native, as impossible as that may be. At the time, I had no idea how much more true that statement would become. In fact, now, whenever I see a *ka-lun* or lion dance performed without the accompaniment of firecrackers it feels ritually incomplete.

At the end of the day one of the more outspoken members of the *ka-lun* group suggested that we might return the following Sunday. That individual was Jim Low, the man who would become my husband. All day he had gone out of his way to offer tips for observing the event. Although he appeared to be a self-appointed tour guide, I learned later his martial arts master had appointed him. When our group had arrived at Wai Jow and people asked why a group of foreigners was present, the martial arts master Wan Chi Ming said he had granted permission for the visit. He turned to Jim and said in Cantonese: "You are the public relations person, relate." Jim was invaluable in helping us understand the event. He told us New Year is a fifteen-day celebration. This was only the first day. He said next week the festivities would be bigger and his group would be going out with lions instead of the *ka-lun*. He assured us there would be more to see. I was thrilled that there would be another opportunity to view the festivities. The event was celebrated with a kind of passion that fascinated me, so I took him up on the suggestion and assembled a group of colleagues to design a team approach to studying and documenting the event. We returned the following Sunday.

Jim agreed to subsequent interviews and gave me his phone number. He was a willing and generous consultant. Seven months after our first meeting on the streets of Chinatown during the New Year celebrations, Jim and I began seeing each other socially. A year and a half later we became engaged. As a consequence of these events, there has been a profound blending of my personal life and professional concerns. Jim's deep passion for the lion and *ka-lun* dance traditions has become part of my life, and my intense academic interest in these customs has become his concern. This close relationship has been a tremendous asset in gaining deeper access to the field, but it also has many drawbacks and has created obstacles that would not ordinarily occur in a strictly professional relationship.

Taking a Role in the Field as Culture Broker and Researcher

Shortly after the 1986 Lunar New Year, a program coordinator at the New York Historical Society asked me to help hire a lion dance group for a public program planned in conjunction with an upcoming exhibition of photographs of ethnic celebrations in New York City. A series of contacts led me to kung fu master Sifu Yee Ji Wai, who was generous with his time and permitted me to interview and photograph his students as well as to join him and his senior students for their regular Saturday morning tea at a local restaurant.

Up to this point, formal information about Chinese martial arts had been carefully parceled out, although sometimes I was permitted to observe practice sessions and attend functions with various groups. It was always at the more informal activities, such as traveling to an event or enjoying a meal at a local restaurant, when valuable information was revealed. At these more casual meetings, a person's guard was usually down, talk was free, and much of the social fabric of lion dance and martial arts was exhibited.[3] For example, a sense of competition and rivalry was apparent when dancers made comparative evaluations of their work against that of others. If protocol had been breached during a performance, rules were disclosed when elders instructed the offending students. In order to do my research, I had to spend a great deal of time hanging out, observing, and listening to idle talk, much of which amounted to gossip. Though there are rules that martial artists must not boast about themselves or belittle others, and that they should uphold the honor of their "adopted" kung fu families, private talk gave evidence to the contrary. Material gathered in this way often helped me formulate questions that I would present to the group, or it could be combined with other information to develop a line of inquiry and shift my perspective.

Take the shopkeeper's role in this event as an example. The lion dance is usually viewed as entertaining and is believed to have ritual efficacy. Shopkeepers throw firecrackers at the feet of the dancers, who are expected to dance for as long as they are exploding. This is a sign of the group's respect for the proprietor and at the same time a demonstration of the members' fearlessness. In exchange for this performance, the shopkeeper gives the group money in a lucky red envelope; in return, the group gives him a printed card. Some display the card bearing the group's name as a public indication of the transaction. If store owners want to underscore their relationship with a particular group, they can provide a grand display of firecrackers or create a puzzle for the dancers to solve. The shopkeeper's role in this event is essential to the continuance of lion dancing at New Year, and how enthusiastically these businesspeople embrace the tradition affects the potency and vitality of the performance.

By observing the New Year procession from inside one of the shops, I discovered that the shopkeepers are perhaps the dancers' harshest critics. Though most stores are closed to the public during the processions, they are open to other members of the business community, and it is customary for the local shopkeepers to visit each other during the festivities and drink toasts to each other. Invariably they discuss the quality of the dancing in the streets; an unfavorable review can have a direct effect on how much money is placed in the envelopes.

Also underlying the excitement of New Year processions is the potential for violence. It is a well-known fact that there are youth gangs in Chinatown, usually connected to adult organizations, which are responsible for widespread extortion in the business community and for dividing the neighborhood into territories. Since some gang members are also students of martial arts and lion dance, the possibility of rivals meeting during this highly charged festive occasion adds a dimension of danger that the event could erupt into total chaos if ritual protocol is not faithfully observed.

One might conclude that the lion dancers' roaming from door to door in search of payment is an institutionalization of patterns of extortion. My findings indicate this is not true. One dance group that has performed in Chinatown for many years refuses to accept payment from some proprietors. The *sifu* (master) said he had been asked by some proprietors to assign some of his students to hang around their shops and provide physical protection in case of gang trouble. Although the proprietors offered handsome sums of money for these services, the *sifu* did not want his students to participate in street fights or expose them to other problems associated with illegal activities. He performed the customary dance and left without accepting a red envelope.

As I got deeper into the social, political, economic, and ritual dimensions of the Lunar New Year lion dances, I began to realize I was gathering information not usually made public. By establishing a wide base of individuals—kung fu masters and students, shopkeepers, police, tong members, and youth gang members—I was able to recognize further complexities in this cultural performance.

My role changed as well. When I was asked to contribute to *The Drama Review*,[4] a performance studies journal, I felt obliged to go back to the people with whom I had spoken and clarify my intentions. Previously, I had been cast as insignificant. Being a woman and not Chinese, I was so far outside the martial arts culture that I was not seen as someone of much consequence.

Yee put no restrictions on the material we had discussed. Jim Low asked only that I use his Chinese name, Lau Doc Keun. Another key figure, Sifu Chan Fai of the Pak Hok (White Crane) School, also allowed me to quote him. In fact, he later inquired if I would consider helping him write a book about lion dancing. Those agreeable to being quoted, who continued consulting with me, were estimating, I think, that they might gain wider recognition as performers or as authorities by appearing in print. This had not been the case with everyone, however. Some community members thought my interest in the social and political aspects of lion dancing and martial arts was inappropriate. Others asked me to assign them pseudonyms in some cases because they had made references to powerful tongs[5] engaged in gambling and extortion. One police officer, with whom I had originally spoken "off the record," denied having said certain things about the informal power structures in Chinatown. He told me if I wanted to quote him I would have to use new statements.

Moving Inside as a Martial Arts Student and Adopted Daughter

Knowledge of lion dancing is acquired through training in, and practice of, Chinese kung fu. In fact, for the martial artists who work the lion, the performance is a demonstration of kung fu skills more than it is a dance. Every move and stance the performers take has its basis in the Chinese fighting arts. It became evident that if I wanted to continue learning more about this Chinese-American performance complex, I had to find a teacher to accept me.

Some kung fu schools featured regular classes open to beginners that I could have attended, but those were not schools deeply committed to maintaining lion dance traditions. The Wan Chi Ming School, of which Jim Low was a member, had the reputation of upholding strict discipline and training in the traditional ways. Some distinguished this school as closed to outsiders. Although I did see a couple of participants in the lion dance procession who were not Chinese, that association was predominantly male and not easily accessible to non-Chinese since admission is by invitation. A member may introduce a non-Chinese candidate, but it is the member's responsibility to apprise the initiate of Chinese customs and behavior expected of students. I thought that if Wan Chi Ming were to accept me as a student, I would have to abandon my role as ethnographer. As a novice student in a strict traditional organization I would not have the freedom to be also its chronicler; that role is the sole privilege of the masters designated as "torch bearers."

After deciding not to pursue membership in three other schools for various reasons, I thought of one more possibility. When I had first visited the Mission Church on Henry Street, Sifu Yee was out of town, and an elderly Chinese man of elfin quality was occupying the premises. Through gestures and Father Kwang's rough translation, he told me that he was very sad. "In China," he said, "I am a famous *sifu*. But here in New York, I am a lowly dishwasher."[6] He tilted his head down slightly and with his forefingers gracefully traced a pattern of tears falling from his eyes. When I asked why he did not start a school, he said, "It takes a lot of money. You must pay the 'Mafia.' "[7] When Father Kwang told him I was researching lion dancing, he said, "The year is not a lot of days, but a wild animal. A star made the lion to meet the year and tame it."[8] I felt a connection with this man, though I did not know his name. In my fieldnotes I called him Mr. Chen. As it turned out, Chen Tai Shan is the name his *sifu* had given him. Our meeting was brief, but it had a lasting effect on me. Chen was the man who would become my martial arts teacher and adopted father and take the role of matchmaker at my wedding.

Through contact with a member of another martial arts association, Sherwin Chow, I learned that Chen Tai Shan was starting his own school to teach Tibetan Lama and Choi Li Fut styles of kung fu. Yee had moved to a new location, leaving the space at the Mission available for Sifu Chen. Chow urged me to visit Chen. He said I should not worry about the problem of our language difference. There were some students fluent in Chinese and English who were going to help Chen with translating. Since our first meeting, I had often thought about Chen. If he would accept me as a student I could observe firsthand how a school is established from the beginning. When I approached him, Chen remembered our brief meeting, smiled, and agreed to teach me. He told me to return the following day with workout clothes.

My meetings with Chen were more than kung fu lessons. He lived in the basement of the Mission, where he taught and had established a traditional Chinese medical practice. After evening lessons, Chen cooked dinner and insisted his students stay to eat with him. During the day he expected me to accompany him on shopping trips through Chinatown. We would always stop for lunch or a snack and inevitably he introduced me to people in the restaurant. Clearly accepting my dual role as academic researcher and kung fu student, he introduced me as a graduate student who was studying lion dance traditions. He seemed proud to have a scholar as his companion.

Kung fu entails many hours of diligent practice and because I was mainly concerned with the overall culture of martial arts, I gradually spent more time in activities peripheral to training. However, I cherish my extended relationship with Chen. He is an exceptional man with many talents. In addition to introducing me to his biological family, he created roles for me in his professional life. He included me as an assistant in his medical practice and has taken me with him to meetings of the Chinese Herbalists Association. He even made me his assistant when he practiced *feng shui* (Chinese geomancy).

When Chen formally adopted me, he visited my father to make his intentions known. My family was receptive to his visit and has welcomed him on subsequent occasions. But this kind of close relationship has built-in problems for continuing fieldwork in a small community like that of Chinatown's martial arts enthusiasts. As a member of a particular school, I no longer had the privilege of traveling freely from one school to another.

Chen moved to Canada and lived there for almost a year. During that time we corresponded and spoke on the phone. Since his return to New York, I have spent very little time with him, although our relationship is still deep. He gave Jim and me his blessing on our marriage, and like a father he instructed us to perform certain rituals on our wedding night. He acted as our matchmaker when Jim's emissaries came to my parents' home to bargain for my bride price. Over time, Chen became more of a relative than my kung fu teacher. The gap between fieldwork and my everyday life has been closed by the deepening of my relationships. But from time to time Chen reminds me of my fieldwork. He insists I have a lot to learn about Chinese ways and he often instructs me by telling stories, drawing pictures, or writing letters. Sometimes he has said I am his biographer. He knows I have saved all his letters, many of which describe episodes of his life in China and the difficulties he has encountered as a recent immigrant and kung fu master in New York.

From Insider to Outsider — Mistaken Identities

While I was working with Chen, my social relationship with Jim Low developed. I frequently accompanied Jim when he went to his kung fu school. Sometimes I went only to socialize; other times I went expressly to conduct fieldwork. Although not everyone in the school was informed of my research interests, Sifu Wan Chi Ming was.

The conflict between my stance as a researcher and my identity as Jim's partner eventually reached a crisis point that forced me to reevaluate the circumstances of and my approach to this work. The crisis was provoked by misrepresentation in the Chinese press of a program scheduled at a small branch library in Queens. Through City Lore, Inc., photographer Martha Cooper and I received a grant to create a slide/lecture depicting the Chinese New Year lion dance traditions. We were to present this as a free program at three locations around the city. I worked a brief performance segment into the slide/lecture. Jim Low was the most likely performer to recruit for three reasons: (1) practicality — he performs the Buddha character, a role in the lion dance that can be done solo to recorded music; (2) talent — his characterization has earned him accolades in the Chinese community; (3) poise — he is a confident performer and experienced in responding to questions from an audience.

The crisis arose when a library publicist, using information from a general letter I had sent to the program office months before, mistranslated into Chinese a claim I had made for Jim's expertise in lion dance traditions. The Chinese term she used, *siwong*, is literally "Lion Dance King," implying that Jim was a master of masters. When the officers of the Wan Chi Ming School, where he is a student, read this, they were outraged. They accused him of promoting himself and berated him for not acknowledging his teacher, master Wan Chi Ming. They threatened to stop the lecture if he dared make an appearance.

All this came as a shock to both of us. His only defense was that he had not made such a claim and he did not know how this misunderstanding evolved. As far as he was concerned, he was only helping me out by providing the performance component and making himself available for questions from the audience. To make matters worse, when the press releases were published, I was in the Midwest and would not return until one day before the library engagement. I was horrified when I got word about this problem. After many long-distance calls, I was able to convince the officers of Jim's school that it was a translation error. But there were other unresolved issues about authority and representation as well.

I had some knowledge that the Wan Chi Ming School was organized around a corporate structure with elected officers, but I had never doubted that the highest authority was Wan Chi Ming. Before Martha Cooper started shooting slides for our lecture, I had approached Wan Chi Ming and he gave permission to photograph when the students were practicing kung fu, rehearsing the lion dance, or receiving medical treatment for injuries. For the New Year, he had arranged for Cooper and me to have special passes to allow us inside the barricades for an unobstructed view. He had also granted permission for Cooper to shoot during a private ceremony conducted to ritually "open the eyes" of new lions. I had recorded interviews with Wan Chi Ming, and he had helped me make a recording of music for Jim's performance in the slide program. To let the members of the school see the work we had been doing, we had arranged a slide preview at the school following a regular class session attended by senior students and officers of the organization. We had publicized this event with fliers on the school bulletin board and in the office. After the viewing, we had presented Wan Chi Ming with a picture album in gratitude for the school's cooperation. At no point did I suspect my intentions had not been clear.

However, after the news release was published, the officers of the school claimed that they had no knowledge of my research interests or of the slide lecture. When I emphasized that my negotiations had always been with Wan Chi Ming, they explained that I had approached the wrong authority. Furthermore, since I was not a member of the school, they would not authorize me to represent their organization.

I did not think of myself as a spokesperson for the Wan Chi Ming School, and the slide lecture we had prepared was never intended to be solely about one institution. Our documentation was more broadly based. However, the Wan Chi Ming School was the most photogenic. Its members perform the most complex routines and strictly uphold traditions of ritual and training. Photographically, this school stood out as a superb example through which I could structure a lecture about the entire lion dance performance complex. But no matter how I tried to explain the situation to the officers, I was met with restrained, polite anger. We agreed that I would meet with them and Wan Chi Ming when I returned to New York.

I alerted Steve Zeitlin at City Lore of these developments. Personally, I was emotionally torn because the dilemma generated by this crisis was difficult for Jim. The officers admitted they had no authority over what I did—I was an outsider, they said—but they forbade Jim to appear in the program. They insisted the problem was Jim's because he should have guided me through the proper channels. However, as project director, I knew I had to bear the responsibility. Under the circumstances I had no interest in going on with the program if the problems could not be settled. Zeitlin agreed with me that if the school officials maintained their objection to the program we would not present it.

The night before the scheduled program I brought the slides and a typed script of my lecture to the school. By that time I had drafted a brief commentary illustrating how a simple error in terminology can have grave repercussions in traditional societies such as this kung fu association. I intended this statement not only as a retraction of the published error, but also as a perspective on the material I was presenting to point to issues of authority and representation.

The secretary/treasurer of the school, Steven Lee, listened to the entire script. He said it depicted the traditions with sensitivity and accuracy. He was relieved I had not revealed any secret information. As for the slides, he remembered them from the preview and said there was no problem with them. He suggested I also discuss details with Wan Chi Ming, and if he had no objections, the slide lecture—including Jim's performance—would be authorized.

Just to be sure there was no misunderstanding about the content of the slides, I pointed out a few sequences that Wan Chi Ming might consider too private for a general audience: traditional medicine, ancestor worship, and details of the setup for and rehearsal of a *choi cheung*, a special lion dance routine that is actually a puzzle the dancers must solve. He confirmed these were not a problem. Wan Chi Ming did, however, want to correct the errors made in the newspaper. He said it was all right to call Jim Low a *sifu* because he has earned that title, but *sigung* (meaning grand master) or *siwong* were titles no one, not even he, would dare claim. He accepted the fact that the error was not generated by Jim or me, since one newspaper had used the proper terminology. But in his estimation there was another error that needed to be remedied.

The publicist had taken information from an earlier article I had written[9] in which I mentioned that the range of lion dance performance traditions included occasional gravesite rituals for the dead that required a white lion and white percussion instruments, all of which are burned on the spot after the performance. Wan Chi Ming adamantly denied the practice of such dances and insisted that I never associate his school with discussions of these performances. I accepted his position, but also went back to my original sources to double-check the accuracy of my information. At this writing I can only speculate that this custom may be practiced only by a very small group of people and is rarely discussed outside the group.

Questions of authority and the power of representation are critical issues every fieldworker must face, and they are of paramount concern when working with more than one organization in the same culture area. In such cases it is essential not to confuse information gathered from one group with the customs and beliefs of another. Where we see patterns and similarities among groups, the members of those same groups may see disorder and incongruity. In a slide/lecture, the juxtaposition of an image and commentary carries the weight of association. Using an image from one group to discuss another easily creates false ideas about the subject of the photograph, no matter how well researched the material or how good the intentions of the presenter.

Members of the Wan Chi Ming School never questioned the content of my article that combined photographs of their group with analysis based on work with many different groups. Yet they challenged my plan to create a general discussion about martial arts and lion dancing based predominantly on slides depicting activities of their group, perhaps because the article was in an academic journal. In response to their concerns about the slide lecture, I revised many of my statements to qualify distinctions between what I had learned through my extended research and what I knew to be true for the group pictured.

Four months after the officers of the Wan Chi Ming School had challenged my authority to speak about the results of my research, the tables were turned completely around. The school asked me to write a descriptive narrative about their organization for a grant proposal, and when they agreed to do a public educational program, they asked me to be the speaker and show slides to enhance their demonstration performance. The irony of that situation was that they also insisted I answer the questions from the audience.

The Collaborative Nature of Research

Fieldwork is an intersubjective enterprise in which the object is to acquire knowledge of the Other and eventually make a report on one's findings. It is commonly expected that the report will characterize some aspect of the Other's reality—ideally, from the Other's perspective. But it is easy to lose sight of the fact that these relationships are not static; they are continuously negotiated throughout the research period. Thus, we are unable to identify objectively the hypothetical reality of the Other whom we study. The reality we construct in our analyses and reports is a product of personal interactions, observations, library research, and the act of writing field notes and other documentation. These elements of fieldwork form a tense but shifting web of influences affecting the final product. Most of all, they affect our own lives by enriching them with new experiences and relationships. But these experiences can also be troubling, for they are no less complex than those we have with our own families and friends. But in the field we are obliged to be reflexive about our work and not lose sight of our ever-changing role in the lives of others we study.[10]

In my reports the event is constructed anew. It takes shape based on a combination of observations and experiences. This is true of any ethnographic work. Through representations we create a sense of intimacy with the events and the people involved in them that is not always true to the experience of the moment as it was lived by any one participant. For the reflexive researcher, who is in the field seeing herself seeing the Other, there is a mirror effect that is forever turning in on itself. The experience is something like twisting a kaleidoscope. Each turn poses different possible relationships, but the whole picture is fractured by mirrors reflecting back different parts of what appear to be the same picture. But it never looks quite the same. Each time I was allowed to see the "back regions"[11] of lion dancing and the martial arts performance complex, I learned that there were always regions farther back to which I could never have access.

In Chinatown my identity is located firmly between two positions: those of researcher and of family member. As Jim Low's wife, I am considered a member of his family. In this role I enjoy having extended access to the everyday culture of his kung fu association. In addition to frequent visits to the school and office, I attend numerous performances and social events. There is no "unnaturalness" about this situation, although now I am forced to balance the two sides of my hyphenated identity—folklorist-wife. It is not that I have two identities, or even a new identity, but the distinction between my working life and social life collapsed.

When I began my fieldwork with Chinese-Americans it was easy to distinguish between my personal life and my fieldwork, between subject and object. There were times when the field experience presented situations that forced me to be reflexive about my relationships, but overall I had not taken an academic reflexive attitude toward my work. When my student/teacher relationship with Sifu Chen evolved into a family relationship, and when my social relationship with one of the "folk" turned into marriage plans, my concerns shifted. For a while, I became totally engrossed in my everyday life. Occasions for lion dances and other martial arts activities were no longer events I asked permission to attend and document. They were on my social calendar, often as obligations. Not every cross-cultural/cross-gender fieldwork experience has these particular problems, but they point to fundamental concerns for every fieldworker.

Epilogue

About half an hour before I was to read a paper about my research on Chinese lion dancing at the 1987 American Folklore Society meeting in Baltimore, I stepped into the lobby to read over my paper one more time to ensure it would go smoothly and be within the twenty-minute time limit. I looked up and saw a stout Chinese man walking toward me dressed in a brown three-piece suit. Over one shoulder he carried a Chinese hoe; under his other arm he cradled a large papier-mâché Buddha mask. I thought I would die right there. This was Jim Low, at the time known to me only as a traditional performer and a generous source of information about the customs of Chinese lion dancing in New York City. "I'm going to perform," he said. "I told you I would come down to help you out with your paper, and I keep my word." I thought this was an elaborate joke. This is his style. But, as much as I tried, I could not suppress him.

"Jim, these are twenty-minute papers. We have strict time limits. I can't just insert a performance. I'm reading a paper word-for-word. I've timed it. It's already got slides and a video clip. How can I possibly incorporate a live performance? There is no time. I'm in the next session." I knew, then and there, my fieldwork had gotten out of hand. I did not know whether to laugh or cry.

In spite of my protests, Jim did perform as part of my AFS presentation. As it turned out, there was a logical place for his Buddha dance.

He entered while I read a transcript of his charming narrative myth explaining why there is a Buddha character in the lion dance. The presentation was well received. No one knew it was not planned.

A colleague expressed concern when I told her how successful the session was and how I would consider including folk practitioners in future talks because it emphasizes the collaboration that is at the heart of any fieldwork experience. My colleague retorted, "When the performers are present, they inhibit the way we speak about them. They have no place in the sessions of an academic professional meeting." Certainly a performer's presence at such a session might inhibit critical analyses, but I do not wholly agree. In many cases, such analysis is more valuable if it is expressed in clear terms to those for whom the traditions are most important, and I question whether a public forum is appropriate if it has not already been discussed in the field. As more folklorists work close to home with people who are not geographically remote or insulated from academic concerns, the nature of the collaboration between researchers and those we study needs to be refined and vigilantly attended to. Whether to include performers in paper sessions or lectures is more than a problem of style. And, I do not advocate this approach as the only way to work. But in the case of lion dancing in Chinatown, individuals who have contributed to my research are articulate and willing to extend the basis for our collaboration into the frameworks of representation where their traditions are recontextualized for purposes they had not previously considered.

Notes to Chapter 4

1. Most Chinese-Americans call the *ka-lun* a unicorn; however, according to Ying-Jen Chang ("The Rise of Martial Arts in China and America," Ph.D. diss., New School for Social Research, 1977), the *ka-lun* is a mythological beast for which we have no equivalent English term. The *ka-lun* incorporates the features of a variety of animals and is often mistaken for the southern Chinese lion, although its head and jaw are distinctly smaller and characteristically different.

2. Wai Jow Association is one of three Chinese benevolent societies in New York City's Chinatown which represent those who trace their ancestry from Tai Pang, an area of Guangzhou, China. They speak the Hakka dialect and often use the *ka-lun* in Chinese celebrations to identify themselves as descendants of this area of southern China.

3. The southern Chinese lion dance in New York City's Chinatown is part of the martial arts performance culture. Instruction in the ways of the lion is included in a student's learning; consequently, kung fu schools in Chinatown regard the lion dance as an emblem of the school's strength and skill.

4. Madeline Anita Slovenz, " 'The Year is a Wild Animal': Lion Dancing in Chinatown," *The Drama Review* 31 (Fall 1987): 74–102.

5. The term "tong" carries the connotation of gangster organization and is sometimes used to signify a Chinese "Mafia." In Chinese "tong" simply means meeting hall and constitutes part of the words for Christian church and dining hall.

6. Tai Shan Chen, interview with the author, New York City, March 4, 1986.

7. Ibid.

8. Ibid.

9. Slovenz, "The Year is a Wild Animal," p. 75.

10. James Clifford and George E. Marcus, editors, *Writing Culture: The Poetics and Politics of Ethnography* (Berkeley and Los Angeles: University of California Press, 1986), and George E. Marcus and Michael M. J. Fischer, *Anthropology as Cultural Critique: An Experimental Moment in the Human Sciences* (Chicago and London: The University of Chicago Press, 1986) critically analyze many of the current concerns of fieldwork and ethnographic writing.

11. I have adopted this term from Dean MacCannell's *The Tourist: A New Theory of the Leisure Class* (New York: Schocken Books, 1976).

II.

Symbolic Responses to Ethnic Tensions

5. The Atlanta Child Murders:
A Case Study of Folklore in the Black Community

In the preface to *The Evidence of Things Not Seen*, his book-length essay on the Atlanta child murders, the late African-American author James Baldwin explains his near-obsession with these crimes by claiming, "It has something to do, in my own case, with having once been a Black child in a White country."[1] Seeking to understand the meaning of the seemingly senseless string of twenty-eight homicides that plagued the African-American community of Atlanta, Georgia, during a twenty-two-month span between 1979 and 1981, Baldwin—like other African-Americans struggling to comprehend the crimes—probed beneath the surface of the Atlanta story as reported in the national media to determine if it revealed some disguised agenda. Indeed, his interest in the case was so strong that he was compelled to return to the United States from his self-imposed exile in Paris. In needing to make sense of the case, Baldwin was not alone. African-Americans much closer to Atlanta than Paris shared his preoccupation with this series of unexplained murders.

The fact that these crimes were committed in the city of Atlanta has a special significance. As Baldwin notes, many blacks proudly identify themselves by employing the adage, "I'm not from Georgia. I'm from Atlanta."[2] The city that Sherman burned during the Civil War, the city where Booker T. Washington delivered his conciliatory compromise speech of 1895, the city that was the setting for several of the bitterest civil rights confrontations, had by 1979 emerged as a particularly comfortable environment for blacks. Desegregation efforts had taken well in Atlanta, and black leaders were visible in the city's highest offices. A large middle-class black community thrived in Atlanta. Many African-Americans believed that Atlanta, the home of five black colleges, offered more educational and economic opportunities than any other city, south or north. While rural Georgia was still beset by racial unrest and hostility, Atlanta seemed to exemplify the potential for racial harmony in the "New South."

This seemingly idyllic situation was shattered in 1979 as a growing number of young blacks disappeared, only to be found dead on the south side of Atlanta. During the next year and a half, the number of victims climbed to twenty-eight and non-Atlantans flocked—some with, some without invitation—to the stricken city. Psychics, the Guardian Angels, Frank Sinatra, Muhammad Ali, and Sammy Davis, Jr., all made the news when they offered their talents to Atlanta's black community. With headlines such as "Terror on Atlanta's South Side" and "City of Fear," national news magazines ensured that their readers kept track of the steadily increasing victim count and the law enforcement community's struggle to solve the crimes. Seeing the possibilities for outside exploitation, the families of the victims formed an organization to protect their own stake in the investigation.

Following a period of haphazard surveillance, law enforcement authorities arrested Wayne Williams, a twenty-three-year-old African-American record promoter, and charged him with two counts of homicide. Alternately proclaiming his innocence and taunting the law enforcement community, Williams's hostility, arrogance, and alleged homosexuality further linked him to the murders. His very public trial was marked by dissension between his own legal advisors and his family. Williams was convicted of two of the murders through circumstantial evidence and the investigation of the remaining crimes was closed. In 1985, a highly controversial television docudrama refocused attention on unanswered questions about the case. Doubts about Williams's guilt were expressed by the organization of victims' families and the community at large, but for six years the case remained closed and the records sealed. Mounting pressure from the media and from persistent family members of the victims caused the case to be reopened in June of 1987. At the time of this writing, Williams is still in prison and no other arrests have been made.

The events in Atlanta constituted an obvious crisis for its African-American community. But the crisis was not limited to black Atlantans; its impact was felt by virtually all of those black adults who had been "Black child[ren] in a White country." The degree to which this tragedy moved African-Americans can be seen in their collective efforts to mobilize, in the coping strategies employed by African-Americans outside of Atlanta during and after the crisis, and especially in orally transmitted explanations about the reasons and motives for the deaths.

African-Americans across the country wore green ribbons to sympathize with the victims, and local churches and organizations dispersed information and solicited funds. These efforts were not mere expressions of sympathy. Throughout the crisis, black Americans feared that racist violence might spread to other parts of the country. Black parents worried about their children's anxiety and about the possibility that children outside Atlanta were at risk. Black children in and outside of Atlanta suffered from bad dreams about potential abductions. One female African-American summed up the attitude of most by claiming that the ribbons were a way of "expressing distress." They provided a vehicle through which wearers could nonverbally testify to their concern for the black community's safety; when their daily conversations or activity reflected another interest, the constant presence of the ribbon on the lapel, hat brim, or collar informed the world of their allegiance and their continuing awareness. The ribbons functioned not as signs of helplessness but as tangible symbols of community cohesion.

As the victim list in Atlanta grew, African-American social, political, religious, and cultural groups used their resources to offer support to their members and to the Atlanta families. Bake sales, fashion shows, raffles, and other fund-raising activities raised money for the families in Atlanta and for programs to give children alternatives to playing in the street. Churches, always reservoirs of African-American solidarity and expression, played a key role during this period. Special services were conducted so that individuals could come together and pray for the victims. Most African-American church pulpits became news sources. Community groups held informational sessions at which individuals who had been to Atlanta would offer whatever information they might have to supplement or counter news being circulated through "official" (i.e., white) channels of communication. Participants in these activities recall the sense of well-being and control that came from opportunities to come together in order to "do something" about the crisis. The helpless feelings generated by the increasingly somber reports from the official channels of information were offset by communal attempts to support Atlanta's black families and the nationwide black community as well.

But it is the unofficial, unconfirmed "news" about the murders—in the form of rumor and urban legend—which caused the greatest consternation among African-Americans. Almost simultaneously with the realization that a series of crimes against a segment of the black population was being committed, speculation about the probable assailants and their motives surfaced. What arose was a cycle of stories which accused anti-black groups of a conspiracy to steal black bodies for medical experiments. As one informant claimed, "I remember hearing that the killings in Atlanta were related to [the] genocide of the black race. The Federal Bureau of Investigation (FBI) was responsible and using the bodies for interferon during research at the Centers for Disease Control."

This form of statement most closely resembles the folklore genre of the urban legend. These modern-day narratives exist in multiple versions and are usually told by the narrators as true or at least believable. Rumors, on the other hand, tend to be more open-ended and unspecific and usually lack narrative chronology. For example, a female African-American reported, "I have heard that the killer or killers were not a black man or men. They said the white people wanted to get back at the blacks in Atlanta by killing off young black males and two females." The differences between the two statements reside in the former's specificity of act, agency, and motive. The latter rumor lacks that precision. But these differences are really quite minor in comparison to the consistency of theme and motivation both contain.

In his seminal study of rumor formation, Tamotsu Shibutani has argued that "rumors emerge in ambiguous situations. . . . If the demand for news in a public exceeds the supply made available through institutional channels, rumor construction is likely to occur; . . . the greater the unsatisfied demand for news, the more likely it is that rumors will develop."[3] Clearly the situation in Atlanta was ripe for rumor formation. Neither possible motives nor suspects were positively identified until the count exceeded twenty victims. Anxious for information to augment the inconclusive data being supplied by the investigators, the community sought its own explanations for the ominous events.

Although some informants recalled rumors in which the crimes were attributed to one individual motivated by some sort of sexual perversion, the more popular rumors attributed the crimes to a conspiracy group. Many felt that a theory based on a single murderer was not credible because the crimes did not follow the same *modus operandi*. Different techniques were used to kill the victims; most victims were male but two females were found dead during these months; the youngest victim was seven, while the oldest was in his twenties. Race and the Atlanta setting were the only constants. A more important reason for such rumors was that African-Americans were all too familiar with organized groups whose expressed or implied agenda promoted anti-black activity. White supremacist groups were prime candidates, especially since they had often been accused of assassinating important leaders such as John F. Kennedy, Robert F. Kennedy, Malcolm X, and Martin Luther King even when single individuals were arrested for the crimes. Indeed, in the initial investigation of the homicides, President Jimmy Carter ordered the FBI to investigate the possibility of a conspiracy headed by white supremacists.

The Ku Klux Klan (KKK) was a prime suspect for the murders, as suggested by the narrators of the legend. Organized in Pulaski, Tennessee, circa 1865–1866, the KKK has a long history of anti-black activity.[4] Since that time this oldest of white-supremacist organizations has frequently emerged as a plausible source of conspiracy in Afro-American folklore, especially on the political assassinations of the 1960s. Gladys-Marie Fry has documented this pattern in her germinal book on the use of supernatural phenomenon as a mechanism of racial control.[5] Rumors even circulated that the KKK controlled a fast-food franchise in order to impede black procreativity through one of the menu items.[6]

Since Wayne Williams's incarceration, it has been discovered that one of the prosecution witnesses testified under a pseudonym. This individual had ties to both the KKK and one of the murder victims. Given these circumstances, the notion that the KKK might have been responsible for one or more of the homicides is completely tenable. When the Klan's phoenix-like ability to reinvent itself just when it is presumed impotent is taken into consideration, it seems prudent to be a bit paranoid about the potential of its hostility.

Less common but still popular were a series of rumors and legends that associated the conspiracy with the FBI, the Central Intelligence Agency (CIA), and/or "the American government." Many of these versions contain an additional motif in which the agency in question is collecting the bodies to perform medical experiments on them. The black community's distrust of the FBI can be traced back to the agency's earliest years. Initially it stemmed from J. Edgar Hoover's reluctance to investigate civil rights violations.[7] Under his leadership, the agency came to symbolize all that was unfair about the law enforcement community: it was always anxious to punish black offenders but never willing to investigate or control anti-black violence. With their conservative suits, haircuts, and cars and their penchant for secrecy, the FBI men (almost exclusively white) visually resembled the KKK. Both groups consisted of hand-picked individuals who enthusiastically embraced a code of conduct that protected white citizens while ignoring or denigrating blacks. By the 1960s the FBI had quite clearly demonstrated itself to be Klan-like in its philosophy.

J. Edgar Hoover's reluctance to follow Robert Kennedy's instructions to protect civil rights advocates, and his desire to discredit the Reverend Martin Luther King, Jr., by publicizing information he had secretly gathered about the civil rights leader's sex life, became well known.[8]

The historically uneasy relationship between the FBI and the black community was further strained by the federal agency's approach to the Atlanta investigation, in which the FBI played a leading and quite controversial role. At the close of the Carter administration, the outgoing president called upon the FBI to investigate the Atlanta crimes in conjunction with other seemingly random attacks on blacks throughout the country. Carter specifically asked the FBI to determine if blacks had been conspiracy victims. He told *Ebony Magazine* that "the possibility exists that there is a conspiracy. . . . The FBI is concentrating on that with the utmost diligence and is making regular reports to me. It's hard for me to form an opinion without having actual evidence to base it on. . . . But, yes, the possibility exists that there is a conspiracy."[9] As the list of victims in Atlanta grew, the FBI's attention focused primarily on finding a person or persons responsible for the deaths and less on uncovering an organized local or national conspiracy.

Although the FBI's involvement began with Carter, most of it took place during the first two years of the Reagan administration. With the shift to a Republican administration in 1980, the FBI's investigation increasingly downplayed motivations induced by social tensions. In April of 1981, FBI director William Webster announced that twenty-three of the murders had been "substantially solved." One of the numerous agents assigned to the case said publicly, "Some of those kids were killed by their parents." He claimed that these murders were committed because the children were a "nuisance." These statements infuriated the local Atlanta investigators, and Mayor Maynard Jackson fired off an angry letter to the bureau.

The local Atlanta law enforcement team was led by and composed primarily of a black group of officers, while the outsiders (the FBI) were predominantly white. The two units also feuded on the strength of the evidence that led to Wayne Williams's arrest. Fulton County's District Attorney Lewis Slaton, a native white Atlantan, was reluctant to arrest Williams when the only evidence was circumstantial. His stalling infuriated the FBI. Of course, all of this was played out in the local and national media. In a rather curt response to a letter of inquiry, an FBI public relations spokesman seemed oblivious to the possibility that the agency's behavior might have been perceived as hostile by the black community.

The posture assumed by the FBI throughout this case was perceived as antagonistic by blacks nationwide. By criticizing the local law enforcement community, publicly accusing the victims' own families, and pushing for the arrest of a black suspect, the FBI of the eighties was conforming to the anti-black pattern established during the Hoover dynasty. These factors contributed to the FBI's emergence as a probable suspect in the minds of some black Americans. Attributing the crimes to the FBI resolved the question of why the murders weren't solved to everyone's satisfaction. Discussing another crime that the FBI had failed to quickly resolve, Martin Luther King, Jr., observed, "You can't explain to a Negro why a plane can be bombed and its pieces scattered for miles around and the crime can be solved, but they can't find out who bombed a church."[10] Since the number of homicides in Atlanta was great and evidence was scarce, people felt that the FBI agents had the skills necessary to commit the crimes and to cover their tracks. These rumors also explain why the supposedly all-knowing federal agency was unable to solve the crimes in a definitive fashion.

Unlike the FBI, the CIA had no direct or indirect role in the investigation conducted in Atlanta and, therefore, informants blamed this agency much less frequently than the FBI. Nonetheless, it is possible to understand why the CIA was mentioned. First, the CIA had also been implicated in rumors about the assassinations of black heroes such as JFK, RFK, MLK, and Malcolm X. Many associated the CIA with anti-black activity in the third world. In their dealings with peoples of color, the CIA had been known to plot assassinations, coups, and other violent acts, ostensibly for the good of the United States. It was easy for people to confuse the "division of labor" between domestic and overseas law enforcement; boundaries and jurisdiction issues became irrelevant. It seemed plausible that the CIA would be willing and able to use its special talents to apprehend black Atlantans if the medical community needed the bodies.

Out of these rumors about the possible conspiratorial roles of the KKK, CIA, and FBI, a group of urban legends emerged. Urban legends require the crystallization of public opinion and the perception of a common anxiety. They encapsulate modern anxieties by commenting on the effects of urbanization, mass society, technology, and ethnic relationships. Clearly these Atlanta events constituted a crisis in the black community which was of interest and concern for blacks nationally. In discussing the development of rumors, Shibutani has argued, "Any crisis, however mild, arouses popular excitement and leads to the formation of a *public* consisting of those who are in some way concerned with an event that has disturbed the routine of organized life."[11] The Atlanta situation was sufficiently volatile to evoke mass public sentiment; the "public" (in this case, black Americans both within and outside of Atlanta) was starved for satisfactory news. The relationship between the white conveyors of official news and the public was so laden with mistrust and apprehension that the rumors that emerged still did not supply enough information for many blacks. In turn, the same legends helped mobilize blacks to become a national community in response to these crimes. Rumor theorist Terry A. Knopf argues: "Like hostile beliefs, rumors create a 'common culture' within which leadership, mobilization, and concerted action can occur spontaneously. Crystallizing, confirming, intensifying hostile beliefs while linking them to actual events, rumors often provide the 'proof' necessary for mass mobilization.[12] Once in the public domain, it was natural for rumors about the Atlanta murders to link up with earlier legends about previous instances of racial tension that supported the theme of racially induced crimes involving body parts.

The element of racial and urban tension in the Atlanta stories has close affinity to the well-known "castrated boy" legend in which a child is abducted and castrated in a public setting. Florence Ridley, Barre Toelken, Jan Harold Brunvand, Michael Carroll, and other scholars have collected and reported numerous versions of the urban legend in which a pre-adolescent male is castrated by one or two males of different race in a public rest room.[13] In the oldest variants of this legend, the victim is a non-Jewish boy whose blood is needed by Jews for Passover. In the Atlanta murders, it is whites who need the black body parts or bodies (depending on the version) in order to perfect a particular "miracle" drug.

The adaptation of these motifs into Atlanta lore was no doubt stimulated by the fact that the medical and business community was making the news with stories about interferon, a drug believed at the time to be a major breakthrough in cancer research. Coincidentally, Atlanta is also the home of the Centers for Disease Control (CDC), a major medical research institution. The most common versions of the urban legend that developed from the castrated boy motif allege that the FBI (or CIA or KKK) committed the murders in order to take the bodies to the CDC so that they could be used for interferon experiments.

Like the FBI, the CDC has a history of weak relations with the black population. It was formerly affiliated with the United States Public Health Service, which conducted a destructive experiment from the early 1930s until the early 1970s on a group of adult black males in rural Alabama. Telling the subjects that they had "bad blood," doctors annually examined them in order to observe the effects of untreated syphilis. No comparable experiment was conducted on white males.[14] Just as other Atlanta-based institutions lent their expertise to the investigation, the CDC eventually offered its services by warning people about the nature of the murders and suggesting ways of preventing them. By employing a paradigm designed to reduce epidemics of disease, the CDC claimed it might be able to prevent the murder "epidemic" from spreading.[15] Unfortunately, and to my mind not surprisingly, outbreaks of murder and outbreaks of disease cannot be controlled by the same measures. Although the CDC was never involved with any interferon research, given its prominence as an internationally respected problem-solving institution headquartered in Atlanta, its ineffectiveness at contributing anything genuinely useful to the solution of these homicides, and its troubled history with the black community, it is not surprising that some interpreted its role in an ominous fashion.

Accounting for the interferon connection requires an understanding of three basic facts. First, no other drug was getting as much media attention at the end of the 1970s and beginning of the 1980s. Second, it was getting media attention in both the medical news and the business news. The latter coverage is important because article after article dwelled on how rich those who invested heavily in this emerging biotech industry would become. In a sense, Gary Alan Fine's theory of corporate dominance sheds light on this component. He argues quite convincingly that a corporation linked with a rumor or urban legend is almost always the best known and largest in the industry.[16] Since interferon was the best-known drug of the era, it makes sense that it would be the one targeted by the folk. Finally, interferon is a drug that is naturally produced by the human body. The furor over its "discovery" focused on the introduction of additional interferon in order to combat a wide range of maladies. At the same time that human bodies were being destroyed, a potentially lucrative substance produced by the human body became the subject of intense scrutiny. Although a CDC representative assured me that the center had not been a setting for interferon experimentation, the fact that such a well-known research facility was based in the city where the homicides were occurring no doubt left an impression on many people. Thus it is easy to see how this particular drug so logically fit into the demands of the legend.

Ties of the murders to the CDC and to the need for interferon subjects were popularized in the media, with many informants claiming to have heard the rumor from a friend or relative. Several attributed it to comedian and social commentator Dick Gregory or to author James Baldwin.

In his book, Baldwin identifies Gregory as his source. Interestingly enough, Baldwin's version of Gregory's story differs from those I have collected from informants who have heard Gregory lecture. Baldwin, with acknowledged ambiguity, states, "He [Gregory] had suggested . . . that the key to the Terror was in the nature of a scientific experiment. I am being deliberately vague, but the nature of the experiment was based on the possibility that the tip of the Black male sexual organ contained a substance that might be used to cure cancer."[17] After claiming that Gregory's suggestion did not convince many Atlantans, Baldwin reflects, "I tend to doubt Dick's suggestion because—apart from the fact that I want to doubt it—it seems such an untidy way of carrying on a scientific experiment. But, then, one is forced to realize that a scientific experiment *must* be untidy: that is why it is called an experiment."[18]

The Atlanta child-murder variant of the castrated boy legend is the latest in a well-established pattern with African-American oral tradition that highlights white attempts to manipulate the bodies of black people. As far back as the earliest days of the slavery era, rumors told by recently captured Africans claimed that their white captors intended to eat them eventually.[19] Gladys-Marie Fry documented the antebellum era's orally transmitted beliefs that emphasize the ways in which southern white patrollers and night doctors wanted to use black slave bodies.[20] In 1943, a full-scale race riot erupted in Detroit after a rumor spread quickly through the black community alleging that whites had thrown a black infant from the Belle Isle Bridge.[21] In the fifties, sixties, seventies, and eighties, countless versions of the castrated boy legend described a black pre-adolescent male castrated by white men in a public rest room. The late seventies and early eighties saw the development of a rumor that held that the Church's Fried Chicken Corporation was owned by the KKK and that the white supremacist group was tampering with the chicken so that eating it would sterilize African-American males. The manufacturers of Troop clothing, a popular line of sportswear marketed at young African-Americans, has had to fight rumors and urban legends that claim that the KKK owns the company and uses the profits to further their antiblack hostility. In all these cases, black bodies are regarded by whites as nonhuman and therefore to be treated with disregard. For several hundred years, this pattern has characterized the most prevalent rumors and legends in the African-American community.

Anthropologist Mary Douglas has argued that symbols of group conflict are frequently revealed in forms that emphasize the human body. Body parts become synechdoches for the body, and the body becomes a synechdoche for the group. Thus, attacks on single black individuals are perceived as affronts to the entire African-American community. To protect their "body parts," African-Americans believe that they must guard themselves as individuals and as a people from white animosity. As Douglas writes, "When rituals express anxiety about the body's orifices the sociological counterpart of this anxiety is a care to protect the political and cultural unity of a minority group."[22]

Circulating these rumors among themselves, African-Americans are seeking to gain some measure of control over threats to their presence and status in a hostile environment. The Atlanta murder spree activated familiar uncertainties for many black Americans. Transmitting rumors and formal and informal activities reflect communal attempts to exert control in the face of these uncertainties. Given the often troubled relationship between blacks and whites, it seems reasonable that many blacks perceived these murders as attacks against them as a people rather than as attacks on individuals. Occurring nearly thirty years after the civil rights movement, these ostensibly racist attacks and the seemingly substandard investigation functioned as clear-cut reminders that racial equality has not been realized. In their folk responses to the crisis, African-Americans used folklore as a means to solidarity and group cohesion in order to combat perceived attempts to destroy the group.

Notes to Chapter 5

1. James Baldwin, *The Evidence of Things Not Seen* (New York: Henry Holt and Co., 1985).

2. Baldwin, 2.

3. Tamotsu Shibutani, *Improvised News: A Sociological Study of Rumor* (Indianapolis: Bobbs-Merrill, 1966), 56–58.

4. Wyn Craig Wade, *The Fiery Cross: The Ku Klux Klan in America* (New York: Simon and Schuster, 1987), 31.

5. Gladys-Marie Fry, *Night Riders in Black Community Folk History* (Knoxville: University of Tennessee Press, 1975).

6. Patricia A. Turner, "Church's Fried Chicken and the Klan: A Rhetorical Analysis of Rumor in the Black Community," *Western Folklore* 46 (1987): 294–306.

7. Wade, *Fiery Cross*, 287.

8. David J. Garrow, *The FBI and Martin Luther King, Jr.* (New York: Penguin, 1986), 165.

9. Walter Leavy, "The Case of the Disappearing Blacks," *Ebony* 36 (December 1980): 136.

10. Garrow, *FBI*, 124.

11. Shibutani, *Improvised News*, 37.

12. Terry Ann Knopf, *Rumors, Race, and Riots* (New Brunswick, N.J.: Transaction Books, 1975), 164.

13. Florence Ridley, "A Tale Too Often Told," *Western Folklore* 26 (1967): 153–56; Barre Toelken, *The Dynamics of Folklore* (Boston: Houghton Mifflin, 1979), 176–79; Jan Harold Brunvand, *The Choking Doberman and Other "New" Urban Legends* (New York: Norton, 1984), 82–86; Michael P. Carroll, " 'The Castrated Boy': Another Contribution to the Psychoanalytic Study of Urban Legends," *Folklore* 98 (1987): 216–25.

14. James H. Jones, *Bad Blood: The Tuskegee Syphilis Experiment—A Tragedy of Race and Medicine* (New York: The Free Press, 1981), 1–15.

15. Martin J. Blaser, Janine M. Jason, Bruce G. Weniger, et al., "Epidemiologic Analysis of a Cluster of Homicides of Children in Atlanta," *Journal of American Medical Association* 251 (1984): 3255–58.

16. Gary Alan Fine, "The Goliath Effect: Corporate Dominance and Mercantile Legends," *Journal of American Folklore* 98 (1985): 63–84.

17. Baldwin, *Evidence*, 87.

18. Ibid.

19. Winthrop D. Jordan, *White Over Black: American Attitudes Toward the Negro, 1550–1812* (Baltimore: Penguin, 1973), 25; Mary Cable, *Black Odyssey: The Case of the Slave Ship Amistad* (New York: Penguin, 1977), 53.

20. Fry, *Night Riders in Black Folk History*.

21. Janet L. Langlois, "The Belle Isle Bridge Incident: Legend Dialectic and Semiotic System in the 1943 Detroit Race Riots," *Journal of American Folklore* 96 (1983): 187.

22. Mary Douglas, *Purity and Danger: An Analysis of the Concepts of Pollution and Taboo* (London: ARK, 1985) and *Natural Symbols: Explorations in Cosmology* (New York: Pantheon, 1970).

6. *Corridos* and *Canciones* of *Mica, Migra,* and *Coyotes*: A Commentary on Undocumented Immigration*

MARIA HERRERA-SOBEK

A large corpus of *corridos* (ballads) and *canciones* (songs) has evolved over the past one hundred and thirty years reflecting the adventures and travails of Mexicans immigrating to the United States.[1] These songs continue to be produced and sung at local radio stations, in bars and restaurants, during fiestas and *tertulias*, and in the privacy of the home.[2] The present wave of migrating undocumented workers provides an opportunity to observe this immigration process firsthand and to note the attitudes and reactions of immigrants as they face innumerable hardships.

This study centers on the metaphoric strategies and artistic renderings of the immigration process as reflected in contemporary (1970s and 1980s) Mexican immigrant *corridos* and *canciones*. Three themes dominant in the discourse of Mexican immigration can be identified: quest for a *mica*, a legal border-crossing card (also called a green card); conflict and tension between *la migra* (the border patrol) and the immigrant; and the role of *coyotes* or guides, who serve as mediators (for a fee they smuggle undocumented persons into the United States). Popular music comment-

*A preliminary draft of this study was read at the "La Frontera: Symbiotic Relationships on the U.S.-Mexico Border" Conference held April 20–21, 1984, at Arizona State University, Tempe, Arizona. I wish to thank Professor Jaime Rodriguez, Director, Mexico/Chicano Focus Research Project; Professor Eloy Rodriguez, Director, International Chicano Studies Center; and the Humanities Research and Travel Committee for their generous grants provided to undertake research on this project.

ing on these themes mirrors the strategies used by Mexican immigrants to circumvent their problems and ameliorate their negative status.

Furthermore, the songs symbolically reflect the struggles of aspiring immigrants by objectifying and parodying situations and persons with whom immigrants come into daily contact. The singing of songs objectifies the immigrants' experiences by articulating their concerns, anxieties, and fears; by historicizing the event of migration to fit it into familiar patterns; and by contemporizing these events to make them meaningful to continuing immigrant experiences. These experiences are made relevant through a series of transformations in which the realities of immigrant life are portrayed figuratively in key metaphors that reverse the hardships of the immigration process. This song tradition reveals the immigrants' awareness of the forces affecting their everyday lives and demonstrates the artistic ingenuity of these twentieth-century folk bards in creating a way of confronting the realities of their world.

The Rise in Mexican Immigrant Songs

The increase in *corrido* production in the last two decades parallels the drastic changes in immigration policy undertaken by the United States in the 1960s. The Bracero Program instituted in 1942 at the request of the American government was finally terminated in 1964.[3] The legal importation of Mexican labor ceased for all practical purposes, although there was a provision (H-2 Temporary Workers Act) that allowed the entrance of a limited number of temporary workers on American farms.[4] The H-2 Temporary Workers Act, however, never equalled the scope and extent of the Bracero Program.

Although the Bracero Program ceased to exist in the 1960s, the demand for workers did not abate and consequently the number of undocumented workers rose dramatically in the last two decades. As immigration from Mexico increased, so did the number of songs commenting on the immigrant experience. Two major factors contributed to the increase of song production. First, César Chávez's efforts to unionize farm workers used *corridos* narrating the grievances and travails of the farm worker in recruiting efforts, in long marches, and in the Teatro Campesino productions. This use of the *corrido* as protest song stimulated the writing and recording of more Mexican immigrant songs. Second, the general popularity and prestige of protest songs during the 1960s and 1970s in the United States—through the folk songs of Joan Baez and Bob Dylan, for example—helped the *corrido* achieve general acceptance as a viable, traditional form of expression. As immigration has continued to increase in the 1980s, new songs continue to be written and sung.

Selection Criteria

Mexican immigrant songs selected for this study were those recorded between 1970 and 1987 and which specifically mention that the immigrant had come from Mexico to the United States, was presently working or residing in the States, and was portrayed as an undocumented worker. Several terms are used throughout these songs to refer to Mexican immigrants and their plight: *ilegales* ("illegals"), *enganchados* or *reenganchados* (contracted workers), *alambristas* (wire jumpers), *mojados* or *espaldas mojadas* (wetbacks), *indocumentados* or *sin documentos* (without green cards or legal documents), and/or *braceros*.[5] These terms are all value-loaded and reflect the symbolic process of labeling the immigrants so as to transform them metaphorically into abstract objects.

Fieldwork for collecting *corridos* and *canciones* about Mexican immigrants was conducted over a span of more than ten years (1976 to 1989). During this period I have collected more than 3,000 texts from various sources. One of the major ones was the Eduardo Guerrero Collection (1924 and 1932) housed in the Biblioteca Nacional de México. Additional library *corrido* collections include the texts found in the Biblioteca de la Ciudad de México and the National Anthropology Museum in Mexico City. Other texts were obtained from pulp *cancioneros* (songbooks) which I collected in flea markets, book stalls, and bookstores throughout Mexico City in the summer of 1979. Another major source was professional recordings made by both well-known singers and groups which target working-class audiences.

Information was also obtained from interviews with *corrido* singers (*mariachi* groups, duets, individual singers) about their repertoires and about the meaning and function of these songs for them. Singers were very much aware of the significance of the *corrido* as a vehicle for commenting on historical events, such as the Mexican Revolution of 1910–1917, and on historical personages, such as Emiliano Zapata, Francisco Villa, Porfirio Díaz, and President John F. Kennedy. During my interviews, I found that both singers and audiences (who consist mainly of working-class and immigrant people) were conscious of the *corrido* tradition in Mexico and in the United States as a viable and significant mode of historical documentation.

Historical Background

The "illegal alien" phenomenon dates back to the third decade of this century. Before that period, no significant restrictions or immigration laws applying specifically to Mexico existed; people crossed the border at will, as had been the custom prior to the loss of Mexican territory. Concern over unimpeded immigration did surface in the 1880s, but it was principally directed at Asian immigration and not at Mexican nationals. The various acts passed during the second half of the nineteenth century—the Chinese Exclusion Act (1882) and the Gentlemen's Agreement Act (1907)—were targeted to stop the flow of Chinese and Japanese workers. Consequently, the Immigration Act of 1907 was not geared toward restricting Mexican immigrants and border officials were lax about enforcing the various provisions of the Act when it came to Mexicans entering the United States.

The decrease in Asian railroad and farm workers, together with the increased labor needs of the Southwest's expanding economy, stimulated American companies actively to recruit Mexican labor in Mexico and at the United States/Mexican border. However, the surge in the population of this ethnic group in the second decade of the twentieth century alarmed certain Anglo-Saxon nativist groups, and again pressure was exerted on Washington to enact legislation to "control" the borders. Responding to these pressures, Congress passed the Immigration Act of 1917.[6] This act provided for the implementation of a literacy test and an $8 head tax for each prospective immigrant. Since many Mexicans were extremely poor and uneducated, these two stipulations proved insurmountable to a large number; the result was that many American farmers paid the legal fees for Mexican workers while other Mexican workers crossed the border without paying the head tax. Some of the older folk songs discuss the immigrants' cleverness at crossing the border without paying the stipulated entrance fee.[7] Again, the border patrol, instituted in 1924, was extremely lax in enforcing the new regulations against Mexican workers since they were sorely needed in the agricultural fields and other areas. As Mexican immigrants began to pose a greater economic threat in the decades that followed, immigration requirements became progressively more stringent and obtaining legal residency became more difficult.

The most traumatic period for Mexican immigrants came during the era of the Great Depression, when Mexicans and American citizens of Mexican descent were forcefully deported or "voluntarily" repatriated to

Mexico. Many songs exist depicting this dark period in American history.[8]

After the Great Depression, job opportunities increased and continued to attract Mexican labor (for example, through the 1942 Bracero Program). The enterprising immigrant throughout these years devised various strategies for entering the United States, but of course the preferred method has always been to acquire a legal resident's card, a "mica."

Circumventing the Law

The word "*mica*" metonymically refers to the resident card issued by the offices of the Immigration and Naturalization Service (INS). Its name derives from a substance that resembles the laminated card. Mica, according to *Webster's New Twentieth Century Dictionary* (1964), is "any of a group of minerals (complex silicates) that crystallize in thin, somewhat flexible, easily separated layers, translucent or transparent."

The dream of all undocumented workers is to legalize their status in the United States so as not to pay exorbitant prices to smugglers for helping them enter the United States, and so as not to fear later deportation. Applying for legal residency is a long, expensive, and arduous affair. There are, however, provisions in the immigration law that facilitate the acquisition of legal residency, one of which is marrying an American citizen.

The recently popular song "Micaela" describes in metaphoric terms the extreme yearning and desire on the part of a man to obtain a "*mica*".[9]

MICAELA

(Hombre):
Tú eres mi Mica, Mica, mi
  Micaela.
Tú representas todo lo que mi
  alma anhela.
Esas visicitudes que se han
  enseñado
por mi pasado las resolveré
si estás a mi lado.

Tú vas a ser mi Mica,
  mi Micaela.

(Male):
You are my Mica, Mica, my
  Micaela.
You represent all that my soul
  desires.
Those vissicitudes that have
  cropped up
In my past I shall resolve
If you are by my side.

You are going to be my Mica,
  my Micaela.

Y esto lo arreglamos con mucha cautela	And this we shall arrange with great caution
sin que nadie se entere de que tú me quieres	Without anyone suspecting you love me
vamos y nos casamos	We shall go and marry
y así todo lo arreglamos.	And fix everything up.
Tienes que ser mi Mica, mi Micaela.	You have to be my Mica, my Micaela.
Verde como los pastos de las praderas.	Green like the pastures in the fields.
Siempre aquí mi esperanza	Always with hope here
la voz primera que serás un día mi compañera	I voice firstly that you shall some-day be my companion
por fin que seas mi Micaela	At last you'll be my Micaela
y todos mis problemas	And all my problems
se irán al demonio	Will go to the devil
sólo con que resuelvas	By your agreeing
lo del matrimonio.	To our matrimony.
Juntos no habrá ya nada que jamás nos duela;	Together there will never be any-thing that'll hurt us;
serás tan feliz que llegarás a abuela.	You shall be so happy you'll live to be a grandmother.
Yo seré tu amor y tú mi Micaela.	I will be your love and you my Micaela.

(The woman repeats the same verses)

This song portrays a man singing a love song to his "Mica," meta-phorically disguised as a woman named Micaela (Michelle). The woman then sings the same words to the man. The suitor suggests that through marriage (or the coming together of the two—man and "*Mica*") they will live happily ever after. The lyrics of this song linking marriage and *mica* together reflect what happens in real life: marriage is one way of obtaining a *mica*. The song cleverly disguises the real nature of the desire by transforming the green card or "*mica*" into a woman—Micaela. The first letters of Micaela provide a clue as to the "hidden" identity of the true desired object. The linguistic play is further enhanced by con-verting the *mica* into a beloved whom the subject wishes to marry.

The first strophe indicates through the nickname "Mica" that there is a double meaning in the lyrics. The plot is complicated by the mention of previous difficulties, "*vissicitudes*," suffered by the singer. The fact that the marriage has to be arranged with "great caution" and secretly, as stated in the second strophe, further underscores the suspicious nature of the proposed marriage.

The third stanza conclusively confirms the identity of Mica. Micaela is not a person; "she" is described as "green like the pastures in the fields." Thus the coming together of the green "Mica" through the metaphor of matrimony resolves all the immigrant's problems. Pain and suffering will "go to the devil" and the two "lovers," Mica and immigrant, will live happily to a ripe old age.

Obtaining a *mica* through marriage occurs sufficiently often to be commented upon by the news media, such as in a 1984 *Los Angeles Times* article bearing the headlines "Scam to Stay in U.S.: Aliens Find Home with Trip to Altar." The report examined the existence of thriving businesses offering sham marriages for a fee.

For illegal aliens who want to live here, marrying a U.S. citizen is the fastest and surest way to gain permanent residency, it is generally agreed. The broker capitalizes on the alien's desire to gain a permanent foothold here, authorities say, while pandering to greedy or gullible Americans willing to pose as spouses.[10]

However, only a comparatively small percentage of Mexican immigrants can take this route to legalizing their status. The $1,000 typical expense is too great for the average Mexican worker. However, even this serious matter is caricatured in the *Times* when a typical "want ad" for prospective spouses is presented:

Wanted: Spouse. Any size or shape. No sex or relationship desired. Must be a U.S. citizen. Will pay $1,000. (p.1)

The ironies implicit in trying to use one law to circumvent another are expressed in the *canción* "La Bracera," in which the search for a prospective mate backfires:[11]

LA BRACERA	THE *BRACERA*
Para conseguir dinero	In order to make money
yo me pasé la frontera.	I crossed the border.
Iba dispuesto a la chamba	I was ready to work
saliera lo que saliera.	Anywhere work was available.
Pizqué limón y naranja	I picked lemon and oranges
subiá y bajaba escaleras.	I went up and down ladders.
Como no era contratado	Because I had no legal papers
yo quise hallarme acomodo.	I tried to find a way to get them.
Pensé que si estaba casado	I thought if I were married
sería más sencillo todo.	Everything would be easier

Me dije este año me caso	I said to myself: "This year I marry
O no me llamo Teodoro.	Or my name isn't Teodoro."
Me enteré en un viejo pueblo	I found out in an old town
de una muchacha cualquiera	About a girl living there.
para en seguida casarnos	I immediately proposed to her
y que ella me consiguiera	Hoping she would get for me
la visa y el pasaporte	My visa and my passport
para cruzar la frontera.	So I could cross the border.
El trato quedó cerrado	The deal was sealed.
y se citó la ceremonia.	We set the date for the ceremony.
Tuvimos mil invitados	We had a thousand guests
y otros quinientos de gorra.	And five hundred party crashers.
Unos eran mis amigos	Some were my friends
y los otros de la novia.	The others were the bride's.
Ya que estábamos casados	After we were married
le digo, "Bueno, mi vida,	I said: "Listen, my love,
ahora que estamos solitos	Now that we are alone
Vas a saber de mi vida.	You are going to know about my life.
Yo soy purito mojado.	I am really a wetback.
Hay tú sabrás si me 'imigras.' "	It's up to you to get my documents."
Apenas oyó mi esposa	As soon as my wife heard
lo que yo le propusiera	What I was telling her.
me dijo, "Ya te amolaste.	She told me: "You are out of luck.
Pues también yo soy bracera.	I too am a wetback.
Me casé por lo mismo	I married you for the same reason
para cruzar la frontera."	So that I could cross the border."

In this song the undocumented immigrant is portrayed in the role of a trickster who tries to hoodwink a young woman into marriage in order to obtain his resident's visa. The Trickster Immigrant, however, following the pattern of many folktales with the trickster as protagonist, is duped in turn. Still, marriage is not the only strategy available to the prospective immigrant. The use of false or fraudulent documents to assume another identity is integrated into the lyrics of "La patera":[12]

LA PATERA

En Texas y en San Francisco	In Texas and San Francisco
me agarró la inmigración	The border patrol caught me

pero a mi no me hace nada	But they couldn't do a thing
yo traigo una mica falsa	I have a false green card
y falsa es mi dirección.	And my address is also false.

Transformation from Person to Animal as Border-Crossing Strategy

A commonly described border-crossing strategy in contemporary *corridos* and *canciones* involves the smuggler who, for a fee, helps the undocumented worker enter the United States. These guides are called *coyotes* or *polleros* ("pollero" = smuggler, meaning one who takes care of the *pollos* or "chickens," the undocumented workers). The smuggling of "illegal aliens" arose out of a definite need. Northern Mexico or "*la frontera*," as it is called in Mexico, has been up to recent times sparsely populated. Immigration to the United States has tended to originate from more heavily populated states in the interior with high unemployment, such as Jalisco, Michoacán, Guanajuato, Durango, Zacatecas, and San Luis Potosí. It is obvious, therefore, that an immigrant traveling from the interior of Mexico will not be experienced in crossing the border illegally nor will he or she be knowledgeable about the best routes. The *coyote* has become an indispensable middleperson (both females and males practice the trade) in helping the uninitiated succeed in crossing over to the United States. As the song "*Yo soy mexicano, señores*" ("I am a Mexican, Gentlemen") states:[13]

Y ay señores no quiero ni acordarme	And, oh my dear sirs, I do not want to remember
los trabajos que pasamos en Tijuana	The hard times we had in Tijuana
cuando ya veníamos cruzando	When we were about to cross
la migra que nos echa pa' trás.	The border patrol kicked us out.
Un coyote tienen que conseguirse	You have to find a good smuggler
nos decía la voz de la experiencia.	The voice of experience told us.
Un coyote que con su buena lana	A skilled smuggler who with money
por fin nos ayudó a cruzar.	Finally helped us cross.

The coyote figure is a staple character in Mexican, Chicano, and American Indian folklore, frequently in the guise of the trickster. In immigrant lore the brutalizing and dehumanizing process of crossing the border has been reconceptualized and restructured poetically through a cast of archetypal characters belonging to the animal world, to the realm of the brutal and irrational sphere. In this capacity, the coyote is a trickster figure who has the reputation of being wily, sly, sneaky, and clever at deceptions; he is the arch-deceiver. Immigrants must rely on their wits to enter the United States, but many times they are duped by the coyote, who relies on the naivete of the immigrant.

The crafty coyote (smuggler) takes advantage of the innocent undocumented workers, the *pollos* (chickens). The coyote is the animal that sneaks into the barnyard at night and steals the farmer's chickens to eat them. The *pollos* waiting to be smuggled across the border are thus perceived in this metaphor as innocent victims who must fall into the claws of the coyote in order to be guided out of the chicken coop. The coyote is the figure who can successfully evade the watchful eye of the "farmer" (read immigration officer) and in the dead of night sneak them into the United States.

Although the *coyote* performs an important service to the prospective undocumented immigrant, he/she suffers from an extremely negative image. Many people view this figure as the lowest form of life on this planet. *Coyotes* are known to pack people into poorly ventilated trucks or garages and expose them to the danger of suffocation. Equally true is the fact that *coyotes* charge high fees to smuggle people. The going rate at present ranges from $300 (for walking illegals through the hills in southern California and then transporting them to their destination) to $600 (for smuggling undocumented workers in the comfort of a car across the Tijuana-San Ysidro inspection station).[14] The general population feels that *coyotes* prey upon innocent, unsuspecting victims, charge them exorbitant fees, and often leave them stranded in the middle of the desert to die.

The goal of undocumented workers is to be rid of the *coyotes* and to be able to cross at will. Many eventually do learn the safest routes to take and no longer need the services of the *coyotes*. This fact is expressed in the song "No necesito coyote" ("I Don't Need a Coyote").[15]

Con esta van cuatro veces	This makes the fourth time
que he visitado Tijuana	I have visited Tijuana
la ciudad más visitada	The city most visited
de mi tierra mexicana	In my Mexican homeland
porque es la puerta de entrada	Because it is the gateway
a la Unión Americana.	To the United States.
Por Tijuana, Mexicali	Through Tijuana, Mexicali
Nogales y Piedras Negras	Nogales and Piedras Negras

no necesito coyote	I don't need a coyote
para cruzar la frontera	To cross the border
Yo no tengo pasaporte	I don't have a passport
y paso cuando yo quiero.	And I cross whenever I please.

The INS vs. the Mojado

If the dehumanizing activity of crossing the border has been reconceptualized by the folk into a world of animals—*coyotes, pollos*, and *polleros* (smugglers of *pollos*)—other songs create a different order of characters. Contemporary *corridos* continue the literary tradition of incorporating within their lyrics formidable heroes who challenge and battle the foe. In the latter part of the nineteenth century, the Texas Rangers ("*Rinches de Tejas*") served as the forces of evil in constant pursuit of the Mexican hero. The "*Corrido de Jacinto Treviño*" and the "*Corrido de Gregorio Cortés*" are examples.[16] During the Porfirio Díaz regime in Mexico, the Rangers found their counterpart in the *Federales* (federal soldiers) who fought against Mexican rebel guerrilla fighters.

During the Depression, the forced "repatriation" of Mexicans and Mexican-Americans created great bitterness toward the INS in the Chicano community. *Corridos* written during this period castigate the border patrol for their heartless disruption of family life and the breaking up of families. In the second half of the twentieth century, the "*migra*" or border patrol again becomes the villain and is portrayed in *corrido* lore as the arch-enemy of the undocumented worker.

It is clear that changes in attitude toward the border patrol have corresponded to political and economic events. In the 1940s, when workers were needed to help in the war effort, Mexican nationals were heartily welcomed to the United States. The INS maintained a low profile and was not a common topic in *corridos*. In the 1950s, when the much-maligned "wetback invasion" occurred, the "*migra*" was not generally portrayed as a malevolent force. Rather, it was frequently the butt of jokes,[17] often linked to the Stupid American motif.[18] In many Mexican folktales and jokes, the Mexican or Mexican-American applies wit and intelligence to get the better of the Anglo in a particular encounter.[19] The Anglo is portrayed as clumsy, dim-witted, and easily duped by the sharp-witted Mexican.

In ballads sung in the 1960s and 1970s, the role of the border patrol changes from "Stupid American" to villain; the patrol is viewed as vindictive, their actions hypocritical. According to several scholars of immigration, such as Julian Samora, the INS has been frequently responsive to the interests of Anglo-dominated communities and has not applied immigration law in an even-handed, objective manner. Thus, during periods of peak harvest, the INS tends to look the other way, allowing "illegal aliens" to harvest the crops; when the harvest season is over, the border patrol descends on fields and ranches and deports the undocumented workers.

An equally pernicious belief undermining respect for immigration laws is that the INS served the interest of employers during the farm workers' attempt to unionize. Many union leaders point out that whenever incipient unionization movements arise, the employer calls the INS to "round up" those working without proper documentation. Jose C. Ortega reports in "Plight of the Mexican Wetback" that "the illegal status of employees also gives the employer other advantages. If any of them complains about low pay or substandard working conditions, the employer merely tips the Immigration Service, which will remove the complaining employee."[20] A 1970s *corrido* details precisely this view:[21]

Policiá e inmigración	Police and border patrol
unidos con los rancheros,	Together with the growers
conspiración contratista	This was the contractors' conspiracy
por el maldito dinero.	For the sake of evil money.
En contra de nuestra gente	Against our people
Parecían unos perros.	They acted like dogs.

The role of *migra* as villain is supported by transforming the INS into another animal, this time a dog. Even the vans used to transport undocumented workers are characterized in terms of animal metaphors: the INS officials, for example, are described as acting like *perros* (dogs) and the vans are called *perreras* (dog-catcher vans).[22] This stereotyping remains necessary as long as the INS is regarded as the villain, even though the INS, according to newspaper accounts, has at times saved the lives of undocumented immigrants.

The Transformation of Anglos from Villains to Wetbacks

The final stage in the process of reducing the pain of immigration is to convert Anglos themselves into wetbacks. The change is represented in the popular song "Superman *es ilegal*" ("Superman Is an Illegal Alien").[23] The most cherished comic-book hero, Superman, is made into an archetypal alien who remains foreign no matter how American he is made out to be. That his foreignness is accepted and the Mexican immigrants is not points to the hypocrisy of the favoritism shown to European immigrants.

HABLADO	SPOKEN:
¿Es un pájaro, es un avión?	Is it a bird, an airplane?
No hombre, es un mojado.	No man, it's a wetback.

(Sound effects of an airplane)

Cantado:	Sung:
Llegó del cielo	He came from the sky
y no es avión.	And he is not an airplane.
Viene en su nave	He arrived in his spaceship
desde Kryptón.	From Krypton.
Y por lo visto	And anyone can see
no es americano;	He is not an American;
sino otro igual	He is just another
como yo indocumentado.	Undocumented [worker] like me.
Así que migra	So, border patrol,
él no debe trabajar,	He should not be allowed to work,
porque aunque duela	Because even though it hurts
Superman es ilegal.	Superman is an illegal alien.
Es periodista	He is a journalist
También yo soy	So am I
Y no "jue" al army*	And he did not serve in the army
¡A que camión!**	What a bastard!
Aquel es güero,***	He is fair-skinned,
ojos azules,	Blue-eyed,
bien formado;	And has a great physique;
y yo prietito	And I am dark-skinned,
gordiflón y muy chaparro.	Fat, and very short.
Pero yo al menos	But at least I served
en mi patria ya marché	In my country's army
Con el coyote que pagué	With the smuggler whom
cuando crucé.	I paid when I came.
No cumplió con el	He did not do his
servicio militar.	Military service.
No paga impuestos	He does not pay taxes
y le hace al judicial.	And practices law.
No tiene mica	He does not have his green card
ni permiso pa' volar;	Nor a permit to fly;

*jue = fue (from verb *ir* = to go)
**camión is a euphemism for "cabrón" = fucker
***güero = fair-skinned, blonde

y les apuesto que ni	And I bet he does not
seguro social.	Even have a social security card.
Hay que echar a Superman	We have to kick Superman
de esta nación.	Out of this country.
Y si se puede	And if we can
regresarlo pa' Krypton.	Send him back to Krypton.
¿A cúal borraron	Whose skin did they whiten up
cuando llegó?	When he arrived on earth?
De un colorcito	Wiping out his native
verde limón.	Lemon-green color from Krypton.
Y no era hierba	He wasn't a green-colored plant
ni tampoco un agripal	Nor was he a _____
más bien agüita	It was probably water
*de'sa que hace reparar.**	Firewater, that is!
Y que yo sepa	And as far as I know
no lo multan por volar	They don't fine him for flying;
sino al contrario	On the contrary
lo declaran Superman.	They declare him Superman.
Hay que echar a Superman	We have to kick Superman
de esta nación.	Out of this country
Y si se puede	And if we can
regresarlo pa' Krypton.	Send him back to Krypton.
¿Dónde está esa autoridad	Where are you now
de inmigración?	Border patrolmen?
¿Qué hay de nuevo	What's new in the
Don Racismo en la nación?	Nation, Mr. Racism?

*De'sa = de esa (that one)

This contemporary immigrant song encompasses in its lyrics several grievances the undocumented worker has vis-à-vis American society's heroes and villains. The question leading off the song, "Is it a bird, an airplane?" symbolically asks, "Who is this Anglo that is so taken for granted?" The answer in "Superman *es ilegal*" is that he himself is a wetback. Equating the all-American hero, emblematic of patriotism, the "American way of life," and American justice, with a wetback who represents the antithesis of the all-American icon elicits laughter.

Superman is unmasked in the various duplicitous actions he is engaged in: he comes from the sky and he *is not* an airplane; if he is coming from Krypton he is a Kryptonite and *not* an American. The song's narrator continues to enumerate Superman's illegal and unethical conduct: he is a journalist without any credentials, and horror of horrors, he is a draft dodger, not having served in the army as most Mexicans and Mexican-Americans do. Even the lowly and unethical coyote is deemed superior to Superman since he, too, did his patriotic duty.

The specter of racism and unequal treatment under the law is raised in the next stanza, where the "superior" racial characteristics of Superman are listed and contrasted with the devalued Mexican ones. Superman is fair-skinned, blue-eyed, and has a great physique; the immigrant is dark-skinned, fat, and very short.

The song further enumerates Superman's unethical conduct: he does not pay income taxes, he practices law without a license, he does not have a legal resident's card (*mica*), a permit to fly, not even a Social Security card!

It is a well-known fact, the song continues, that Superman as a resident from Krypton was not really a white man but was carefully made up to look white. The original color of his skin—like all good Kryptonites—was yellow-green.

Given Superman's illegal status, immigration laws should apply equally to him and he should not be allowed to work. The poetic voice concludes that he must be an illegal alien. The only fair action to take would be to deport Superman from the United States and send him back to his planet of origin, Krypton. The final stanza ends with two rhetorical questions: "Where are you now Mr. Border Patrolmen?" and "What's new in the nation, Mr. Racism?" Both questions invite the audience to participate in structuring an answer. The only possible answers are that the INS does not apply immigration laws equally and objectively but favors European immigrants, and that the United States of America continues to engage in racist actions.

In a complete inversion of status, the INS is frequently devalued in status through the Spanish slang word "*migra*." By using this designation, the immigrant effectively deconstructs the INS's official status. "*Migra*" is an epithet that divests the agency and its personnel of its status and power; at the same time it confers on them ridicule and disdain. In this process of deconstruction of power through naming, "*migra*" and "*mojado*" become equal entities in a chess game in which each player tries to outwit the other. In the end, however, each participant knows that it really does not matter who wins, because the game will continue to be played indefinitely. In "Superman," the singer—who is an immigrant—confidently exposes the American icon as a wetback and urges the "*migra*" to accept this fact even though "the truth hurts" ("*aunque duela*").

At times the *migra* is victorious and thoroughly routs the *mojado*, even taking away his very existence, as in "*Los que cruzaron*":[24]

Cuando tocaron la orilla	When they touched the river's edge
los guardias les dispararon	The guards fired at them
y se rifaron la vida	And they pitted their lives
contra los americanos,	Against the Americans
y allí quedaron regados	And they ended up dead
como si fueran gusanos.	As if they were worms.

On other occasions the undocumented worker defeats and eludes the "evil forces" and even mocks them, as in "*Los mandados*."[25]

La migra a mi me agarró	The immigration caught me
300 veces digamos	about 300 times, let us say.
pero jamás me domó	But they never broke me down
a mí me hizo los mandados;	I sent them to do my bidding;
los golpes que a mi me dió	The blows I received from them
se los cobré a sus paisanos.	Their countrymen paid dearly for them.

In his bolder stance, the immigrant seriously confronts the "*migra*." It is as if, with each successive historical period, he/she gains historical perspective to unmask the evils of a system which is harsh and hypocritical. This confidence comes about only through successive transformations where the focus of attention shifts from the self-pity of the immigrant clinging to his *mica* to confrontation, as when the illegal immigrant becomes locked in a moral struggle with the *migra*.

But as in the case of blacks during the slavery period or Jews during settlement in the United States in the early 1900s, the illegal immigrants' victories are pyrrhic. The *corrido* does not submit to the "they lived happily ever after" formula but is more attuned to reality where the axiom "win some, lose some" predominates.

Conclusion

The metaphors created in *corridos* and *canciones* not only allow negative feelings to be vented, but symbolically transpose hardship into victory through parodying the immigrants' plight. When historical consciousness leads to symbolic reversals, as happens in the *corrido*, a powerful tool is created for dealing with crises.

The *corrido* in the nineteenth and early twentieth centuries was used to denounce injustices suffered at the hands of the Mexican *federales*, the Texas Rangers, and the *patróns* (bosses). In the last two decades it has likewise continued to serve as a vehicle for airing grievances. The charismatic and skillful United Farm Workers Union organizer César Chávez in the 1960s grasped the importance of the *corrido* as an effective tool for bringing to the attention of farm workers the many injustices existing in the agricultural fields of California and the nation.

The *corrido*, through its continued announcement of injustices, gives the plight of the immigrant greater attention. The politics of metaphorization valorize the immigrant experience and eventually force society at large to reevaluate and revise negative views of the immigrant. Song writers exploring the immigrant experience believe in the mediating power of their lyrics. This affirmation of self through song writing transforms the immigrant from low social status into a figure of heroic and epic proportions. Viewed in this light, it is easy to comprehend the great popularity and lasting appeal of *corridos* and *canciones*.

Notes to Chapter 6

1. See Américo Paredes, *A Texas-Mexican Cancionero: Folksongs of the Lower Border* (Urbana: University of Illinois Press, 1976); Paul S. Taylor, "Songs of the Mexican Migration," in *Puro Mexicano*, edited by J. Frank Dobie (Dallas: Southern Methodist University Press, 1935), 221–45; María Herrera-Sobek, *The Bracero Experience: Elitelore Versus Folklore* (Los Angeles: UCLA Latin American Center Publications, 1979); and Manuel Gamio, *The Life Story of the Mexican Immigrant* (New York: Dover Publications, 1971).

2. I am presently writing a book-length study on Mexican immigrant songs entitled "Northward Bound: The Mexican Immigrant Experience in *Corridos* and *Canciones*," and I have collected more than one hundred and fifty.

3. There are numerous works detailing the Bracero program. See for example Ernesto Galarza, *Merchants of Labor: The Mexican Bracero Story* (Santa Barbara: McNally and Loftin, 1964); Richard H. Hancock, *The Role of the Bracero in the Economic and Cultural Dynamics of Mexico: A Case Study of Chihuahua* (Stanford: Hispanic American Society, 1959); Robert C. Jones, *Mexican War Workers in the United States* (Washington, D.C.: Pan American Union, 1945); Peter N. Kirstein, *Anglo Over Bracero: A History of the Mexican Worker in the United States from Roosevelt to Nixon* (San Francisco: R and E Research Associates, 1977); and my study of the bracero experience cited in footnote 1.

4. See Kirstein, *Anglo Over Bracero*.

5. The Mexican press used the more neutral *espaldas mojadas*, a literal translation from the English "wetback," but which did not carry the sense of hostility implied by the term "wetback." The general Mexican population, on the other hand, used the term *mojado*, which carries a connotation of disparagement and opprobrium as well as feelings of superiority toward the "lowly" immigrant worker. In California the term *alambrado* (wire fence) arose because Mexican nationals cut holes or jumped over the wire fences erected along the California-

Mexican border. Other terms such as *ilegales* (illegal aliens), *indocumentados* (undocumented workers), *braceros* (from the word *brazos* — arms) have also been used at one time or another.

6. Mark Reisler, *By the Sweat of Their Brow: Mexican Immigrant Labor in the United States, 1900–1940* (Westport, Connecticut: Greenwood Press, 1976), 12.

7. See Herrera-Sobek, *The Bracero Experience*, 1979.

8. See María Herrera-Sobek, "Northward Bound: The Mexican Immigrant Experience in *Corridos* and *Canciones*" (manuscript in process).

9. Guillermo de Anda, "Mi Micaela," 1981, Profono Internacional, 45-79-063.

10. *Los Angeles Times*, 10 Aug. 1984, p. 1.

11. Estevan Navarrete, "La bracera," n.d., Anahuac AN-1048 (collected in 1978).

12. Magdaleno Olivia, "La patera (Juana la patera)," 1979, Odeon MST 24312.

13. Juan Manual Valdovinos and José Cruz Carrera, "Yo soy mexicano, señores," *Corridos y Canciones de Aztlán*, 1980, XALMAN SBSR 102980-B.

14. This information was gleaned from various interviews conducted during 1982 to 1984 for a study I am presently researching on the undocumented *Mexicana*. See my article "Crossing the Border: Three Case Studies of Mexican Immigrant Women in Orange County in the 1980s," in *Second Lives: The Contemporary Immigrant/Refugee Experience in Orange County: The Shaping of a Multi-Ethnic Community*, edited by Valerie Smith and Michael Bigelow Dixon (Costa Mesa, California: South Coast Repertory, 1983), 83–86.

15. Jesús Zermeno, "No necesito coyote," 1981, Luna Records, L-278-B.

16. Américo Paredes, *"With a Pistol in His Hand": A Border Ballad and Its Hero* (Austin: University of Texas Press, 1978).

17. Herrera-Sobek, *The Bracero Experience*, 92–95.

18. See Américo Paredes, "The Anglo-American in Mexican Folklore," in *New Voices in American Studies*, edited by Ray Browne (Lafayette, Indiana, 1966), 113–27, and José E. Limón, "Folklore, Social Conflict, and the United States-Mexico Border," in *Handbook of American Folklore*, edited by Richard M. Dorson (Bloomington: Indiana University Press, 1986), 216–26.

19. María Herrera-Sobek, "Verbal Play in Mexican Immigrant Jokes," *Southwest Folklore Journal* 4 (1980): 14–22.

20. George C. Kiser and Martha Wood Kiser, eds. *Mexican Workers in the United States: Historical and Political Perspectives* (Albuquerque, New Mexico: University of New Mexico Press, 1979), 189–90.

21. Francisco García and Pablo and Juanita Saludado, "Las voces de los campesinos," 1976, UCLA Folklore and Mythology Center. FMSC-1.

22. Ibid.

23. Jorge Lerma, "Superman es ilegal," 1982, Profono Internacional, PI 3088.

24. Victor Cordero, "Los que cruzaron," 1983, *Los mejores corridos mexicanos* (México: El Libro Español, 1983), 40.

25. Jorge Lerma, "Los mandados," 1978, Columbia Broadcasting Company 8065.

III.

Realigning Ethnic Boundaries:
Strategies of Adaptation

7. Strategies of Ethnic Adaptation:
The Case of Gypsies in the United States

CAROL SILVERMAN

For years, scholars and laymen alike have predicted that Gypsies would be assimilated in the New World.[1] They base their claim on an increase in intermarriage between Gypsies and non-Gypsies and on a decrease in the Gypsy's nomadic lifestyle. Those who view these phenomena as signs of assimilation, however, are considering only the more visible manifestations of Gypsy participation in American society: purchase of homes, enrollment of children in public schools, and entrance into occupations not previously practiced by Gypsies. Beyond these instances of adaptation remain a system of values and a body of adaptive strategies that actually contribute to reinforcing Gypsy identity in America.

Rom are Gypsies who speak the *Romanes* language, a member of the Indic branch of the Indo-Aryan languages. After leaving India around the year 900, these nomadic peoples reached the Balkan peninsula in the fourteenth century. There they remained for several centuries, developing the Vlach dialects. By the late nineteenth century, *Rom* were dispersed throughout Europe and began emigrating to the United States. Estimates place the current *Rom* population in the United States between 20,000 and 200,000.[2] Census data are not reliable because *Rom* do not usually report themselves as Gypsies. In the United States there are at least three subgroupings of *Rom* often referred to as tribes: *Kalderash*, *Machwaya*, and *Lowara*. This essay examines the adaptation strategies of the *Kalderash* and *Machwaya*, because they are the more populous of the three subgroups and because they are homogenous enough to be considered a single ethnic entity.³ My use of "Gypsy" here refers to this population.

Outsiders to Gypsy culture are not privy to the adaptive strategies of Gypsies. I entered Gypsy culture only because I was willing to commit my time to participating in Gypsy life. I discovered that when Gypsies adapt to American society they do not by and large assimilate. On the contrary, they adapt by using American values and society to their advantage, in the service of maintaining a viable Gypsy culture.

My fieldwork with Gypsies began in 1974 as a teacher in the Philadelphia "School for Gypsy People." Housed in a fortune-telling-parlor storefront, the school provided classes for Gypsies of all ages and all levels of literacy. In 1976, I became a tutor for the children of a New York City Gypsy family, who then recommended me to other families. The role of tutor grew to include housekeeping, cleaning, baby-sitting, chaperoning, and photographing, and involved me in the daily maintenance of three households. As a maid, I was carefully instructed in the rules of cleanliness, which alerted me to the complexity of the taboo system.

I spent about two years living intermittently with one family, the Millers, consisting when I met them of a father, mother, three children, aged 14, 12, and 7, a grandmother, and two cousins. At first I was treated like an outsider, served food on special dishes, and made the butt of jokes. However, my willingness to perform services for the family, such as reading and answering the mail and chaperoning the teenage girls to ensure that they did not socialize with non-Gypsy boys, made me an asset, and I was taken along to feasts and ceremonies. After a few months, the father suffered a heart attack and the resulting crisis threw us closer together. The family relied upon me more for child care, and the grandmother asked me to move in with them. In the spring of 1977 I traveled with the family to Florida, Georgia, South Carolina, Virginia, and Washington, D.C., as they visited kin and explored business possibilities. I thus had the opportunity to see how Gypsies perceive the world and the different attitudes they hold about other Gypsies and non-Gypsies (see Table 1 for a set of distinctions). I also traveled alone to California numerous times from 1977 to 1979 to visit branches of the families with whom I worked. Because I traveled so much and brought news and photographs, I became a link in their communicative network.

As my fieldwork progressed, I realized that I could use my own status in the family as a measure of the validity of my analytic findings. The more I learned about appropriate Gypsy behavior, the better I could myself behave as a Gypsy. My transformation from outsider to insider

TABLE 1: Relations of Gypsies to Insiders and Outsiders

To Insiders	To Outsiders
1. Sociability, hospitality, respect, commensality	1. Absence of sociability, hospitality, and respect, or faked sociability; absence of commensality
2. Cooperation	2. Exploitation
3. Money exchanged (e.g., bride price)	3. Profit sought
4. Lying prohibited	4. Lying permitted
5. Speak *Romani*	5. Speak the *gazhe's* (non-Gypsy's) language
6. Deal with deviance by public monitoring and *kris* (*Rom* court)	6. Deal with deviance through *gazhe* authorities; may break *gazhe* laws
7. No absolute leadership; leadership and respect fluctuate	7. "King" is leader
8. Demonstrate ethnicity and folk beliefs, especially taboo adherence	8. Conceal ethnicity, pass as other ethnic groups, demonstrate local religion
9. Demonstrate chastity and modesty	9. Demonstrate fake promiscuity and exaggerate sex appeal
10. Demonstrate wealth and status	10. Conceal wealth and status

can be traced on two levels: the access granted to me and the way in which I was treated. For example, initially the Miller children gave me the "dirty glass" to drink from. After a couple of months the same children told me, "Don't drink from that glass—it's dirty—it's for the customers." At first the children tried to prevent my finding out about Gypsy affairs and family problems; later they were the first to inform me. Little by little, the children confided in me their past and present secrets, including much they kept concealed from their elders. Similarly, all the fortune-telling activities were initially kept hidden from me. Whenever there was a customer, in person or on the phone, I was sent to another part of the house. Gradually these preventive measures ceased, and I was given the responsibility of answering the fortune-telling letters.

A change which signaled the beginning of my transformation was the attitude of the female children. They began to show an interest in me, to talk to me, to ask me questions, to ask me to stay longer. At first their biggest interest was my appearance, which they thought was pitiful: "You dress corny, your earrings are odd, you gotta get some nice clothes."

"Come on, let me fix you up, tweeze your eyebrows, cut your hair, put makeup on you. The main thing is to catch the boys. They'll be runnin' after you. It's about time. Carol, you're twenty-five years old!" An afternoon's activity would sometimes consist of the teenagers' "fixing me up," during which time we would talk. They wanted to remake me into their ideal of an available woman, Gypsy style: one who wears makeup, gold jewelry, mod clothing, and platform shoes. They offered advice about what to wear and gave me gifts of clothing. This ideal also had a nonphysical aspect: an unmarried woman should know how to sing, dance, walk, cook, clean, and tell fortunes; thus my informal instruction began. They would correct my singing and teach me (and each other) how to dance, walk, and put on makeup. The older women instructed me in cooking, cleaning, and in other practices such as chaperoning the teenagers.

My reputation was a big concern to the Millers, for it affected theirs. When I traveled alone to California, I was given explicit instructions as to the Gypsy rules of conduct:

> You got to watch out for the men in California. Don't go to the houses alone. . . . Be careful when they say, "Come over to tutor or baby-sit—I give you $20." Leave the house in the daytime—don't spend the night. Because, you know what I mean, you get a bad name for us and then you can't come here. Be careful when the men smile and laugh and especially at parties when they're drunk.

I was given these directions not only for my protection, but also for theirs. Similarly, I was advised to stay away from some relatives where the men were "fooling around." I was told, "It's too dangerous. What might the people say?" If I did something wrong, I could no longer associate with the family who had sent me. As an outsider who learned how to cross the outsider/insider boundary to act as a Gypsy, I was, in many ways, treated as one. Note, however, that I was never labeled a Gypsy; one must be born into that status.

Out of my personal knowledge of and socialization into Gypsy culture, I became aware of the underlying values which informed their behavior and the implicit strategies used to reinforce those values. The Gypsy worldview is lodged in the dichotomy between insider and outsider, or *Rom* (meaning man, Gypsy, or husband; plural *Roma*, meaning people) and *gazhe* (meaning non-Gypsy; by implication, nonpeople or subpeople). See Table 2 for a set of distinctions.

Gypsies view the world of the *gazhe* as separate, inferior, and polluting. The only extended contact with non-Gypsies occurs in the eco-

TABLE 2: Differences between *Rom* and *Gazhe*

Rom	Gazhe
1. Superior	1. Inferior
2. Clever	2. Gullible
3. Clean; maintain *Rom* taboos	3. Dirty, polluted; unaware of taboos
a. source of health	a. source of disease
b. modest and chaste	b. promiscuous
4. Member by birth (at least one *Rom* parent)	4. Both parents *gazhe*
5. Speak and understand *Romanes*	5. Do not speak or understand *Romanes*
6. Adhere to *Rom* kinship and social organization	6. Lack *Rom* kinship and social organization
7. Self-employed	7. Work for others
8. Derive profit only from outsiders (*gazhe*)	8. Derive profit from their own kind
9. Abide by *kris*	9. Abide by *gazhe* legal system
10. Nomadic (as the ideal, have freedom to travel)	10. Tied to location
11. Flexible in organization of time	11. Adhere to schedules
12. Display *Rom* physical appearance and nonverbal behavior	12. Do not look or act like *Rom*
13. Display *Rom* material possessions (dress, houses, jewelry, cars)	13. Do not display *Rom* material possessions

nomic sphere where self-employed *Rom* provide goods and services, such as used cars, body and fender repair, and fortune-telling for non-Gypsies. Profit results from these exchanges.[4] The separation of *Rom* and *gazhe* is grounded in the taboo system which defines polluting or defiling persons, objects, foods, body parts, and topics of conversation.[5] Cleanliness is associated with Gypsiness, males, superiority, health, luck, and success. Pollution is associated with non-Gypsies, Gypsy women, disease, death, bad luck, and failure. Non-Gypsies are by definition polluted because they are ignorant of the rules of the taboo system.

The center of ritual purity is the head or, more specifically, the mouth. The woman's lower body is considered *marime* (ritually unclean, polluted) and everything associated with it is potentially defiling, such as contact with genitalia, inappropriate sexual activity, bodily functions, the bathroom, clothing touching the lower body, and topics of conversation alluding to sex and pregnancy. Strict washing regulations are enforced, including the use of separate towels, soaps, and wash basins for the two body zones. In addition, objects from the environment are classified by status; mops and brooms, for example, are *marime*. Anything entering the mouth, such as food, and anything touching the head, like a pillow, is carefully screened.

The most potent danger of pollution emanates from the woman's lower body zone. A woman can deliberately defile a man by touching him in public with an article of clothing from her lower body, like a slip or a stocking. Although the act of defilement rarely occurs in actual fact, the knowledge that it *could* happen is sufficient to guarantee elaborate precautions. When a man is defiled, he himself becomes *marime* and is excommunicated. He is cut off from commensality and sociability with other Gypsies. This is the greatest shame a man can suffer. Defilement may result from other transgressions, such as having sexual contact with *gazhe* or stealing from a Gypsy. For example, a stepson of the Miller family was *marime* on the East Coast for one year because he had an affair with a non-Gypsy woman. During this period, he could not attend any public Gypsy gatherings, such as weddings, baptisms, or funerals. The only way *marime* status can be revoked is by convening a *kris*, an arbitration council composed of respected men.

Men and women are segregated at public events. A woman monitors her movements so that she does not pose a threat to males by appearing physically or symbolically higher than they. She does not step over or through male territory or intrude in the public domain dominated by men. At one home gathering, I was told that I could not enter a room full of men even for a moment to retrieve my purse; I had to send a prepubescent girl seven years of age to do it for me.

The Millers gave me specific instructions for observing the taboos so I could pass as a Gypsy. I avoided referring to the bathroom and pregnancy. At first I was prevented from preparing food, but as I learned the rules of behavior, I was permitted to cook. On one occasion while traveling, Mrs. Miller introduced me to our Gypsy host as her daughter. The host showed interest in me as a bride for his son. Mr. Miller, worried that the host would press for the match, then changed my status to *gazhe* tutor. To drive home the point, he told the host that I drop towels on the floor and step over them. He added that I use the same cloth for drying my body and my face. It was untrue, but it proved I was a *gazhe*.

Judged by this elaborate system of purity and taboo, Gypsies consider non-Gypsies to be ruleless, orderless, promiscuous, dirty, inferior, and totally undesirable. This view is substantiated not only by avoidance codes, but also by oral tradition.[6] *Gazhe* who eat in *Rom* homes are often provided with their own cup, plate, and silverware, as I was initially. These objects are *marime* and are often treated with disgust; a six-year-old child warned another child, "Don't use that glass—*gazhe* drank from it." Mrs. Miller remarked, "I used to be crazy, I was so particular about being clean. I used to carry my own glass around in my bosom, even at weddings. I still drink from paper in a restaurant. I don't use their forks; I use my hands. Their plates are okay because they didn't touch their mouths. Sometimes I imagine that they go to the bathroom and don't wash."

The criteria for membership in the group *Rom* are primarily aspects of behavior once descent has been established. In other words, to be *Rom* it is not enough to be born *Rom*; one must also act *Rom* and display *romania* (*Rom* traditions) to other *Rom*. Displaying *Rom* social organization involves enacting lineage (*vitsi*) affiliations and obligations such as hospitality and aid, age and gender roles, and marriage customs (including the paying of a bride price). Furthermore, if a male *Rom* disobeys the decisions of the *kris*, he is formally relegated to outsider status for a certain amount of time. The impact of public opinion enforces *kris* decisions. In a more general sense, the *kris*, by monitoring deviant behavior, helps to maintain *Rom* traditions and the Gypsy/non-Gypsy boundary.

Conditions of Adaptation

How does such a strong value system fare in a heterogeneous, multicultural society? Some observers of Gypsy life predict the breakdown of Gypsy culture as a result of the clash of that culture with that of the United States. As one observer stated, "To them it must be terrible, not merely to live cooped up in a city, but to see their old trades and skills become obsolete and many of their customs die out under the pressure of modernity."[7] But change does not necessarily lead to total absorption of Gypsy culture. Gypsies may change external traits, but their core values remain intact, especially with regard to such phenomena as urbanization, travel, employment, and technology—forces most often recognized as contributing to change.

Rather than being a threat to Gypsy culture, urbanization has acted to support and strengthen it.[8] Gypsies have always voluntarily passed through cities, finding business opportunities plentiful and convenient in the urban environment. They have sometimes settled in lower-class neighborhoods because Gypsy practices may not be tolerated in upper-class areas. Although they considered moving to an upper-class neighborhood in Manhattan, the Miller family ultimately decided to remain in Flatbush, Brooklyn (a lower-class neighborhood), because the rents would be higher in Manhattan and the street population and police would be more hostile to fortune-tellers. In the United States, busy shopping streets offer Gypsies the greatest business advantages: location, accessibility, and a sizable population of potential customers. Gypsy used-car and fortune-telling establishments fare well in cities. Rules of territoriality have been established to deal with the problem of competition for fortune-tellers in areas of dense *Rom* population. In New York City, for example, a three-block rule was in effect between 1976 and 1979, stipulating that no *ofisa* (fortune-telling parlor) could operate closer than three blocks to an existing *ofisa* without the consent of the *Roma* involved.

Because of urbanization, the physical distance between Gypsy and *gazhe* has narrowed significantly. Prior to the 1930s, when Gypsies camped outside cities and traveled in caravans, contact with fortune-telling customers — and non-Gypsies in general — was established by entering the city or by setting up a booth at a carnival where non-Gypsies were sure to congregate. Today, customers enter Gypsy territory for readings. A curtained-off "reading room" has emerged for Gypsy/non-Gypsy interface. This space is manipulated by the fortune-teller in constructing her image and establishing her credibility.

Increased contact with *gazhè* has also created new opportunities for fortune-telling and its advertisement. The Miller children distributed handbills on buses, on subways, and at busy street corners. Mrs. Miller's sister always gives a handbill to her taxi driver and to the nurses and aides in the hospitals she visits. She remarked, "I like to go and pay bills at the telephone company because there are lots of people there. I pass out [hand]bills in line."

American cities have, then, become havens for Gypsies. Those *Roma* who live in small towns are often pitied by urban *Rom*. Of the tiny town of Wildwood, Florida, Mr. Miller remarked, "These poor *Roma*, they're really out in the sticks." Not only is their *gazhe* customer pool small, but they are isolated from the sociability of other *Roma*. Such isolation is nearly equivalent to cultural stagnation in a society that depends so much on face-to-face communication. Urban life also offers many locations for in-group *Rom* gatherings such as weddings, baptisms, and saint's day celebrations. Like their *gazhe* neighbors, *Rom* now rent banquet halls for these occasions. Far from hampering Gypsy life, then, the social conditions of American cities favor it. Cities are quite anonymous, and it is possible to slide through the bureaucracy untraced and to remain unnoticed for long periods of time. For example, it took the business-license agents six months to discover that there was a fortune-telling business operating in Mrs. Miller's sister's apartment. Moreover, the United States does not require multiple settlement, registration, and citizenship documents, as do many other countries, especially those of Eastern Europe. Some elderly American Gypsies, having been born in campsites, do not have birth certificates or Social Security numbers.

Finally, the mobility of the United States is ideally suited to Gypsy life. Although nomadism has declined somewhat among the *Rom*, it is still a strong cultural concept. Mrs. Miller's mother, for example, believes that getting on the road when you feel an illness approaching will help keep the illness away. In actuality, a Gypsy may be nomadic or sedentary as the situation requires and as the environment changes. Whereas many earlier studies labeled entire groups as either nomadic or sedentary, in reality the Gypsy's residence is chosen according to the requirements of the situation. Nomadism and sedentarism are alternate strategies for negotiating social and economic niches; the amount of time spent traveling is inconsequential. What is really significant is that the option to travel is constantly present in the minds of American Gypsies, in spite of the fact that they may remain sedentary for long periods of time. For example, one *Rom* family has "lived" in a home in Pomona, California, for eleven years, but still spends three to four months a year traveling and would consider "moving" at a moment's notice if the right opportunity—such as a good business venture—arose. While they travel, their home is rented to *Rom* relatives. This family, like many others, has accumulated a great deal of expensive furniture, but they do not hesitate to leave their home for travel. The status in owning an opulent home or furniture comes from spending the money and from the oral circulation of legends and rumor about the opulence. It matters little that the family is not occupying the home. Thus, lavish furnishings are typical of *Rom* households, but the objects do not make the *Rom* sedentary.

Travel is necessary to find brides, attend Gypsy celebrations, be near ill relatives, and find profitable business locations. Gypsies think nothing of traveling 600 miles by car in one day to attend a Gypsy wedding and then traveling home the next day. A Gypsy funeral may draw people from thousands of miles away within a few hours. Travel is also a viable means of physically removing oneself from sources of conflict back home. The conflict may be with *gazhe* authorities or with other Gypsies. If the police, for example, are cracking down on fortune-tellers in a particular area, Gypsies may move temporarily until "things quiet down." Similarly, a Gypsy who is *marime* (ritually polluted) in one state may travel to another state or take a trip for the duration of his excommunication. The Miller's stepson, *marime* for a year on the East Coast, went to California where he could socialize with *Roma*.

Modern means of transportation have actually helped keep nomadism viable. The passing of the horse and caravan and the coming of the automobile, rather than forcing assimilation, have simply increased the Gypsy's speed and rate of travel. Not only is automobile travel easier, faster, and more comfortable than caravan travel, it is also "the American Way." Upon returning to New York City, seven-year-old Ephram Miller explained his nomadism to an outsider in commonplace American terms: "I just got back from vacation." The "vacation" was actually a three-month-long trip to numerous southern cities taken in a brand new Cadillac Eldorado Biarritz, with plush red carpeting, AM-FM radio, air conditioning, eight-track cassette player with four speakers, make-up mirror, and many other accessories. The purpose of the trip was to visit relatives, gather news, investigate marriage possibilities for the teenage daughter, and explore future business ventures. Mrs. Miller also told fortunes at every possible opportunity. She passed out handbills while waiting in line at Disneyworld, and at the motel at which we were staying she tried to interest the maids and waitresses. "I'm a famous fortune-teller from New York—I've been on radio and T.V. Come to my room for a reading." They indeed did come to the room, and she sometimes worked two or three hours a day. Even while shopping she found opportunities to tell fortunes: "This carpet wasn't too expensive because, when we went to Atlanta to the factory to get it, I told a couple of fortunes to the salesladies in the waiting room, and so they knocked off $100 here and there." Change in means and frequency of travel, then, has not altered the basic relationship of Gypsy to *gazhe* but has rather provided more opportunities.

Similarly, modern methods of communication, such as the telephone, have actually contributed to the vitality of *Rom* networks. The telephone is a constant source of news concerning marriages, elopements, bride prices, deaths, and feasts. Through the telephone grapevine, people and events are endlessly discussed and evaluated, reputations are established and lost, and the kinship network is activated. Telephone conversations also provide data about the non-Gypsy world, such as business locations, weather reports, and the reputation of doctors, hospitals, lawyers, school and welfare officials, and the police. The monthly telephone bill for the Miller household was usually over $300 in the late '70s, indicating frequent use. A contemporary urban innovation is the use of the telephone for fortune-telling. A separate number is usually used for this purpose; it is answered only by women in the language of the customer population. The family may also have a second number for car transactions; it is answered by men. A third number is the "*Rom* phone," the number known only by other *Rom* and answered in *Romanes*. In sum, the telephone has encouraged the orality of *Rom* culture.

Occupational innovation is another indication of successful adaptation to changing environmental conditions. During the early years of the twentieth century, the North American *Rom* continued their European trades of horse trading, horse doctoring, carnival work, and metal work, such as replating vats and mixing bowls for institutions like hospitals and bakeries. Women often begged or told fortunes either at carnivals or in rented storefronts. In the post-war years, horse trading and metal work have been replaced by used car trading and body and fender repair. The switch from tinkering to automobile repair has been viewed by some as the loss of a traditional Gypsy trade. But body and fender repair can also be seen as a creative adaptation of metal work to a new situation. Rather than indelibly labeling a certain occupation "Gypsy," it is important to consider the larger structural view of Gypsy economics. Throughout the years, certain occupations have become typical or "traditional" because they are lucrative and fill the needs of time and place while not compromising basic *Rom* values such as self-employment, mobility, independence, and the restrictions of the taboo system.[9] In North America, for example, as the *Rom* became more urbanized, fortune-telling became the major source of income, with male income viewed as supplementary. The fortune-telling niche serves the *Rom* well since "reading and advising" seem to strike a responsive chord with many American customers. Whenever fortune-telling is not profitable, *Rom* easily switch to another trade. When the Millers moved to Los Angeles, for example, the family's major source of income switched from fortune-telling to car sales. The choice of occupation is extremely flexible, and a Gypsy man or woman usually engages in many occupations during his or her lifetime. Mr. Miller, for example, has dealt in used cars, toys, retinning, and carnival work during his thirty adult years.

Strategies of Adaptation

Given the many exchanges between Gypsy and non-Gypsy in vital areas of urban life, how do Gypsies maintain social and cultural independence? The answer is that Gypsies have developed sophisticated social strategies for pretending to be acculturated while actually remaining fiercely loyal to the Gypsy community. Successful interaction with non-Gypsies is crucial for survival because *Rom* depend economically and materially on non-Gypsies. When Gypsies interact with non-Gypsies, they have various motives for influencing the impressions others may have of them. To a lawyer, they may be interested in demonstrating their credibility as American citizens; to a welfare worker, their victimization as an afflicted minority; to a restaurant audience, their flair for music; to a fortune-telling customer, their spirituality. Switching among these roles has made Gypsies expert in the arts of "impression management." In general, the more skills a Gypsy accumulates, the better off he or she is; Gypsies prefer strategies of survival that offer multiple opportunities. Thus, they learn many trades and many languages and absorb information about diverse aspects of the surrounding cultures. They are equally facile at employing these skills.

It is often necessary for Gypsies to submerge their Gypsy ethnicity because it is a social stigma. Quite deliberately, Gypsies pass as members of other ethnic groups, as Puerto Ricans, Mexicans, or Greeks, when they wish to avoid harassment by such *gazhe* authorities as landlords, tax officials, truant officers, welfare workers, or the police, or when they wish to seek housing, jobs, or welfare services. Passing involves adopting the personal front of a non-Gypsy, including appearance, demeanor, use of the English language, and adoption of American names. When the Miller family was scouting for an apartment among real-estate agents, the mother dressed like a non-Gypsy: she used pale makeup to lighten her skin, she wore a blonde wig, she took off her traditional head scarf, and she wore an "American" dress, which was shorter, more tailored, and more subdued in color than her usual clothing. In addition, she spoke only English, not *Romanes*. When this strategy failed to conceal her Gypsiness, I was sent (with a teenage daughter) to procure an apartment for the family. Mrs. Miller told me: "Tell them you're sisters, you're Jewish, and give them your name. Don't tell them where we live. They're prejudiced against Gypsies." In this case, a non-Gypsy was used as a front. Furthermore, I was often warned by the children and the parents not to tell the neighbors, the fortune-telling customers, or the local storekeepers that the family was Gypsy. I was also warned not to tell the black maid for fear she would quit. "Don't tell the customers we're Gypsies. They don't trust Gypsies. Say we're Greek."

On the other hand, Gypsies sometimes perpetuate and exaggerate the common *gazhe* stereotypes of themselves. For example, Gypsy fortune-tellers advertise themselves as spiritual, psychic, religious, foreign, erotic, and exotic healers, gifted with supernatural powers. Gypsies encourage this stereotype not only because it promotes business by fulfilling *gazhe* expectations, but also because it serves to conceal the in-group culture. In effect, the outside world is presented with a surrogate Gypsy culture. Furthermore, Gypsies perpetuate misconceptions that *gazhe* have of them, such as using the appellation "King of the Gypsies" to deliberately inflate the power and romance often attributed to Gypsies. Using the titles "king" and "queen" is also helpful in securing privileges, such as when obtaining private hospital rooms, requesting extended visiting hours, and seeking permission to bring food into funeral homes and cemeteries. Ratso Ephram, a middle-aged *Rom*, said, "Any Gypsy who enters a hospital is automatically a king. They get better treatment. . . . There's no such animal in the Gypsy race as a king. . . . It's just some person who wants to be glorified. But you go to the newspaper morgues in New York and get old papers and every time a Gypsy died he was king. There has got to be 1,000 kings. . . . He could have been penniless, didn't have a dime, but when he died he was king. . . . That's just garbage." In reality, the "king" holds no absolute authority within the community; he is a public relations man whose main task is negotiating between non-Gypsy authorities and Gypsies.

Naming is another strategy that Gypsies use for passing. Gypsies use a multiplicity of common American names to avoid visibility; there are probably hundreds of Gypsies named John Miller, George Adams, and Dora Stevens. When a truant officer entered the home looking for John Miller, six males ranging in age from two years to eighteen years claimed that name, hopelessly confusing the case. Furthermore, the Miller family listed their apartment under one name, the telephone under another, and their fortune-telling business under yet another. Because many *Rom* are semi-nomadic, addresses change continuously. This multiplicity makes Gypsies hard to identify and trace, producing precisely the effects Gypsies seek. In Western society, a name is an indelible mark which rarely changes. For Gypsies, on the other hand, changing American names is a strategy they use to remain invisible, concealed, and untraceable. Among themselves, however, they employ kin designations.

Another perpetually important skill is linguistic agility. While virtually all American Gypsies have learned to speak English, they also retain *Romanes* because both languages are functional. As Anne Sharp recently reported, "The mixing of Romanes and English . . . is not due to the imperfect learning of either language, but is a beneficial way of insuring that all members of the community know both languages from an early age. While English is essential for economic survival, *Romanes* continues to be important for cultural solidarity. The mixing of the languages follows rules which show that mixing is not random and does not lead to general confusion of the grammar of either language."[10] Wherever Gypsies live, they learn the languages of the area in addition to retaining *Romanes*. In the Hungarian district of New York, local Gypsy women tell fortunes in Hungarian. They are, at the very least, bilingual and usually multilingual. In southern California and New York City, for example, many Gypsies speak Spanish as well as English. Gypsy women may command use of a greater number of languages than Gypsy men because they service many ethnic groups through fortune-telling. A marked specialization exists in the function of non-Gypsy languages. There are Gypsy women who can tell fortunes in nine or ten different languages without being able to speak fluently in any of them. Multilingualism has always been an asset to the Gypsies and has not interfered with the retention of *Romanes* as an exclusive in-group language.

Conclusion

By thoroughly understanding and creatively using the environment around them, Gypsies have been able to adapt well to American society without giving up the essentials of Gypsy distinctiveness. They are able to maintain their identity as Gypsies while appearing to be assimilated. Extrinsically, Gypsies are Americanized: they speak English, dress in the latest American fashions, live in apartments, drive cars, and furnish their homes with American goods. Indeed, they may be considered highly "American" because they have adapted so well to the American context. They interact to a high degree with Americans, who may be unaware that they strongly identify themselves as Gypsies. Yet the basic values of Gypsy culture are extremely important to Gypsies, who wish to remain distinct from Americans and American culture. In this pluralistic society, to be an American does not require shedding one's cultural heritage. An ethnic may be quintessentially American while simultaneously remaining loyal ethnically. Members of ethnic groups develop values and strategies for ensuring that the identities "American" and "ethnic" complement each other.

Notes to Chapter 7

1. The following is a sample of sources which predicted the assimilation of American Gypsies: James K. Reeves, "A Gypsy Settlement," *Chautauquan* 10

(1890): 446–50; Victor Weybright, "Who Can Tell the Gypsies' Fortune?" *Survey Graphic* 27 (March 1938): 142–45; Stephen Murin, "Hawaii's Gypsies," *Social Process in Hawaii* 14 (1950): 14–38; Georgina Traverso, "Some Gypsies in Boston, Massachusetts," *Journal of the Gypsy Lore Society* 37 (1958): 126–37; M. W. Clark, "Vanishing Vagabonds," *Texas Quarterly* 2 (1967): 204–10; Katherine Esty, *The Gypsies: Wanderers in Time* (New York: Meredith, 1969); Marilynn Preston, "Destiny Is Closing in on Today's Gypsies," *Chicago Tribune*, 9 June 1975.

2. Werner Cohn, *The Gypsies* (Reading, Massachusetts: Addison Wesley, 1973), 23.

3. Matt Salo, ed., *The American Kalderash: Gypsies in the New World* (Hackettstown, N.J.: Centenary College, 1981), iii. Deciding who is *Rom*, however, depends *primarily* on who is doing the deciding. As Salo has aptly demonstrated, ethnic labeling is highly problematic when dealing with Gypsies; each group defines "Gypsy" as its own group and contrasts itself not only with non-Gypsies but with other Gypsy groups. See Matt Salo, "Gypsy Ethnicity: Implications of Native Categories and Interaction for Ethnic Classification," *Ethnicity* 6 (1979): 15.

4. For the economic organization of *Rom*, see Salo, "Kalderash Economic Organization" in *American Kalderash*, 71–97.

5. See Anne Sutherland, "The Body as Social Symbol Among the *Rom*," in *The Anthropology of the Body*, edited by John Blacking (New York: Academic, 1977), 375–90; Carol Silverman, "Pollution and Power: Gypsy Women in America" in *The American Kalderash*, edited by Matt Salo, 55–70.

6. See Matt Salo, "The Expression of Ethnicity in *Rom* Oral Tradition," *Western Folklore* 36 (1977): 37–39.

7. Traverso, "Some Gypsies in Boston," 136–37.

8. See Carol Silverman, "Everyday Drama: Impression Management of Urban Gypsies," *Urban Anthropology* 11 (1982): 377–98.

9. See Salo, "Kalderash Economic Activity"; Don Boles, "Some Gypsy Occupations in America," *Journal of the Gypsy Lore Society* 37 (1958): 103–11; Traverso, "Some Gypsies in Boston," 137–38.

10. Ann Sharp, "The Relationship between Romanes and English as Spoken by the Portland Gypsies," M.A. thesis, Portland State University, 1983, 2.

8. Iranian Immigrant Name Changes in Los Angeles*

BETTY A. BLAIR

When it comes to names, you never quite know what you're in for as a foreigner, especially if your own language is very different from the main culture's. It's like trying to play football when you've practiced soccer all your life. Suddenly, the ball is headed straight towards you, and you don't know whether you're supposed to kick or carry. No one cares that you've never played the game before, never had a chance to read the official rule book, and that there's no coach prompting you from the sidelines. Yet everyone expects you to play the game as well as the next guy. And you better believe, if you want to make the team, you'll have to play a whole lot better than everybody else.

— An Iranian Immigrant Living in Los Angeles

Iranians, like millions of others who have immigrated to the United States, are often confronted with the question of whether or not to change their foreign-sounding names. For many, the choice is difficult because their names are packed with emotional significance, identity, and meaning. The Iranian expression "Prove me wrong and I'll change my name" underscores the strong belief in the importance of names in their culture.

In the States, however, foreign names are often perceived as complicated, harsh-sounding, and strangely unfamiliar. An immigrant's ability

---

*This chapter is based on data originally collected in 1987.

to succeed may be dependent upon using a name acceptable to and understandable by others. Choosing a new name may affect one's potential friendship network and the ability to obtain suitable employment, as well as the development of a positive self-image and identity in the host society. Thus, the reality of one's continued residence in a new country often makes dealing with one's name a harsh, unavoidable reality.

Researchers have sometimes concluded that when immigrants adopt names similar to those used in the host culture, they are expressing a desire to assimilate.[1] Data from my research suggest that acquiring new names should, at least for the Iranian immigrant in the American context, be viewed not as a denial of one's ethnic identity but rather as an adaptive strategy.[2] The decision to change one's name should be viewed as a dynamic and deliberate response to current needs rather than as a departure from past traditions. For Iranians, name changing is a conscious attempt to acquire more power, control, and access in a cross-cultural context and may function in at least three different ways: (1) to facilitate acceptance by members of the host culture—socially, psychologically, and/or economically; (2) to serve as a barrier against embarrassment, intrusion, insult, and conflict; and (3) to distance or dissociate oneself from political conditions in the home country.

The Iranian community in Los Angeles, although almost nonexistent 20 years ago, is today fairly sizable and well established. Though accurate statistics are not available, it is estimated that between 300,000 and 400,000 Iranians live in the city, which they themselves sometimes jokingly refer to as "Tehrangeles."[3] Evidence of the community's substantial population, especially on the more affluent west side—such as in and around Beverly Hills—is apparent from school enrollments, which are estimated to be as high as ten percent Iranian. According to the current 700-page *Iranian Directory Yellow Pages*, now in its seventh year of publication (1987), the community supports more than 200 practicing physicians, 69 dentists, 25 restaurants, 34 food markets, 47 insurance brokers, and 28 travel agencies. Perhaps the most influential and cohesive force within the community is the Iranian media, which broadcast and publish daily in Farsi. There are more than 35 hours of television and radio programs each week, a daily newspaper, 6 weeklies, and several political and literary magazines published monthly.

The majority of Iranians living in the United States left their home country just prior to the Shah's being ousted from power in 1979. With the Ayatollah Khomeini's establishment of the Iranian Islamic Republic and the subsequent involvement of Iran in a devastating and seemingly endless war with Iraq, many Iranians have been reluctant or unable to return home, at least for the present. The dilemma is further complicated by the fact that in contemporary history, there are no precedents of permanent emigration from Iran. The last major mass exodus occurred nearly ten centuries ago when Persian Zoroastrians (Parsees), fearing religious persecution from the Arab invasion, sought asylum in India, where today they remain a thriving community. What this means in terms of Iranians coming to the United States is that they have no model upon which to pattern their lives, either in terms of the major practical issues in life or in terms of symbolic issues such as name practices. Much of their energy is spent on "finding their own way," as one Iranian expressed it.

My interest in the subject of Iranian name changes began at a party several years ago when I was the only American among more than a dozen Iranians. During the course of the evening, I inquired of the whereabouts of a woman whom I knew as Kathy, only to be met with blank stares, as if I had named a person totally unknown to the group. No one seemed to know who Kathy was. Finally, in desperation, I mentioned her husband's name, to which they all chorused, "Ohhh! You mean Atusa." In other words, the woman who had previously introduced herself to me as Kathy was known only as Atusa to her Iranian friends, and neither the Iranians nor I realized that she also went by another name.

As I began questioning other Iranians about the names they used, I soon discovered that it was common to have different names for Iranian and American audiences. Everyone who had adopted a new Americanized name claimed to use it only with non-Iranians while retaining his or her original name within Iranian circles. As in the case of Atusa/Kathy, even close Iranian friends did not necessarily know of the existence of the second, more Americanized name.

I decided to study the problem more systematically to determine the extent to which Iranians were adopting new names and to identify their motivations for making such changes, as well as to record their attitudes toward other members of the community who had opted for change. In January 1987, I developed a ten-page questionnaire and distributed it among members of the Iranian community.[4] My research differs from most previous studies of immigrant name changes in that I focused on personal names rather than surnames or family names and asked the immigrants directly for opinions and impressions about the process and impact of name changing, rather than obtaining data from official documents.

Differences in Naming Traditions
Between Iranians and Americans

Iranians bring to the United States a strong tradition of using names to mark social distance in relationships with others. The original personal name is reserved for primary relationships. A different name is used with secondary relations; typically, surnames are combined with appropriate titles, such as Mr., Mrs., Professor, Engineer, Doctor, or Hajji. Children in public school, from kindergarten onward, are addressed by their family names without a title, with a title (Mr. or Mrs.) being added at the university level. I am suggesting that when Iranians adopt Americanized versions of their first names and use them only within non-Iranian circles, they are employing a similar pattern of interaction based on social distance in their homeland.[5]

Furthermore, in Iran, personal names of women are more carefully guarded in public than are men's names. Just as there is a tradition of veiling women physically, shielding a woman's personal name from men outside the family is perceived as a form of protection. Evidence for this phenomenon still exists in Iranian rural settings.[6]

In America, however, different naming practices place pressure on the traditional Iranian patterns. Many Americans use personal names to address older people as well as individuals not previously known to them. Iranians who marry Americans often comment about the dilemma they face in deciding how to address their new in-laws appropriately. From the Iranian point of view, to call one's father- or mother-in-law by his or her first name seems disrespectful because it ignores age and status. For the same reason, Mom and Dad, the terms often adopted by American couples, seem uncomfortable. But to address them, as is customary in Iran, by Mr. or Mrs. along with the surname may seem too formal from the American point of view.

In addition, other studies indicate that Americans favor shorter names, viewing them as more potent and more active than names of greater length.[7] This custom often presents difficulties for the Iranian, whose name may extend to eight or nine letters. Americans also give preference to common names over less common ones.[8] Except for names such as Ali or Mohammed, most Iranian names do not meet this criterion. The issue is further complicated in that three sounds in the Persian language — an aspirated /h/ and the guttural sounds /kh/ and /gh/ — do not exist in English, and many, if not most, Iranian names include at least one of these sounds.

A final difference in traditional naming practices is that Iranians select names largely because of their meanings, while Americans concentrate primarily on the euphony created by the combination of the first and last names.[9] Iranian names are generally selected from the following categories: prominent religious figures, classical historical personalities; heroic literary characters; natural phenomena (such as names of flowers, birds, and celestial bodies, all particularly popular for female names); and positive attributes such as the words "fortunate," "precious," and "happy." More recently, a new category of experimental names that recall abstract concepts, such as "hope," "message," and "belief," are being used. In other words, Americans emphasize phonology while Iranians seem more concerned with semantics.

Ironically, names which once had so much significance in Iran are not only totally stripped of their original meaning in America, but they may take on pejorative or obscene interpretations. For example, Simin means silver in Persian but becomes totally inappropriate in English because of its phonological proximity to the word "semen." Negar means lover but could easily be misconstrued for the ugly slur "nigger." Nazi conjures up the atrocities of Hitler during World War II, rather than a charming, lovable girl. Poopak refers to an Iranian bird, but may evoke the act of defecation for English speakers. Asal means honey but one Iranian mother perceived it dangerously close to "asshole" in English. Faced with such negative association, Iranians have little choice but to select a new name or else experience derision and ridicule. (The identical situation would occur were an American girl named Ann to go to Iran; in Farsi Ann means shit.)

Occasionally Iranians suffer embarrassment when Americans mispronounce their names resulting in an offensive meaning in Farsi. Though the mistake may be recognized only by the name-bearer, the situation can be very frustrating. For example, English speakers invariably pronounce Khosrow as Kosrow, not distinguishing the guttural /kh/ sound from the /k/ sound. As a consequence, Khosrow, which names an ancient king, inadvertently recalls the Persian equivalent of cunt. One man named Khosrow recalled that at parties, after the Americans had left, his Iranian friends would tease him all evening about the way the Americans had pronounced his name—"Kosrow! Kosrow!"[10]

Name Change as a Means Toward Facilitating Acceptance

Iranians who often come into contact with Americans, such as in businesses and schools, are especially vulnerable to the effects of mispronunciation. Within the business world, many Iranians have determined that having a name that is easy to pronounce is crucial to being accepted by others.[11] The vast majority of respondents in my survey were highly educated professionals competing for jobs against non-Iranians in fields such as medicine, engineering, computer technology, architecture, teaching, administration, accounting, and business. Iranians recalled experiencing embarrassment when attempting to conduct business with American clients who focus on their strange-sounding names. As a result, many regard their foreign names as a handicap in freely entering the marketplace. To facilitate communication in the business world, Iranians often initiate what might be considered a "rite of passage" in which the immigrant sheds the liabilities brought about by his original name.

Many found that adopting a new name increased job opportunities; in some cases, it seemed to be the determining factor. One woman, Sarvnaz, commented:

> If you're trying to get a job and the person evaluating your resume can't even pronounce your name, much less determine if you are male or female, chances are you won't get an interview. They'll ignore you. I want people to be able to pronounce my name correctly; but more importantly, I want them to remember me.

Another young man, named Sayeed, was so convinced that his name had prevented him from obtaining the job he wanted that he adopted the name Andy, the first part of his last name Andalibian:

> Three times I interviewed for jobs for which I was well qualified. Each time I was rejected; the employers simply could never remember how to pronounce my name. When I changed my name, I got the job I wanted on the very next interview.

Since then, Andy has opened his own office in one of the most prestigious sections of town.

Another man found the need to camouflage the religious connotation of his Iranian name:

> I really love my name, Ali, but at work, I call myself Alex because I'm in the jewelry business and my colleagues are Jews. I don't want them to think of me as a Muslim before we even have a chance to establish a relationship.

Predictably, women who did not adopt new names complained more than others that their jobs did not make good use of their education. Typically, 60 percent of the respondents in the other groups (males who had adopted new names, males who had retained their own names, and females who had adopted new names) felt that their "jobs made good use of their education" compared to only 9 percent of the women who had retained their Persian names. This difference seems to illustrate the economic advantages of selecting a new name.

In schools, Iranian children meet non-Iranians daily and are greatly concerned about how to fit in and be accepted. Children are especially sensitive to being perceived as outsiders. One young girl, who had experienced years of frustration with her Iranian name, remarked, "We look so different as it is. Having a strange name makes it so much harder." Schoolmates are often cruel in their use of nicknames, and many Iranian children have modified their names to ease anxiety. For example, although Fatimeh, the name of Mohammed's daughter, may be one of the most revered and sacred names in Islam, on the playground she may be easily targeted because of the phonological proximity of her name to the word "fatty." In another example, eight-year-old Farahnaz (meaning "exhilarating" or "cheerful") was called "fart" while classmates giggled and pranced about her making what they thought were appropriate sound effects. Banafsheh (violet) suffered the humiliation of Banafshit, and Farokh (happy, joyful spirit) had to cope with "fuck." A five-year-old girl, Pantea, was already feeling the effects of her classical Persian name as early as kindergarten where classmates proudly brandished their knowledge of the alphabet at her expense by calling her, "Panty-A, Panty-B, Panty-C." Kayvan (Saturn), an eight-year-old boy, was teased by others who picked up on the rhyming pattern and called him "Sav-On," the name of a chain of drug stores in the area.

Even when children manage to escape ridicule, they are very sensitive to differences between their names and those of Americans. One mother observed that her child's awareness of names seemed to be much like his growing consciousness of race:

> When my son was young, he didn't even recognize that there were differences in either skin color or names. But now that he's eight, he's very conscious of both and perceives his name (Bardia) to be so different from the other children's that he wants to change it to Brad.

Name Change as Protection from Unwarranted Intrusion and Conflict

In addition to changing one's name to facilitate acceptance by the host society, adopting a new name can serve to distance or shield the individual from intrusion and insult. This is especially true for Iranians since the United States Embassy Hostage Crisis in 1979. Iranians are extremely sensitive to the way in which they are perceived and blame television for a great deal of discrimination and misunderstanding. One man remarked, "When people watch programs like 'America Held Hostage!' you bet, not only do I detect an uneasiness in the way people respond to me, but I feel a great need to watch my butt."

As foreigners, Iranians are conscious of subtle nuances and shifts in the verbal and nonverbal behaviors of others. Ninety-seven percent of the respondents believed Americans have very negative opinions of Iran. Forty percent indicated that they had been deliberately discriminated against at work. Nearly fifty percent of the respondents commented that whenever they mentioned their nationality, they detected that others felt somewhat uneasy. Some deliberately attempted to divert attention from the subject of nationality. One man frequently contrived jokes when asked his nationality: "I just tell them I'm from the moon and my father is Neil Armstrong, and then we both laugh and they forget to ask again." Some say they are from Persia rather from Iran, incredulous that many Americans do not know that both words refer to the same country.

Names can also serve as a barrier against outside intrusion in the business world. One woman claimed that changing her name allowed her to get more work done in her fast-paced telephone dispatch job. It shielded her against infringements on her time:

> Using an easier name helps me skip over the repetitive questions that people always ask. It helps me to get down to business quicker. Besides, I get tired of answering the same questions over and over again, such as, "How do you pronounce your name again?" "How do you spell it?" "What does it mean?" "What kind of name is that?" and "Where do you come from?" It saves an incredible amount of time when I use a different name.

Another man, Hushang, had a similar experience and found it financially necessary to make the change:

> I'm a salesman and do most of my business by phone. If I tell people my name is Hushang, that's the end of my sale. I might as well hang up and save myself the time and effort because people interrupt and ask questions and the conversation gets sidetracked. On the other hand, when I tell them my name is Michael, they never question me and even though I have an accent, I can continue directing the conversation the way I want it to go.

The importance of having a "value-free" name is emphasized by students as well, as when a teenage girl who had recently arrived from Iran remarked, "I chose a different name to use at school because I didn't want people to change their opinion about me after I told them where I was from." In other words, she preferred establishing her own reputation rather than taking the chance of being prejudged by others.

Adopting new names can also serve to mask psychological pain and give outsiders the impression that "everything is fine." Common among Iranians is the expression, "Keep your face pink even if you have to slap it" ("*Ba sili seuraetra sorkh negaehdashtaen*"), indicating that it is advisable to maintain an appearance of physical and psychological fitness, even if one must suffer physical pain to produce the effect. In other words appearances are often viewed as more important than realities. A line from the well-known Iranian poet Saadi of the thirteenth century suggests, "Better a wise lie than a conflict" ("*Dorugh-e maslehaet amiz beh keh raste fetne angiz*").[12] Most Iranians consider themselves exiled from home and privately mourn their forced separation from family, friends, and culture. Many admit to being psychologically wounded. Under different political circumstances, if given the choice, many would opt to return to Iran rather than live abroad. Choosing a new name to use with non-Iranians can serve to provide a means of escape from constant reminders of a world left behind.

Iranians attempt to avoid conflict with non-Iranians whenever possible. Many Iranians prefer to ignore an affront or to tolerate an error, especially during initial encounters, rather than correct it. In Persian culture, it is acceptable to misrepresent oneself or tell a "white lie" in order to avoid potential conflict.

One might compare the Iranian's nonconfrontational style to that of a gracious host who anticipates potential conflict and prevents guests from experiencing difficulty and discomfort. Iranians pride themselves on being among the most hospitable and courteous people in the world. Despite the media's depictions to the contrary, Iranians have a cultural regard for foreigners that can be traced historically to the role Iran played as a hub for the dissemination of ideas in science and philosophy, the arts, crafts and technology, architecture, military science, travel, and exploration.[13]

Being gracious and polite is a highly refined art in Iran, and children from an early age are taught the nuances of appropriate expressions and behavior. A proverb from the Azerbaijani, one of Iran's ethnic groups, reminds one to fulfill these expectations despite cultural differences: "It is your duty to respect your guest, even if he is Armenian (Christian)." Turning this analogy around, one male respondent likened his residence in the States to being a guest and concluded that it was his responsibility to ease life for Americans since they were his "hosts." Changing his name seemed appropriate behavior for the role in which he perceived himself.

Name Change as a Reaction to Political Conditions in Iran

In their choice of names to use in America, Iranians are responding not only to changes in their contemporary situation in the United States but also to their own past. Iranians continue to cultivate strong ties with their own culture even while attempting to succeed within American society. Some observe that because they may never be able to return to Iran, they identify even more closely with their homeland. Some Iranians admit to reinstituting cultural traditions in America which they once rejected while growing up in Iran.

Reinvigorating Iranian roots is evident in the choice of names for children born in the United States. Nearly all Iranian parents in Los Angeles assign first names to their children at birth that are distinctly Persian in origin, refusing to select either American names or Arabic (Islamic) names, as would be encouraged in present-day Iran. As one informant observed, "We want names for our children that are uniquely Iranian — that is, names that can only be found in Iran and no place else in the world."

Historically, religious names have played an enormous role in the naming practices of Iranians. Before the Pahlavis came into power in 1925, it has been estimated that approximately ninety percent of Iranian parents selected religious names of Arabic origin for their children.[14] During the Pahlavi reign (1925–1979), about half of children's names were derived from these Islamic sources. Now, however, with the establishment of an Islamic Republic, parents in Iran are once again feeling pressure to choose religious names for their children and are doing so as much as eighty percent of the time. Radio and television public service messages admonish parents to choose religious names for their children. To the contrary, however, most Iranians living in the United States consciously distance themselves from anything associated with such pressure. The majority of them reject Islamic religious names in what may be considered a silent but deliberate protest against the Islamic government.

A joke currently circulating (in 1987) among Iranians in the United States expresses their disdain of any association with Khomeini:

A man went to the appropriate government office seeking to change his name.

"You can't change your name. It's impossible," the officials said, denying his request.

"But it's absolutely necessary," insisted the man. "I really can't live with this name. It's really a bad name."

"Well, what is it?" the official wondered. "How could it be such a bad name that you insist on changing it?"

The man replied, "My name is Ruhollah Sendekhor." (Sendekhor translates to something like "shit eater"). The official nodded sympathetically.

"Well, then," the official asked, "what name did you have in mind to change it to?"

"Well, sir, I'd like to be called "Bijan . . . Bijan Sendekhor," the man replied.

The joke hinges on the fact that the joke teller's first name Ruhollah is the same as Khomeini's, while Bijan is a very popular secular name of a Persian hero. Despite the obscenity of the last name, the man chooses to retain it and focus on the predicament of having to share his first name with someone he despises.

Most Iranian immigrants blame Khomeini for their forced exile and the intolerable conditions that now exist in their country. The government he established is considered by many to be the main obstacle preventing their return home. Clearly, the choice of names for children reflects both the anguish of attempting to link their children with Iran while disassociating themselves from anything connected with Khomeini as symbolized by the Islamic religion.

Processes Involved in Name Changing

Adopting a new Americanized name rarely appears a random decision. Several criteria seem to affect the choice. Invariably, the original Persian name becomes the basis for the new name. One man named Jaafar adopted the American name Jeff, explaining that it was the "closest English name to his real name." As if to seek reassurance that he had not strayed far from his Iranian identity, he wrote on the questionnaire I circulated, "Don't you think so?" Americanized names tend to be shorter and, of course, conform to the phonemic structure of English. Invariably the new name begins with the same initial letter or sound as the original Persian name. The most frequently adopted American names in my survey were Faye and Fred. Faye was used in place of Fa'ezeh, Fahimeh,

Fariba, Farideh, Farahnaz, Farnoush, Farzaneh, Fereshteh, Firouzeh, and Farough. Fred was substituted for Farajolah, Faramarz, Farhad, Fariborz, Farid, Farokh, Farshad, Feridoon, and Firouz. Exceptions in adopting identical initial sounds tended to occur most often when individuals directly translated the meaning of their Persian names into English, such as when they asked to be called Lily instead of Niloufar or Violet instead of Banafsheh.

Another pattern that emerges is the tendency for many Iranians to experiment with several names before finally settling on one—like trying on pairs of shoes to see which fits best before finalizing the purchase. Such a process gives the individual the added advantage of proving the receptivity of members of the host culture toward the name. Often, the new name is suggested by others, leading the newcomer to assume that if the name is, indeed, appropriate, the individual will himself be more readily accepted by members of the host culture. Switching names typically occurs when an individual changes school or job or moves to a new community.

For example, one man named Farokh has changed his name four times during his ten-year stay in the United States. Except for his latest choice, all names had been suggested by others. When he first arrived in the United States, he worked in a shoe store owned by a Chinese who called him Fred. Later, while attending a university, he conducted research in a Chicano Studies program and was promptly dubbed Francesco. Upon graduation, he taught school and permitted the children to shorten his last name Nakhjavani to Mr. Javani. Presently, he manages apartment complexes where he tells non-Iranians to call him Frank. This last choice, he proudly explains, is composed of the dominant letters of both his first and last Persian names, Farokh Nakhjavani, and serves to satisfy non-Iranian tastes while remaining close to his ethnic identity.

Parents, too, are concerned with giving their children Persian names that will be successful in a cross-cultural context. Invariably they restrict the Iranian name to four or five letters within the English phonological structure. As discussed earlier, parents try to anticipate names that might have pejorative meanings. Often they consult with American mothers and sometimes even check the English dictionary for words in close proximity to the desired name. Despite their extreme attention to this question, their children often experience considerable problems when this occurs, and many parents respond by immediately taking steps to Americanize the child's name. If, however, a child is unable to convince his parents of the seriousness of the problem, he may take matters into his own hands and adopt a new name without telling his parents. For example, one teenage girl changed her name, Banafsheh, to Lisa. Her parents discovered it only when other children started phoning the house and asking for Lisa. A young boy who suffered considerable anxiety from his name Sibouyeh took it upon himself to tell others his name was Seeby. His parents became aware of his decision while checking returned homework papers.

Conclusion

Decisions about selecting the most appropriate name reflect the active control immigrants exercise in determining how they wish to be perceived by others. Newly adopted Americanized names function (1) to allow Iranian immigrants to become more socially, psychologically, and economically accepted; (2) to shield themselves from unwanted embarrassment and intrusion, successfully warding off potential conflict with strangers; and (3) to distance and disassociate themselves from the political scene at home. Personal name changes are not necessarily evidence of loss of ethnic identity; rather, a closer examination reveals that they are clearly rooted in the Persian culture and provide evidence of the dynamic interaction and creative strategy employed by immigrants to confront the demands of social interaction in their new environment.

Notes to Chapter 8

1. Immigrant name studies within the United States have been conducted with Chicanos by Lurline Coltharp, "Dual Influences on Chicano Naming Practices," *Names* 29 (1981): 297–302; with Chinese University students by Tai S. Kang, "Name Change and Acculturation: Chinese Students on an American Campus," *Pacific Sociological Review* 14 (1971): 403–12; with Hispanics by Richard D. Woods, *Hispanic First Names: A Comprehensive Dictionary of Twenty-Five Years of Mexican-American Usage* (Westport, Connecticut: Greenwood Press, 1984); with Germans by Frederick Walter Hilbig, *Americanization of German Surnames and the Related Process of Changes in Europe*, Master's Thesis (Salt Lake City: University of Utah, 1958); with Greeks by James E. Alatis, "The Americanization of Greek Names," *Names* 3 (1955): 137–56; and with Jewish refugees from Central Europe by Ernest Maass, "Integration and Name Changing among Jewish Refugees from Central Europe in the United States," *Names* 6 (1958): 129–71. In Canada, studies on Slavic immigrants have been undertaken by Robert Klymasz, "The Canadianization of Slavic Names," *Names* 11 (1963): 81–105, 182–95, 229–53.

2. In this study, Iranians who adopted new names claimed to speak Farsi at home just as frequently as did Iranians who continued to use their Persian names

(eighty-five percent). They were equally firm in their resolve to give Persian, not American, names to children born to them in the United States (ninety percent). They were also equal in claiming (eighty-five percent) that their three closest friends were Iranian by nationality.

3. The 1980 United States Census identifies 122,890 Iranians as permanent residents. Of these, 42,608 were said to be living in California. Besides being outdated, these statistics are considered to be significantly unreliable since the majority of Iranians in the United States in 1980 were students, many of whom had overstayed their visas and would not have wanted to draw attention to their ethnicity for fear of being deported by the American government, perhaps in retaliation for the hostage crisis in Teheran. See Jamshid Momeni, "Size and Distribution of Iranian Ethnic Groups in the U.S., 1980," *Iran Nameh* [A Persian Journal of Iranian Studies] (1984): 2, 16.

4. In general, I found the Iranians to be incredibly supportive of my study; of 115 questionnaires distributed, 95 (eight-three percent) were completed and returned, 78 of which came from first-generation Iranians, upon which I base my analysis.

A general profile of the respondents would include the following: (1) approximately sixty percent were male, forty percent female; (2) most had achieved an extremely high level of education: forty-one percent had earned master's or doctor's degrees; only two had no education beyond high school; (3) nearly fifty percent had arrived in the United States before they reached the age of twenty; (4) most respondents were in the prime years of their adult lives: eighty percent were then between the ages of twenty and thirty-nine; five percent were age nineteen or younger, fifteen percent were in their early forties, the oldest respondent being forty-four; (5) nearly seventy percent had lived in the United States for a minimum of seven years, the majority having arrived during the years of the OPEC oil boom (1971–1977); (6) the majority claimed to have come to the United States to further their education, fully intending to return to Iran upon completion; (7) ninety percent were competing for jobs in the mainstream culture, the remaining individuals being employed in Iranian shops and businesses.

5. One of the most frequent complaints made by Iranians who had adopted new names was that they forgot to respond when others called them by these new names. In other words, they still generally considered their true identity bound to their original Iranian names.

6. In villages, a mother's name is rarely mentioned. Instead, she may be referred to by her husband's name, e.g., "Ali's wife," or by a technonymic name (usually that of her first son's), e.g., "mother of Babak." As a married woman, if she has not yet given birth to a child, she may even be known as "mother of the hidden one." One may still observe young boys trying to blackmail and pressure their friends by claiming to know the names of their sisters. Many immigrants, even those who grew up in Iranian cities, recall how common it was to tease each other about knowing the names of female family members.

7. Edwin D. Lawson, "Men's First Names, Nicknames, and Short Names: A Semantic Differential Analysis," *Names* 21 (1973): 27.

8. Ibid. 22.

9. See Jane Morgan, et al., *Nicknames: Their Origins and Social Consequences* (London: Routledge and Kegan Paul, 1979), 21.

10. In this study, four men had the name Khosrow. Each had opted for a new name in the cross-cultural context and each had chosen a different way to solve the problem of maintaining a semblance of identity with the original name. One man chose the name Ken after purchasing his first car from an American with that name (in itself, perhaps, a rite of passage into American life). Two chose some form of the name Kay—one as a first name and the other as Mr. K. (Interestingly, Kay Khosrow was the name of an ancient Persian king.) Another man drew upon his Jewish heritage and Americanized his middle name, which was Hebrew, changing Natan to Nathan.

11. In response to my survey, an average of forty-one percent of the respondents (forty-seven percent female and thirty-seven percent male) admitted to using a second name when interacting with non-Iranians. Although it is beyond the scope of this paper to discuss gender differentiation in relationship to name changes, studies by Piaget and Chodorow would support the likelihood of observing such statistical differences. They found girls more tolerant in their attitudes toward rules, more willing to make exceptions, more easily reconciled to innovations and, in general, more likely to define themselves in relation to and connection with other people than males. See Jean Piaget, *The Moral Judgment of the Child* (London: Kegan Paul, Trench, Trubner & Co., 1932), 83, and Nancy Chodorow, "Family Structure and Feminine Personality," in *Women, Culture, and Society*, edited by M. Z. Rosaldo and L. Lamphere (Stanford: Stanford University Press, 1974), 43–44.

12. Reza Assadi, "Conflict and Its Management: Persian Style," *Anthropological Linguistics* 24 (1982): 202.

13. Suniti Kumar Chatterji, *Iranianism* (Calcutta: The Asiatic Society, 1972), 33.

14. Personal conversation with Dr. Hassan Khanlou, dean emeritus of Tabriz University, Iran.

9. Ethnic Selection and Intensification in the Native American Powwow

BARRE TOELKEN

Although American Indian ritual and celebratory dances have enjoyed close examination and analysis through the years, Native vernacular dances have not been taken so seriously. Perhaps because the social dances lack those impressive magical or ritual goals which make, say, the Hopi Snake and Antelope, the Zuni kachina, or the Navajo *yei-bi-chei* dances so fascinating to whites; perhaps because dramatic elements like blood, trauma, pain, and self-denial (such as might be witnessed in a Sun Dance) are not central to them; perhaps because their participants seem to be having fun instead of playing to the white stereotype of Indian stoicism, the social dances, especially those of an intertribal nature, have remained outside the experience and ken of mainstream Americans. One result is that, for whatever reason, the contemporary intertribal powwow, an increasingly popular vernacular dance expression among Native Americans, has not been given much attention by scholars, even though it has become one of the most common articulations of "Indianness" among Indians today.[1] Indeed, for many Americans, the recent film *Powwow Highway* may provide the first (and only?) exposure to a cultural phenomenon which is occurring around them practically all the time. Perhaps the powwow's very contemporaneity, its dynamism and rapid spread in recent years, and its participants' unhesitating use of modern forms, colors, and implements run so contrary to our stereotypes and assumptions about the Vanishing American and stand so in opposition to the way we think tribal people ought to behave that we have been inclined to see the powwow as a mishmash of leftover ideas no longer seriously functional in the world of the Indians. Perhaps the old notion of *gesunkenes Kulturgut* is still alive and well when it comes to how we think about Native Americans: we think the older, more "pure" customs have died out, and we see little remaining beyond a modern nostalgia for a vanished way of life perpetuated in exercises which lack their "original" meaning and seriousness.

This myopic view has allowed us to ignore one of the most rapidly growing expressions of ethnic awareness and identity to be found anywhere in the world today, and to overlook an important concept about the transmission of cultural reality as well: an idea may be phrased in a number of ways, and indeed it may survive more successfully if it is susceptible of continuous reassessment and retranslation into newer and more functional modes of expression. The Navajos, for example, whose principal cultural and linguistic "leitmotiv" is *movement*, were happy to encounter the horse, for the horse made movement even faster and more efficient; they were even happier to get pickup trucks, for—far from abandoning older cultural ideas—they were able to maintain and intensify an essentially Navajo idea about mobility when the world was closing in around them. We need to inquire if the powwow offers some parallel intensification which might account for its increasing popularity: is there something about the idea of dance per se that articulates or embodies something important for Native Americans today? Does the intertribal nature of the powwow illustrate a reassessment of older tribal allegiances vis-à-vis modern Indian identity? It is the thesis of this essay that the powwow phenomenon can be viewed as a decodable kinetic statement about the realities of life for ethnically aware Native Americans, as well as a tableau scene of intense cultural meaning within hostile surroundings. The dynamic relationship between tribal and intertribal concerns, as well as between intertribal and mainstream ("immigrant," in the view of many American Indians) cultures, is played out and articulated by the powwow in the spatial and temporal arrangements of activities, in the similarities and differences between tribal customs, in the specific styles of dance and their continually developing meanings, in the respective roles of men and women, in the delicate balances between cooperation and competition, and in the overlapping of secular and sacred concerns.

The powwow in its current form is an outgrowth of earlier social dances held by almost all tribes for their friends and allies. As far back as the written histories of Europeans in America go, there are good records of such occasions being held regularly. The difference today is that these dances are held for members of all tribes and not just for allies. That is, they provide for the expression of common interests now felt by virtually all Indians, who see themselves as living surrounded by a hostile and domineering culture. The intertribal connections brought about and nurtured by powwow dancing are of political as well as ethnic importance for Native Americans. Often, powwows provide the occasion for Native Americans to develop political and legal ways to survive in the modern world. The value of intertribally shared interests—in contrast to tribal differences that might have existed from ancient times—is expressed vividly in the powwow. Thus, even though the political issues discussed at powwows are quite modern, the use of the dance as symbolic of reciprocation and cooperation is certainly testimony to the continuing function of older modes of thought and expression.

The term *powwow* seems to come from one of the Algonquian languages (northeastern America), where it originally meant a medicine man or conjurer. The term was borrowed by white Europeans to refer not only to a medicine man but to a meeting at which curing took place. Eventually it was used by the whites to denote virtually any gathering of Indians, especially where singing was central. Indians have borrowed back this term (and several others used in the powwow like "war dance") from English usage.

Today a powwow is essentially a social gathering at which Indian people from several tribes dance together, using a few basic patterns that all the tribes recognize. The music is highly stylized, and the dancing goes on most of the afternoon and evening, with the dancers resting occasionally while particular groups (young men or older women, for example) compete for prize money. From time to time, the hosts or a visiting group will demonstrate a particular dance from their own tribe while other participants watch. Visitors are welcome, but non-Indians are sometimes asked to pay an entrance fee to support the cost of the event and to help pay for the prizes.

The comments in this essay are based mostly on my observation of, and participation in, three different powwows: the huge, nationally known annual celebration held outdoors on the Crow Indian Reservation in Montana called "Crow Fair"; the relatively smaller Arlee Powwow, held outdoors on the Flathead Indian Reservation in Montana each July; and the Native American Student Union (NASU) Powwow, held indoors each year by the Native students at the University of Oregon, Eugene.[2] Although all powwows today are similar in many details, each has its own characteristics. Student powwows often include honor dances and awards for student leaders and recent graduates; tribally based powwows honor local leaders or old-timers. But the ethnically weighty matters taken up in dance and social form by the powwow are very much alike the country over. The regularity and system with which certain events and activities occur at virtually all powwows—rural or urban, indoor or outdoor, whatever their size and their tribal affiliations—are testimony to the existence of a growing body of custom, observance, belief, propriety, and awareness which have superceded the specific tribal customs that once underscored the differences (often the open enmities) among the participating tribes. The emergence of this larger body of custom and observance, which overarches and to a large extent subordinates older differences, is an indication that specific tribal identity is being reassessed by many Native Americans and being replaced by a powerful synthesis of related traditions that can articulate Indianness.

Whether held indoors or out, powwows on or near reservations pull Indian people "home" from wherever they may be working or living; on the other hand, urban powwows call people from the reservations to join their city cousins on neutral ground (a school gymnasium, a rodeo arena) for reestablishing family and social ties. The outdoor event often features a large encampment with tipis, wall tents, modern campers, and mobile homes. The urban, indoor event, on the other hand, requires housing to be located and meals to be supplied.

Crow Fair is so large that thousands of Native Americans spread themselves over many acres in family camps; in a parallel to olden times, a crier (with a public address system mounted on a pickup truck) circulates announcements and camp rules, and lets people know which dances will be coming up in the large central arena where the action takes place. At the Arlee Powwow there is no need of a circulating crier, for the dancing arena in the center of the camp has a public address system that can be heard everywhere. At the University of Oregon NASU Powwow, held usually in the university's field house, a p.a. system suffices for making announcements at the powwow itself, but a detailed mimeographed sheet listing the various contests and the overall order of events must also be distributed to all who come; participants overnighting in various parts of town tend to stay in the field house area all day and evening in order not to miss anything.

The physical arrangement of these events mirrors intertribal attitudes about order and spatial harmony. Crow Fair is full of traders' stalls (people selling raw materials, such as beads and supplies for Native artists who produce items for powwow outfits), booths selling books about Indians and tapes of Indian music, booths where Indians sell and trade other items of interest, stands where churches and veterans' groups sell burgers, fry bread, and cotton candy. Arlee Powwow is surrounded by similar booths, as well as a hall where the teenagers can gather and dance to more recent music if they wish, a covered pavilion where several avid stick games are constantly in progress, and rows of small rooms where card games are played. But the arrangement is not haphazard: both Crow Fair and Arlee Powwow look like concentric circles when viewed from above: in the center a dancing arena, then a circle of booths and stands (some of them mounted in mobile homes or camper vehicles for easy transport to the next powwow), then a larger and more amorphous circle of tents, tipis, and campers. The pattern is essentially the same as it was 200 years ago in villages of the Plains Indians, though content and detail have changed considerably.

For urban, indoor powwows like that of NASU, the pattern is still recognizable, though it takes form within another framework; here, within the confines of a cavernous field house, the gym floor is the dance arena, and it is surrounded (as is the dancing area at outdoor events) by a circle of seated participants and observers. Outside that circle, usually in the hallway surrounding the basketball court, is a ring of concession tables, traders' stalls, book and tape booths, and the like. And around that—in the gridded, anonymous town of Eugene—is an imagined circle of homes whose owners have agreed to let some Indian visitors stay for a couple of nights. "It's a strain on you to turn a square into a circle," says Larry Calica, a yearly visitor from Warm Springs reservation to the NASU powwow, "but you can do it if you concentrate."

The dancing area in all cases is viewed as circular or oval, no matter what shape the actual room may be, for most tribes see the circle as the normal pattern of nature. In the center of the area, from one to five (sometimes more) drums are situated, and the dancing takes place around them, with the prevailing motion usually being "clockwise," or sunwise. Each drum (the term includes the drum itself and the group of singers gathered around it) will alternate with the others in singing, although a particular drum might be asked to perform out of sequence to provide the song for an honor dance.

The most important initial development as the powwow gets under way is the gathering of people around the drums. Among those invited to a powwow will be several groups who are expected, perhaps specifically invited, to bring a drum. A drum group from the local area may be honored by the planning committee by being asked to serve as "Host Drum." But people have often not decided ahead of time exactly who will drum, and a drum may not begin drumming until the proper number of drummers have come forward (the number varies in different tribes). When such a "critical mass" has gathered, the people around a drum will begin to sing and to practice (to "warm up"), and it is not until two or three of the drums have tested a few songs that dancers will move onto the floor and begin dancing. When it is clear that there are enough drums to allow for a sequence of dances to take place, the master of ceremonies announces the opening processional. This juncture arrives naturally as an aspect of the process, not in response to the clock, and it indicates vividly the temporal assumptions of Indian life.

Indeed, all three powwows discussed in this paper start and end on "Indian time"; that is, in spite of detailed planning, both indoor and outdoor powwows unfold according to generalized Native American attitudes about time in relation to event. Rather than starting exactly at the advertised moment of 7:30 p.m., the NASU powwow actually gets under way long before then as people from out of town arrive, meet each other, get their outfits together, wait for the drums to gather, get a bite to eat, and so forth. At 6:00 p.m. there will be a few people on the gym floor, talking, and a drum or two will be setting up and trying a song. By 8:00 p.m. the grand entry might or might not have occurred, depending on whether everyone who is expected to be in it has shown up yet. By 9:00 p.m. the entry will already be behind us, and the floor will be crowded with dancers; by midnight there will still be a few diehards, but most of the people will have left in search of their host families or a stick game. It would be difficult to time any of this by the clock, for these actions are responsive to the internal dynamics of the event far more than to the arbitrary measurement of elapsed time.

Similarly, Crow Fair and the Arlee Powwow have their advertised days and times for beginning and ending, but in fact people start showing up days in advance. Some move in with relatives or friends, others set up tipis, others park their recreational vehicles somewhere near the dance pavilion, then start the visiting, trading, outfit repair, political discussion, and food preparation that characterize life at the large outdoor powwows. At Crow Fair, women are busy setting up family cooking areas, finishing up beaded moccasins and vests for their family's dancing, renewing their acquaintances with people from distant tribes. At the Arlee Powwow everyone is busy looking for clever partners for the stick game (or for cards and other gambling games that go on virtually without letup on all sides). At the NASU Powwow, visitors are attending classes with their children, seeing the town, and visiting with their hosts. In all cases, the event, essentially a social one, is driven by the dynamics of sociability. People start by attending to the broader demands of friendship and kin, then move toward an intense celebration of their shared ethnicity in the medium of dance, then move back to the general level, and finally go home. Since the timing is internal, the event is more like a flower blooming than like an airplane leaving; the schedule is created, so to speak, by the passengers, not the company.

The opening ceremony includes at least a "flag dance" in which national flags of the United States and Canada are paraded around the arena, along with the Indian warriors' flag, actually a staff festooned with eagle feathers honoring Indian people who have died in warfare. Many Indian people are veterans of World Wars I and II, of Korea and Vietnam, and many of them belong to official veterans' groups. But it is made very clear during this processional that the warriors' flag represents all warriors who have fallen in all wars, a very pointed reference to the number of people who died while fighting against European invaders. The tableau of the American, Canadian, and warriors' flags in procession around the pavilion together is somewhat ironic on the political level, but it is also a reminder of the ways in which American Indians have survived culturally by amalgamating many of their interests with those of the countries which have surrounded them. It also stands as a symbolic cameo of the syncretic, inclusive, centripetal force of the powwow itself.

After the opening "flag song," there is often an invocation or pipe ceremony, then an "intertribal war dance," not a dance that has anything to do with war, but a dance whose steps are celebrative (which led early white observers to assume that it was a dance done only in the case of victory in war). The first half-dozen dances or so are all of the intertribal "war dance" variety and are often referred to as "warm-up dances" because they draw everyone into the festivities and help the drummers get into good voice.

Drummers are expected to know their songs thoroughly. Not everyone is allowed to approach the drum, and no one under the influence of drugs or alcohol is allowed anywhere close. Menstruating women are not to sing around the drum or dance, but they may attend the powwow as spectators. Each drum receives payment to cover transportation expenses, but if one drum has been asked to sing an honoring song during the powwow, the family of the person honored will donate an additional gift of money to the drum. While these sums of money are usually quite modest, for an honoring dance—particularly for someone recently deceased—the amount can be as much as $100. The gift is almost always announced publicly as well. Singers usually spend the entire powwow gathered at their drum. Since in a powwow of five drums there is ample time to rest one's voice between songs, some drummers will get up and join the other dancers, especially toward the end of the evening. Whenever a round dance is called, in which all spectators and participants are expected to take part, two or three of the drummers will be seen moving through the crowds gesturing at people with their drumsticks to come to the floor to dance. As the evening goes on the drummers sing louder and louder, and there is a tremendous strain on the voice. For this reason, a number of traditional Indian medicinal plants, such as yarrow root, are used to protect the throat.

Although there are demonstrations of particular tribal dances during pauses in the powwow schedule, the bulk of dancing being done by participants falls into two large categories: war dances and round dances. In the former, dancers dance alone according to their own variation of accepted powwow style (although one often sees friends dancing near each other); everyone who wants to dance will be on the floor, but there is no attempt to dance in unison except for the fact that everyone is using the same drum beat. The round dances, on the other hand, place everyone in the same (or in concentric) circles, and everyone must use the same step, usually a side-step in trochaic meter. The result is several hundred people surging around the arena in unison and in one pattern.

In the war dances, there are two principal styles marked by clothing as well as by execution. The "straight" or "traditional" dancers wear more conservative clothing (often reflecting styles of early contact times) and dance their own unique step (often suggested by their name, or by the prominent animal or bird in their outfit, or even by the theme of their vision quest); the "fancy" dancers wear more modern adaptations of earlier styles, featuring more color, more feathers, more fringe, more moving parts. Fancy dancing tends to be faster and more energetic, and the moving elements in the dancers' outfits help to accentuate their athleticism.

Men are expected to dance energetically, and most of them have noise-makers attached to their legs: sleighbells, various kinds of shells, even large cowbells. The men's role in the war dance is to maintain and extend the heavy pulse of the drum, which holds all the people together in dance. The women, on the other hand, dance very lightly, some of the best seeming almost to float over the ground, for their role in these dances is to symbolize the dignity and the delicacy of the woman's position in nature.

Most of the women dance a style of war dance that would be called "traditional," both in outfit and in dance step. Some of the younger women, however, dance a fancy dance called the Shawl Dance, which features a large shawl with long fringes that wave back and forth. The shawls of the 1800s were buffalo hides; later, woolen blankets were used, and recently fringed polyester has become popular. The footwork is spectacular and the dance is so athletic that hardly anyone over the age of twenty does it.

Fancy dancing derives mostly from the Plains Indians but is done by members of virtually all tribes attending a powwow. It is especially common in competitive events because of the demanding footwork. Lately, however, the straight-dance style has become popular again, and in larger powwows today, the traditional dancers have increased to the point that they are, in some cases, more numerous in contests than the fancy dancers.

In recent years, the Arlee Powwow has had about equal numbers of straight and fancy dancers, although the Crow Fair still has a predominance of fancy (perhaps because of the large cash prizes which attract the most spectacular dancers in the country). The NASU Powwow at the University of Oregon usually has more traditional dancers than fancy, in part because the students, who are young enough to do the fancy dancing, are out of practice, while their elders, visiting from the reservation, are at the age where they naturally tend toward the traditional orientation.

In the fancy dancing, there is a greater obligation to know the songs, for the dances are faster and the dancers are dancing so energetically that it is very difficult to stop. During the competitive fancy dancing, the drummers try to trick the dancers by stopping suddenly in the middle of a song. The drum, however, can stop only at certain traditional places, at the end of a particular musical phrase. Normally, the song might go on at this point, but the drum has the option of stopping momentarily and then starting up again. When the drumming and singing stop, the best of the dancers will also be ready to stop on that same beat. Any dancer who takes another step will call attention to himself because of the sound of his bells. Through such trick stops as these, the less proficient dancers are eliminated from competition and the best of the fancy dancers remain. Obviously, even though part of the competition judging is based on how energetically and how well a dancer performs the steps, only those who know the songs and the song traditions thoroughly can possibly remain in competition until the end. Thus the knowledge of tradition is valued more than the competition itself.

In addition, those who win the top prizes (which may range from $50 to $1,500) almost always share their money with the other competitors and with the drums. This redistribution of prize money is a standard feature of Indian concepts about competition and selfishness: anyone who gains riches or power by his own means and does not share them with his family and friends is thought by many tribes to be a witch. Thus the tendency is not to keep money and goods but to redistribute one's own belongings as far as possible. The powwow provides a continually functional modern context where this may be done openly.

Both the intertribal nature and the secular function of the powwow are illustrated by the clothing worn. One seldom if ever hears the term "costume" from Indian people and the term "regalia" is rare; powwow clothing is seen as something to dress up in, but not in the sense of changing identity or "putting on a show." Outfits avoid tribal-specific details one would expect at a tribal ritual or religious observance. For example, a Navajo who dances in a ritual *yei-bi-chei* dance would never wear his mask and ritual sash to a powwow, but if he were to enter a fancy dance competition he would put on an assemblage of feathered wings and bustles which would have seemed totally foreign to his Athabascan ancestors (and, admittedly, hyperbolic even to the well-feathered Plains Indians from whom the motif comes). In feathers, bells, shells, hot colors, satin gym trunks, and perhaps sun glasses to boot, he would look unlike any Indian of 200 years ago, but he would look just like thousands of other powwow dancers today. For the men, whether dressed in fancy dance feathers or in deerhide and Hudson's Bay blanket, the outfit functions as a recognizable badge of intentional involvement.

On the other hand, the women's clothing at a powwow is often the same as they would wear at home on any Native occasion. Many Indian people feel that this consistency is further indication of the extent to which the dignity, grace, and power of women are demonstrated. That is to say, women do not have to wear special clothing for a powwow because they take their own tribal dignity with them wherever they go. Indeed, in many tribes it remains the women who continue to pass on language, religious belief, and other cultural instruction to the younger generation, especially since it is the custom among many tribes for the grandmother to raise the children.

Whatever the style of the outfit, straight or fancy, the production of the clothing (often made as gifts for friends, relatives, or lovers) is based on beliefs and assumptions about its symbolic function. Outfits should include something from the Wingeds (birds, who, being two-legged like humans, are considered close relatives), especially the feathers of an eagle. The Four-leggeds, who supply us with food and provide hides for moccasins and dresses and fur for decoration, are also represented in the outfit, along with decorations placed by human hands and supplied by creatures from the waters in the form of shells. The outfit is thus said to honor all that gives life on earth, all that provides humans with food, warmth, and sacred power. Wearing symbolic clothes, the dancers are one with all the living beings who share the world with them as their relatives. As people create their outfits for the powwow, stories are told and significances explained that strengthen this symbolism and pass it on to younger people, who are very much incorporated into the creative process. Thus, the outfits worn at the powwow provide an occasion for the material and oral articulation and transmission of traditional values.

Because the various items constituting the powwow outfit may be very special in nature, there has grown up an extremely complex way of dealing with loss, destruction, or deterioration of accoutrements. The one most immediately apparent to a powwow spectator is the Lost Item or Lost Feather dance.

Any time a major article of clothing from a dancer's outfit is lost or dropped on the floor, its return to the owner must be ritualized. Minor items such as a bell or a pair of glasses may simply be turned in or reported to the master of ceremonies, but something like an eagle feather calls for an ornate and serious ceremony. Naturally, there are regional and tribal variations on this ritual, but as it is typically seen in the West, the Whipman—one of the chosen officials on the dance floor—stands by the feather to make sure no one dances on it. After the conclusion of the dance in progress, the lost feather is announced, and a Lost Feather dance is quickly arranged. It usually calls for the four best male dancers (who must usually be war veterans) to surround the feather and dance around it and up to it almost as if they were hunting an animal. Just before they reach the feather, the changing beat of the drum calls them back to the perimeters of their circle, and the hunting starts again. Finally, after some minutes of dancing, one of the dancers (sometimes the person who actually noticed the feather first, but nearly always a war veteran in any case) dances up to the feather, picks it up and holds it over his head with a triumphant whoop, and then all dancers circle the pavilion sunwise. The owner is asked to come forward and claim the feather, then narrate a story about how it was first obtained and what relationship it bears to the dancer's outfit or character. The owner will often sing a song or play a drum to honor the person who found and recovered the precious feather. In some powwows, all lost objects are dealt with in this way, partly to show publicly that a missing item was not stolen or misused, and partly because it calls the loss to the attention of the owner who, in a large crowd, may not have noticed a part of his outfit falling and might not have heard an announcement over the loudspeaker.

Although locals and visitors participate together in these dances, there are other elements of dance protocol which must be observed in order to maintain the dignity of the individual tribes, even in the midst of intertribal celebration. One duty of the hosts, beyond supplying the arena and the housing, is to provide occasions for the expression of tribal identity (including their own), but in a way that will not place undue attention on any particular one.

For example, the local hosts of a powwow, if it is being held in "Indian country," may begin the event with one of their own special dances by way of welcoming participants. Every eight or ten years at the Arlee Powwow, the Flathead people do their Snake Dance, a long processional dance that begins far out in the tipi village surrounding the dance area, moves single-file through the tipis, and eventually arrives at the powwow grounds. Only Flatheads take part in this dance, which is said to derive from a time when a Flathead who had been bitten by a snake was cured when the whole tribe danced the snake's dance. Occasionally this dance is done in celebration of the relationship between Flathead Indians and the snakes (whose appearance and disappearance during the year are also calendar signs indicating when certain stories may be told or not told).

But since the hosts may not culturally dominate the event, it is also their duty to find out which visitors would like to present a specialty dance representing their own tribal affiliation (for example, a young man visiting from the pueblo country did a southwest Hoop Dance at each of the powwows reported here). At the NASU Powwow in Eugene in 1976, a group of eight teenage girls from Warm Springs presented a Butterfly Dance, in which they danced a very limited step with their blankets wrapped around their shoulders and heads with their bodies bent over. In this part of the dance, they represent the worm or the cocoon of a butterfly; later, when the dance's rhythm becomes more energetic, the girls do a much more active step. They throw their arms and blankets back, using the blankets as if they were wings, and whirl around in large circles celebrating the movement of nature from cocoon to butterfly, and also, of course, symbolizing the movement of a young girl to womanhood.

Just two years earlier, the Tolowa Indians of northern California had come to the same powwow to do their Deer Dance, in which the dancers simply stand in a line and bend rhythmically at the knees while small deer hooves attached to their costumes click together in rhythm. The dance is done today as an exhibition and only the Tolowa do it. The women in the group danced "topless" the first night, resulting in a large crowd of non-Indian spectators on the second night of the event. But the Tolowas, not wishing to sensationalize their contribution, added bras to their outfits. This immediate adjustment in the interests of harmony at the powwow is characteristic of the participants' attitudes. Were they to present sacred or ritual dances of their own tribes, such changes would be difficult if not impossible. All of these tribes have sacred dances tied deeply to certain areas of land or particular villages which cannot be performed elsewhere, but in any event—since they are considered a form of worship—these would be considered inappropriate for public display at a secular event like a powwow. The Butterfly Dance is done almost every year at the NASU Powwow, but to my knowledge the Tolowa Deer Dance has never been repeated because of its sensational effect on white people.

But intentional humor is another matter. At the Arlee Powwow, almost every year sees another enactment of the Wanabi initiation dance. The announcer—often Bearhead Swaney or Colonel Doug Allard—asks all Indian people to leave the center of the arena so that non-Indian visitors can be honored by induction into the Wanabi society. Hippies in beads, German and Japanese tourists festooned with cameras, elderly California matrons heavy with Navajo jewelry, grandpas on vacation in Hawaiian shirts and sandals are all dragged into the arena and given basic instructions on how to stamp their feet in time to the drums, and then, as they dance in a mixture of honor and embarrassment, they are told they are now the possessors of the Wanabi Dance, the special ritual dance for those who "wanna be" Indians.

At the NASU Powwow and occasionally at Crow Fair, the elderly ladies from Warm Springs Reservation in Oregon volunteer to put on an "Old Women's Dance." It starts with several ancient women hobbling around the arena on their canes, stumbling and sometimes bumping into each other. Then one pretends to take offense and swings her cane at one of the others, who in turn ducks the energetic blow and tries to strike back. Then follows a melee in which the old ladies try to hit each other in the shins or on the side of the head, all the while jumping over each other's blows, ducking, swinging their canes, all in time to the relentless drums. The battle lasts until everyone is laughing too hard to swing anymore.

At each of the three powwows, and at an increasing number of other powwows across the country, someone who knows the dance will be asked to lead the "Oklahoma Two-Step." The lead couple, holding hands, runs around the arena followed by other dancers, also in couples. The lead couple may stop and dance in place, may jump up and down, may run backwards, may split off with the men and woman going in different directions to come together at another part of the pavilion, and so on, all to a very rapid beat. All participants must follow the actions of the lead couple, and usually the dance dissolves in laughter as people begin tripping over each other and falling to the ground.

One of the most difficult aspects of Indian life today concerns competition, for in nearly every tribe it carries a negative connotation and may be seen as related to moral decay, selfishness, and even witchcraft. In some tribes, competition may be expressed in play or in games, but not in everyday life. Even in games there is a polite avoidance of serious personal competitiveness (a Navajo woman, watching a basketball game on television, asked me, "Why don't they give each of those teams a ball, and then they wouldn't have to fight over it all the time?") The powwow allows for a mediation between the competitive demands of mainstream society and the cooperative demands of Native culture. Thus, while personal competition in and of itself is seen as offensive, competitive demonstration of one's abilities at culturally meaningful expressions, carried out in a culturally determined context, is seen as a positive sign of belonging to, and accepting, one's own cultural value system. Moreover, winning a powwow competition brings cash prizes which, in turn, allow good dancers to afford the continuous travel to powwows. Most Native dancers, then, have learned to view the dance competition as similar to other kinds of competitive interplay that take place at the same event, such as gambling, stick games, and even courtship. As a game, the competition is conceivable and allowable, and it functions to enhance excitement and attendance.

The bigger the prizes, the more likely a powwow will attract the best of dancers; if everyone expects the finest dancers, the powwow will draw more people, both Indian and non-Indian. The Indians will expect to see (and perhaps participate with) the leading exponents of a cultural art form of deep significance to them; the non-Indians, while they do not share the deeper cultural values on which powwow symbolism and deportment are based, do nonetheless understand competition, and will enjoy the event for that and for its exotic and exciting colors and rhythms. The bigger the crowd, the better the powwow committee can pay its bills and plan a bigger event for the coming year.

The competitors are, however, evaluated at all times by Indian standards and not by the applause of the crowd. The women's dancing, for example, is judged by other Native American women who look for certain highly valued abilities that relate to Indian custom including authenticity of outfit, delicacy and style of footwork in the dance, and knowledge of the dance tune (indicated by stopping precisely when the singing stops). Similarly, in the men's traditional dancing, the dancers are judged on their knowledge of the songs, the authenticity of costume, and the forcefulness with which they portray the vision of the animal or process they are symbolizing in their dance. This evaluation encourages younger dancers who aspire to do the traditional dance steps to learn the traditions thoroughly before they dare place themselves in competition. From the Indian point of view, then, it is the strengthening of general tradition rather than the competition for money, trophies, or personal acclaim that is the central feature of the powwow. And thus, a potentially corrosive possibility is converted to a positive dimension of intertribal contact.

How does it come to be, however, that it is *dance* which plays this all-important role for Native Americans? Other ethnic groups have used food, language, music, clothing, liturgy; even for those for whom dancing is important as a medium of expression (say, the Greeks in America) the dance does not seem to have had such a complex function. Nor does dance seem to provide for other groups such an all-encompassing metaphor for cultural reality. Perhaps the Native American attitude toward the dance genre itself can provide us with part of the answer (keeping in mind that every tribe will have its own particularities on the subject). As the previous discussion implies, and as one can learn by asking almost any Native American who knows about dancing, both ritual and social dances in Native American cultures are seen as far more than ritual gesture, entertainment, or artistically motivated motion.

Dance is a dynamic dimension that one enters into intentionally, a kinetic model of personal involvement by means of which one places his or her body into the active, ongoing processes of cultural life (sort of like raising one's hand at an auction). In the words of Vanessa Brown, a Navajo/Sioux who is a consummate powwow dancer, "When we dance, we experience the rhythms of nature, like our heartbeats, like seasons, like gestation periods. When we dance with other people, we use our bodies like living gestures and symbols in patterns that relate us to those other people who are there, and to all the other people everywhere."[3]

Whether or not this is a common attitude among the various tribes whose members have become powwow dancers, it is clear from powwow custom that it has developed into an abiding and deeply emotional model for those who now participate in its logic. The following examples illustrate this functional model more fully.

During any powwow, several honoring dances may be done which call attention to the survivors of calamities, to the anniversary of some well-known person's death, to the services and values of old people, or to graduates of local high schools and colleges. During an honoring dance, one drum is asked to play a slow war dance, and the person or persons being honored dance sunwise around the pavilion all alone. On the second time around, close friends and family members may join in behind, and as the dance continues all dancers fall into place until the entire pavilion has become a parade. At Crow Fair in 1979, such a dance was held to honor Tom Yellowtail, leader of the Crow Sun Dance. At Arlee in the same year, the dance was used to welcome back a young man who had been unjustly jailed. At the NASU Powwow in 1983, Vanessa Brown asked everyone assembled to join in her celebration of reunion with the family she had been out of touch with for thirty years.

The concept of dancing with people as a symbol of supporting them, agreeing with them, or honoring them extends to a number of other very important events in the lives of Indian people. For example, at Arlee there was a special dance in which a young son who had come of age and was about to go off to school danced around the arena with his father. On the fourth time around they danced down the middle until they reached the halfway point; then they turned and danced in opposite directions. At this point, both dancers and their families were in tears, for the dance symbolized the separation of father and son as the son moved away from the reservation area.

Similarly, when middle-aged people move back to the reservation from the cities, as is often the case, they may request that the master of ceremonies at a powwow ask the people for "permission" for them to move back. Actually, they need no permission, but they are looking for the emotional and cultural support of their people. Such a couple, along with their children, may then dance alone in a round dance formation around the entire arena side by side. Then, one by one, other members of their families, friends, and even people who have never met them before will move out and join the dancing until the entire arena is full of concentric circles. Usually at this point the family who has asked for "permission" to be reabsorbed in the tribal system is in tears because of the powerful symbolic meaning of this action.

When someone in the family has recently died, it is the custom for relatives *not* to participate in the dancing of the powwow, or even to attend. But after a year has gone by, a memorial dance may be held, often at a powwow, in which the deceased person is praised and relatives dance in commemoration. Often a younger person in the family will wear some of the traditional clothing that once belonged to the deceased, or items belonging to the deceased will be displayed in a processional.

At all three powwows, as concentric circles of round dancers moved around the powwow area, people shook hands with others who were passing in the other line, whooping loudly as they did so. On occasions like this, the whooping or yelling is often directed especially at a non-Indian who seems to be dancing for the first time. If the person smiles and whoops back, this is greeted by whooping from all present, but if the outsider seems embarrassed and looks away in confusion, another Indian will reach out and try to shake hands. The idea here is not to embarrass outsiders but to force them to become participants, to enclose them within the same circle. Most visitors to a powwow find this an extremely warming custom.

The reason for this is quite clear: the dance genre for American Indians is one which brings about engagement, integration, and re-integration. In the fullest sense of the term, dance *embodies* cultural attitudes which cannot readily be articulated today in other ways. Just as the Hopi kachina dancer actually becomes a part of the sacred by interacting with sacred processes through the medium of dance, thus actually participating in, and embodying, the fertile powers which nurture the people; just as a Navajo *yei-bi-chei* dancer, by putting on his mask and sash and by dancing, actually embodies the live powers of healing which bring about the recovery of the sick patient, so do the dancers of a secular round dance actually form a living picture of the integrated group with which they seek connection. Today the various Native American communities are beset with pressures thought to cause disintegration, dissolution, depression, alienation, and separation. No matter what their tribal differences may have been in the past, their contemporary reality is one of a commonly experienced, commonly perceived corrosive trauma. One of their only ways of dealing with this shock has been to select those features of their various cultures which give them a way of sharing the experience of holding on and maintaining what they have.

The powwow, then, provides Native Americans with a dynamic arena in which the potentially conflictive elements of contemporary life are mediated in an ethnically rich (and therefore meaningful) environment. Associative diads such as female/male, insider/outsider, old/young, Indian/non-Indian, host/guest, group/individual, cooperation/competition, tradition/change, straight/fancy, Christian religion/tribal religion, and so on, are seen by most American Indians not as diametrically opposed but as overlapping and interactive qualities. Viewed as competitive opposites, these qualities can produce friction and disharmony; integrated and embodied in the gestural commitment of dance, however, they have the capacity to promote wholeness and well-being, even between tribes that were once deadly enemies. The powwow can reintegrate alienated individuals with their larger ethnic community without pretending that it is possible to lead a pristine tribal life unaffected by the disaster of invasion and plunder. In other words, the fact that powwow culture is different from the older tribal cultures is not a sign of cultural slippage but of selective, intensified ethnic tenacity. This is an activity which promotes a pride in being Native while not ignoring the fact that there are other tribes, other values, other religious views; it expresses Indianness without ignoring the confusing framework in which that condition must be experienced.

The powwow provides a living context in which young people learn older patterns and experience a tremendous range of expressions based on worldview assumptions that remain important to Indian people. In addition, the process takes place surrounded by the whole family and tribe, the idealized model of cultural and ethnic stability for American Indians.

During the powwow there is a conscious nurturing and intensification of generally shared tribal attitudes that exist outside language and ritual, as well as a deference to the cultural differences which still exist among the various tribes. Such ideas as circularity, time as an outgrowth of event (rather than vice versa), models of reciprocation, competition within culturally acceptable and meaningful contexts (a way of controlling a white idea that otherwise causes trouble), the importance of the family as a unit, all are seen by Native Americans as promoting stability while the absence of these factors is seen as erosive and corrosive to Native American culture. The powwow, with all of its dancing patterns and reciprocal modes of operation, provides a living model of tribal attitudes; it can be planned and integrated into the everyday lives of Indian people without endangering their livelihoods or their survival in a sometimes hazardous and aggressive world.

There is of course a certain amount of nostalgia for an older way of life, and the widespread use of the tipi at the larger outdoor encampments is one way of recapturing this older way. But Indians acknowledge today that the old way has indeed changed forever and that to survive they must now combine aspects of their older customs with realities of the world in which they live. No one believes, in other words, that the Europeans will move back to Europe and the Indians back to tipis. Nonetheless, no one believes that an Indian needs to stop being an Indian in order to live in his own country. Thus, while most Indians take jobs when they can in the American economy, and while most have generally adopted American styles of clothing for everyday life, what they have done with the powwow is to intensify and solidify an occasion through which they can celebrate the continued existence of Indian ways of life.

When Anglo-Americans do such a thing, it is often labeled "Living History"; when Indians do it, it is often called "going back to the blanket." But the issue is far more delicate and complicated (not to say ironic) than that: since taking a job or going to school often necessitates leaving one's family and learning to compete, thus setting up an instability in the family and tribal system, the powwow functions as a way of bringing people symbolically back together for the encouragement and nurturing of their ethnic lives and their continued existence as sane people. In this sense, the new way of life does not replace the old; the old survives by rising to the new demand, by adapting and intensifying. The pow-wow is one dynamic example of how ethnic selection and intensification function to preserve cultural values even under the most trying of circumstances.

Notes to Chapter 9

1. Two descriptive articles appeared in the 1987 issue of *Folklife Annual*, edited by Alan Jabbour and James Hardin (Washington, D.C.: Library of Congress, 1988): "American Indian Powwow" (pp. 46–69), by Barre Toelken and Vanessa Brown, gives a general overview of the powwow phenomenon and is the basis for many of the observations developed in the present essay. The author wishes to thank the American Folklife Center for permission to quote portions of that piece here. The other, "Celebration: Native Events in Eastern Canada," (pp. 70–85) by Michael Sam Cronk, Beverly Cavanagh, and Franziska von Rosen, describes analogous celebrations in Canada.

2. I visited Crow Fair most extensively in the summer of 1979, during a fieldwork survey of Montana by the American Folklife Center. I am indebted to Michael Crummett not only for excellent fieldwork and photography on that occasion, but for introductions which allowed us to interview the White family and to stay overnight in their tipi. As well, Tom Yellowtail and his family were extremely helpful, as always. I have visited the Arlee Powwow a number of times. For information about the powwow and its meaning to the inland Salish people, I am indebted to Mrs. Adelaide Matt (an excellent beadworker), Willie Wright, Victor Charlo, Agnes Vanderberg, Johnnie Arlee, Bearhead Swaney, and Betty White. During my twenty years on the faculty of the University of Oregon, I often had the opportunity of helping with the NASU (Native American Student Union) Powwow. Native American students most involved over the years were George Wasson, Dick Wilson, John Wasson, Ed Edmo, Robert Bojorkas, Dennis

deGross, James Florendo, Larry Calica. Traditional visitors from Warm Springs Reservation usually included Verbena Green, Matilda and Louis Mitchell, Prosanna Williams, and their families.

3. Vanessa Brown, the author's daughter, was born on the Navajo Reservation and raised traditionally in the Shonto area. Later, after attending reservation schools, she married an Ojibwa from Canada and lived for several years on the Roseau River Reserve near Winnipeg. During that time she entered the powwow circuit and came to know people from a number of Midwest tribes; eventually she announced herself for a Sun Dance, and fulfilled a vow of dancing four years in that ritual at the Pine Ridge Reservation in South Dakota, during which time she was given the name Wanbli Ota Wi (Many Eagles Woman). She lives today with her five children in Tuba City, Arizona, where she is active in cultural education and in encouraging Navajo and Hopi participation in the powwow.

IV.

Contracting and Expanding Ethnic Networks and Communities

10. The Celebration of Passover among Jewish Radicals

DAVID SHULDINER

Around the turn of the twentieth century, conflicts arose among East European Jewish immigrants who had brought with them to America a heritage of political activism. As in the case of members of other ethnic groups who made their mark in the political arena, these Jews established political ties with other Jews in American trade unions, activities that contributed greatly to improving conditions for the working class. Although these Jews were associated with an international working-class movement and had inherited socialist symbols and forms of protest to espouse their political cause, many also sought to make their mark as Jews and so looked for appropriate symbols for their Jewishness.

Yet their basic socialist and antireligious beliefs made it difficult to incorporate elements of Jewish religious tradition, especially because the rabbinic leaders of traditional Jewish communities tended toward political conservatism. Indeed, Jewish radicals widely held that any form of identification with Judaism was a liability in the general workers' movement. Nonetheless, many of them did "return" to the Jewish community, if only to organize those co-workers who also happened to be co-ethnics. They sought to work these dual sources of commonality to their advantage by stressing points of unity between Jewish tradition and movements for social change. Though "internationalists" on one level, they felt both a practical and a personal need to be culturally identified with a specifically Jewish component of the larger working-class movement.[1]

Within the labor movement in the United States, Jewish trade union and political activists, like their East European counterparts, developed and maintained a subculture grounded and expressed in the folk ideology of Yiddish radicalism, a synthesis of Jewish culture and proletarian politics. It was an attempt to weld the communal feeling of ethnic ties with the collective mood of working-class solidarity. Through Judaic imagery, Yiddish song and story, and transformed ritual, the political ideology of Jewish immigrant radicals was articulated. What emerged from this process of cultural refraction was a politically defined ethnicity. While ideology may have conditioned the selection of aspects of Jewish tradition to define an ethnic and class consciousness, it was symbols of ethnicity that were pressed into service as compelling symbols of political engagement. Karl Marx may have articulated the conditions under which the working class labored and struggled, but for many Yiddish radicals the prophetic voice of social revolution was just as Mosaic as it was Marxist.

Such manipulation of traditional symbols has been recognized as a common strategy of ethnic groups which seek to meld cultural heritage with political activity. Cultural symbols are noted for their ability to mediate between potentially antagonistic ideologies. As Barbara Myerhoff has pointed out, ambiguous and often contradictory elements are frequently incorporated into the ritual process.[2] In her work among retired Eastern European Jews at a senior citizen's center in Venice, California, Myerhoff demonstrated that these elderly immigrants blend reminiscences of a glorious past with the realities of a more fragile and contradictory present through the rituals and ceremonies they create. Among these older Jews, whose lives enclose tradition and modernity, are those whose political activities have fused universal revolutionary ideals with particular Jewish concerns.

Similarly, participants in the Jewish labor movement reconciled their need to be progressive with their need to remain at least nominally within the general Jewish community. They were able to relate their political ideology to Judaism by fusing visions of a utopian future with the imagery of an ancient, Biblical past. In the words of Beatrice Weinreich, radicals wished "to renounce the religious context of Judaism while retaining affiliation with Jewry on an ethnic-cultural basis."[3] This fusion's historical and symbolic development can be vividly seen in the Passover seder, a ritual traditionally used by Jewish groups of all persuasions to dramatize and legitimize their religious and ideological beliefs.[4]

The Jewish labor movement's views toward Jewish tradition in general and ritual observances, such as Passover, in particular, developed unevenly.

The initial response was to reject tradition as the enemy of progress, custom as a barrier to social change. Many revolutionaries simply remained aloof, while others felt obliged to deride tradition in order to wean potential activists away from those customs—and, by inference, that communal authority—that held them in sway. Yom Kippur balls were held, mocking the Jewish Day of Atonement with feasting and merry-making instead of fasting and solemn reflection. Jewish revolutionaries also held a "red seder" on the first and second nights of Passover. Jews are prohibited from eating any food containing *hametz* (leaven) during the week of the festival, but those attending a red seder were served cake and bread along with wine, while speeches were made and songs sung against religion. This was not only an act of defiance, but a way of forcing activists to make a choice between politics and religion.

Eventually, some Jewish trade-union and political activists recognized that to win people over to new ideas, it was not necessary to reject the old offhand. Chaim Zhitlowsky, an instrumental mover in the Yiddishist movement (which sought to forge a Jewish socialist identity on secular grounds) wrote an essay at the turn of the twentieth century, "*Poetishe vidergeburt fun der yidishe relige*" ("Poetic Renaissance of Jewish Religion").[5] In it, he urged nonreligious Jews to recognize the importance of certain values in Jewish religion, and not discard those values to achieve some kind of assimilation. Many leftists were reared with this duality of radicalism and tradition. Ruth P., who was born in New York City of Jewish immigrant parents, commented that, on the one hand, she learned to question cardinal Jewish beliefs:

> I want you to know that the Workmen's Circle schools had . . . an anti-religious outlook. We did not celebrate seders, we did not celebrate holidays; it was not considered a sin to eat on Yom Kippur. We learned all of the things [about Jewish culture] through our study of Jewish history. . . . We understood . . . that a lot of the [religious] things were man-made, and put into the mouth of God, so to speak.[6]

Ruth's maternal grandparents, on the other hand, exposed her to traditional observances that they retained from the old country:

> From childhood on, we had *sedorim* because my grandmother and grandfather came from Europe . . . and we all lived together. . . . My grandmother went to *shul* [temple]. . . . All through my life—my grandmother lived to be way past ninety—so we had the benefit of that. We used to visit with her in *shul* when she went [for] Rosh Hashana, Yom Kippur, and she would go other times, too. We lived in New York, and on our

street was a *shul* there, so when they had *simchas torah* [fall holiday climaxing the Feast of Booths] and all that, even though we were not members of the synagogue, we participated in all of those things. So I knew about all of these things, even though, as I grew up, I understand that I was not a part of it.[7]

In the search for aspects of Jewish tradition that could be modified to suit the needs of "Jewish-identified" radicals, a potent symbolism was rediscovered in the Passover seder—a rite commemorating the Biblical account of the Exodus of the Jewish people from Egypt. The seder is marked by the reading of a special text and the eating of symbolic foods. No other Jewish holiday is as rich in the imagery of social struggle, as suggestive in the structure of its observance, or as potent in its potential elaboration of that imagery for political purposes. Through a process of secularization, the seder became the single most important calendrical ceremony of the Jewish working-class movement. Yet the road leading to the appropriation of Passover symbols was a long and tortuous one, affected by shifting political perspectives and reflecting tensions between class and ethnic allegiances.

Those who chose alternative ways of celebrating Passover in an affirmative manner needed rationales to justify the adaptation of an elaborate religious ceremony. They had to find ways of distinguishing their secular and radical orientation from the sacred character of the holiday in Jewish tradition. Some found a tradition of dissent and adaptation within the story of Passover and the history of its observance. Morris N., a veteran of the anarchist branch of the Workmen's Circle in New York and Los Angeles, commented on the roots of this tradition of dissent:

> Let me explain [to] you. To begin with, I imagine, you know, the basic principle of celebrating the seder in general—the emancipation of the Jewish people from Egypt . . . around 3,000 years ago. And it became a tradition . . . the main thing—religion second—because our freedom we desired too much, we were freed from slavery by fighting the Egyptians who were a big power at that time, a world power.
>
> Moses—that's how the legend goes—he freed the Jewish people and they marched to the Promised Land of Canaan, after forty years in the desert. . . . At the same time, there were people at that time, Korach, critics of the particular leadership of Moses and his brother, Aaron.[8]

Judaism's adaptability to changing circumstances made this tradition of dissent relevant to different times and places. The *seder* merely embodies these changes. Morris N. explained:

And after so many years—the first destruction of the Temple, the second destruction of the Temple—the Jewish people wandered in different countries in the Near East, in Asia, and in Europe and the Far East. And they wanted to—besides changing their religion many times—as they could interpret [their] religion in conformity of the people they lived with. . . . As they traveled from one land to another, they had to adapt themselves to the conditions that they lived in at that time.

Slowly, slowly, in the different countries, they changed the form of conducting the seder—the seder, that means order, a way to conduct. Some people told when lately they escaped to Russia during the Holocaust, they were shipped out to the very Far East [the Soviet Union evacuated many Jews from the Eastern Front during WWII] where people at that time [who] considered them[selves] Jews, nobody knew exactly what they believed in, but knew they were Jews [probably Jews from Turkmen or Uzbek, S.S.R.], they conducted a seder in different ways—[you] couldn't even recognize it.[9]

The historic flexibility in seder observance allowed many Jewish radicals to avoid confrontation with religious tradition and to preserve for themselves the spirit, if not the actual observance, of those Passover celebrations that were a part of their childhoods. It was precisely this duality of community and polity that laid the groundwork for the celebration of Passover as a prominent expression of the political culture of Jewish radicals.

Among the first to organize a seder for Jewish labor and political activists was the Workmen's Circle (Arbeiter Ring). Officially chartered in 1900 as a mutual aid society, it was also a center of the Yiddish socialist movement in the United States. For those who joined it, it often served as a secular substitute for the community of tradition. Yet these Yiddish activists remained strongly Jewish-identified and sought ways of reconstituting their ethnicity on new, political grounds, as well as methods of passing on their distinctive outlook to their children. The celebration of Passover was viewed, within this context, as a means of grounding Yiddish socialism in traditional roots, roots that had been severed for many activists. In the words of Joseph Mlotek, director of the Education Department of the Workmen's Circle:

We recognized that there were those who did not celebrate this holiday at all. We felt that it is essential to give the students in our schools—many of the second generation—a stronger Yiddish identity. Thus, Yiddish teachers, together with Yiddish writers, sat down and took the old traditional *Hagadah* [sic], translated it into Yiddish, added new material to make it more contemporary and thus both parents and children were able to realize that this was an eternal, timeless battle for Freedom. That it did not begin nor end with Exodus from Egypt.[10]

The seder was held during Passover week after the first two nights, in order to complement rather than confront the traditional services. The first of these Workmen's Circle "third seders" was held in New York sometime in the early 1920s. It was essentially a celebration for the children attending the Workmen's Circle schools. It also set a precedent for the third seder as an organizational rather than family affair. In subsequent years it was held at different locations until it arrived at the Waldorf Astoria, where for the past forty-five years or so it has been a catered affair of grand proportions, including readings of the *haggadah*, presentations by guest speakers, and professional entertainment.

Another group within the Jewish labor movement whose members sought to alter the Passover ritual were the Labor Zionists. They shared with many Jewish revolutionaries a fascination with traditional Jewish symbolism, but like other Jewish radicals they were strictly secular in their orientation. Less emphasis was placed on the Biblical theme of redemption, more on the theme of national liberation and the yearning for a Jewish homeland. A renewed Exodus would make resettlement possible.

The Labor Zionists and the Histadrut campaign (the latter representing the emerging Jewish labor movement in Palestine) held a joint third seder in the late 1920s in Providence, Rhode Island. According to J. Katzman, a participant in this early seder, the service was conducted in Yiddish and included motifs from the traditional *haggadah* with much singing in both Yiddish and Hebrew. Songs in Yiddish were folk songs with traditional themes. Among these were "*In dem land fun piramidn*" ("In the Land of Pyramids") and "*Zog maran*" ("Tell us, Marrano"). The latter recounted the lives of "secret" Jews who concealed their identities during the Inquisition in Spain. Songs in Hebrew were mostly by or about the *halutzim*, those who intended to join Jewish agricultural settlements in Palestine. Katzman's view of the Passover holiday was that it signaled "the birthday of the Jewish people." The class-consciousness of this birthday was very evident in the seder, as Katzman's father, a Farband (Yiddishist Labor Zionist) activist, explains: "The holiday of *Pesakh* [Passover] records the first strike in human history of Jewish bricklayers (against) their pharaoh oppressors."[11]

The third seder of the Labor Zionists and that of the Workmen's Circle tended to be similar in form: a grand catered affair replete with references to the Jewish socialist struggle. Given the pro-Zionist view of the Labor Zionists and the anti-Zionist view of the Workmen's Circle, the main difference was the mention of Israel. The "*Hatikva*" (the national anthem of present-day Israelis), and other songs in Hebrew about Jewish colonization in Palestine/Israel were central features of the observances of the Labor Zionists; they were conspicuously absent from the Workmen's Circle, which refrained from such references until well after the establishment of the state of Israel in 1948. Then, following a general trend in the Jewish community at large, they warmed up to the new Jewish state. Songs in Hebrew and references to Israel were then added to the Workmen's Circle *haggadahs*.

The Workmen's Circle *haggadah* demonstrates a creative blend of sacred and secular elements also present in the traditional *haggadah*. The activist observance contains many traditional motifs but eliminates rabbinical commentary and replaces prayers and hymns of praise with Yiddish poetry and songs relating to the general Passover theme. Among the traditional motifs retained in the first and subsequent versions of the Workmen's Circle *haggadah* were:

1. The drinking of four ceremonial glasses of wine (accompanied by dedications rather than the blessings of the traditional *haggadah*;
2. Descriptions of the special foods placed upon the seder table to which symbolic significance is attached. Among these are: a. *matzoh* (unleavened bread), identified as "the bread of affliction which our forefathers ate in the land of Egypt" (Deut. 16:3); b. *maror* (bitter herb—usually horseradish), a reminder of the bitterness of slavery; c. *haroset* (a mixture of chopped nuts, apples or raisins, and wine), representing the mortar used by the Israelite slaves in laying bricks for the Pharaoh; d. *karpas* (mildly bitter herb, such as parsley), interpreted as a symbol of spring or renewal; e. the shankbone of a lamb, standing for the paschal sacrifice that was the central event in ancient Passover celebrations; and f. a roasted egg, representing an additional sacrifice offered in the ancient Temple, also said to symbolize the continuity of life.
3. The recitation of four questions by a young child concerning the significance of the Passover celebration, prefaced by the general question: "Why is this night different from all other nights?"
4. The description of four sons—wise, wicked, simple, and unable to ask—who provoke different explanations as to the importance of the Passover celebration.
5. The story of the Exodus itself, including an account of the plagues visited by God upon Egypt for the Pharaoh's refusal to release the Hebrew children from bondage.

The differences from traditional observances are most instructive. The reader is presented, in the opening section, not with a *kiddush* (blessing)

over the first cup of wine, as in a traditional seder, but with a poem by
I. I. Schwartz entitled *"Kiddush,"* which recalls the enslavement of the
Israelites thousands of years ago and calls for a blessing of the first cup
of wine in the name of justice and freedom. Appropriately, those gathered say in unison:

> *Far undzer folk, un far zayn zukunft,*
> *Far zayn volyzayn, far sayn glick.*
> *Far a velt a libtik-heler,*
> *Fray fun keyt un fray fun strik.*
> For our people and for the future,
> For happiness and good fortune,
> For a bright and better world,
> Free of chains and free from ropes.

The four questions are recited in Yiddish, exclusively. Hebrew is eliminated entirely from this *haggadah.* The story of Passover is interspersed
with Yiddish poetry on relevant themes like *"Oyfn nil"* ("On the Nile"),
relating the story of how Pharaoh's daughter found the infant Moses,
and *"In dem land fun piramidn"* ("In the Land of Pyramids").

An important addition to this *haggadah* was a memorial to the heroes
of the Warsaw Ghetto. On the first night of Passover 1943, a group of
Jewish partisans, among those walled into the Jewish quarter of Warsaw
by the Nazis, staged a revolt with smuggled arms, and eventually held
off the German army for several weeks. The uprising became a powerful
symbol of resistance, "proof that freedom . . . and liberty [have] to be
won—fought for and rewon time and time again.[12] Following the seder
meal, the story of *"Pesach* [Passover]— *Varshe* [Warsaw]—1943" was told;
included in this section were poems of martyred writers from the Warsaw
Ghetto, and others on the theme of the uprising. The seder ended with
"Zog nit keynmol" ("Never Say"), written by Hirsh Glik, himself a par-
tisan. Sung with great reverence—and always while standing—it has
become the anthem of the Jewish left.

The first third seder in English of the Los Angeles Workmen's Circle
was largely patterned on the 1948 Yiddish version. However, the English
haggadah begins with a short introduction outlining the origins of the
festival and summarizing the Biblical account of the Exodus and prefaced in turn by a brief statement on the Workmen's Circle's view of the
haggadah:

> This suggested "Hagodah" is an attempt to put the traditional Passover
> Seder into a modernized form. It utilizes the English and Yiddish lan-
> guages in order to convey the fullest meaning to Jews in America, and to

the historical and legendary moments of Jewish life which have more recently become part of our experience and tradition.[13]

Some of the Yiddish poetry is eliminated, but the two most popular of the traditional Hebrew Passover songs, *"Dayenu"* and *"Chad Gadyo,"* are added in Yiddish translation. In subsequent versions, the prophet Elijah (for whom a place is traditionally set at the seder table in anticipation of his eventual heralding of the Messiah) is greeted with a bilingual Hebrew-Yiddish version of *"Eliyohu Hanovi"* ("Elijah the Prophet"), a song usually associated with *havdalah,* the ceremony marking the end of the Sabbath.

The plagues visited upon Egypt have their contemporary counterparts in the English version of the Workmen's Circle *haggadah:* "aggressive war, communism, fascism, slave labor, genocide, disease, famine, human exploitation, religious bigotry, and racial discrimination."[14] Here we have reference not only to important issues raised by Yiddish socialists, but also a reflection in the mention of the second "plague" of the enmity between members of the Workmen's Circle and the Yiddish left, who parted company over the question of support for the Bolshevik Revolution in the land of their forebears. The latter, whether supportive of the Soviet Union today or highly critical of it, are uniformly loath to attack communism itself as a system.

As with the Warsaw Ghetto uprising, new historical events important to the Jewish people are added to the observance. References to the state of Israel appeared in the English version in the late 1950s, and tributes to Soviet Jewry became a staple of the Workmen's Circle *haggadah* in the 1970s.

The Yiddish left (those who split from the Workmen's Circle in the 1920s and 1930s in the aftermath of the Bolshevik Revolution) maintained an antitraditional stance somewhat longer than the Labor Zionists and the Workmen's Circle. But by the 1930s and 1940s, Yiddish-speaking members of the International Workers' Order (IWO) were becoming reconciled to those Jewish holidays laden with the symbolism of the struggle for freedom and social justice. Teachers in the Progressive Children's Schools (the schools of the Yiddish left) devised guidelines in the late 1940s for the celebration of Passover. Their format closely paralleled that of the Workmen's Circle third seder, with one notable exception. Although updated and liberally interpreted in broad political terms, themes of social justice in the Workmen's Circle *haggadahs* referred almost exclusively to the Jewish people. The compilers of the left's third seder *haggadah* made a point of generalizing the lessons of the Exodus account to include references to the struggles of other oppressed peoples. A *haggadah* of 1958 states: "Though the sacrifice be great and the hardships many, we shall not rest until the chains that enslave all men, Jew and non-Jew alike, be broken."[15] The Workmen's Circle English *haggadahs* did, in fact, incorporate the spiritual "Go Down, Moses" as a permanent fixture of the third seder repertoire for its poignant depiction of the Exodus theme, though without indication of its source in African-American folk tradition. The left's *haggadah* also includes this song, but a connection is drawn in the reading between the plight of the Jews and those for whom the Exodus theme also strikes a resonant chord:

> The story of the Exodus was an inspiration to another group of slaves, the American Negro, in their struggle for freedom. Both the content of their songs and the symbolism disguised to fool the brutal masters were taken from this period of Jewish history. *Avadim Hayinu* — we were slaves — we the people of the earth; our name is Jew and our name is Negro.

Subsequent *haggadahs* of the Progressive Children's Schools in Los Angeles have contained specific references to the civil rights movement and to striking farm workers led by César Chávez in the fields of central California.

A number of reasons have been offered for the development of the third seder. One is the longing of first-generation immigrants for the rituals, if not the religious messages, associated with their childhood in the Old Country. Another is the desire to reach the Jewish masses with a message bearing a familiar, and therefore accessible, cultural coding. A third argument — and perhaps the strongest — for the creative construction of the third seder among Jewish-identified political activists is the need to reconcile their strong attachment to their Jewish identity with a sense of engagement in a world containing a multiplicity of pressing issues transcending their own ethnicity. The third seder has also enabled secular Jewish activists to experience a sense of ethnic communality while still maintaining lines of demarcation from traditional Judaism.

Subsequent generations have also discovered the potent symbolism of Passover. In the 1960s, young Jewish activists who had participated in the civil rights movement attended third seders celebrating the ties between ancient and contemporary liberations struggles. New *haggadahs* were used, such as Arthur Waskow's *Freedom Seder*. In the wake of ethnic "consciousness" movements in the 1960s and 1970s, a number of Jewish groups emerged to counter the growing conservative trend in the mainstream Jewish community. Prominent among them was New Jewish

Agenda, a left liberal organization initially formed to criticize the political conduct of the State of Israel. It has continued to press this and other issues of concern, as well as to support other movements promoting peace and social justice. Wishing to reach a wider Jewish audience for whom Agenda's views are potentially alienating, they have embraced aspects of Jewish tradition as a means of demonstrating ethnic unity while reinterpreting them to reflect their more progressive stance. Many local chapters have conducted annual third seders, and several have prepared their own *haggadahs*, which have received wide circulation.

The "tradition" of the third seder has, indeed, served as an effective overture to the mainstream Jewish community. In recent years many traditionalists have borrowed the idea of the old Jewish socialists of representing contemporary themes in the *haggadah*. Conservative and reform synagogues and Jewish community centers now conduct third seders. While the Yiddish-speaking, working-class activists who spawned these creative political celebrations of Passover have become a historical footnote largely unrecognized by the mainstream Jewish community, the innovations they introduced have contributed to the repertoire of many contemporary Jews who struggle to bridge the waters between ethnic loyalty and broader social concerns.

Notes to Chapter 10

1. This essay is based on my Ph.D. dissertation, "Of Moses and Marx: Folk Ideology within the Jewish Labor Movement in the United States" (UCLA, 1984).

2. Barbara Myerhoff, *Number Our Days* (New York: Simon and Schuster, 1978).

3. Beatrice S. Weinreich, "The Americanization of Passover," in *Studies in Biblical and Jewish Folklore*, edited by Raphael Patai, Francis Lee Utley, and Dov Noy (Bloomington, Ind: Indiana University Press, 1960), 355.

4. There are surprisingly few studies of the secular Passover seder. In addition to Weinreich's pioneering study of the "third seder," two recent articles are noteworthy. Linda Lehrhaupt, "The Organizational Seder in American Jewish Life," *Western Folklore* 45 (1986): 186–202, compares the secular seder in a senior citizens' home, a restaurant, and a hotel. The last of these is a leftist seder at the Waldorf Astoria which is perhaps the largest and most famous of these seders because, in addition to a meal and the recitation of the *haggadah*, there is a musical presentation by a choir and the performance of a skit for the 1,000 people who attend annually. Anita Schwartz, "The Secular Seder: Continuity and Change among Left-Wing Jews," in *Between Two Worlds: Ethnographic Essays on American Jewry*, edited by Jack Kugelmass (Ithaca: Cornell University Press, 1988), 105–27, describes the special function which the third seder had for

members of the Workers' Cooperative Colony of New York. When the cooperative broke up, former members continued to come together for the seder to remember their group history and identity.

5. Summary provided by Itche Goldberg, director of the Zhitlowsky Foundation, New York, in a telephone conversation with the author 6 September 1983.

6. Interview with Ruth P., 19 September 1983.

7. Ibid.

8. Interview with Morris N., 19 September 1983.

9. Ibid.

10. Masha Leon, *Conversation with Joseph Mlotek* (New York: Workmen's Circle, n.d.).

11. Interview with J. Katzman, 6 September 1983.

12. Interview with Ruth P., 19 September 1983.

13. A *"Third" Seder: Passover* (Los Angeles: Workmen's Circle, English-Speaking Division, 1955).

14. Ibid.

15. *Hollywood Kindershule Pesach Hagadah* [one of the Progressive Schools] (Los Angeles: N.p., 1961).

11. Weddings among Jews in the Post-World-War-II American South*

CAROLYN LIPSON-WALKER

Jewish affinity, the sense of family among Jews, is a worldwide phenomenon. And yet Jews, like any other group, are diverse—culturally, economically, occupationally, politically, socially, philosophically, and geographically. In the United States, Jews divide themselves and have been conceptually divided into many subgroups. One such group is made up of the Jews who live in the eleven states of the Old Confederacy— Alabama, Arkansas, Florida (northern Florida only),[1] Georgia, Louisiana, Mississippi, North Carolina, South Carolina, Tennessee, Texas, and Virginia, plus Kentucky. New ways of being Jewish and new cultural expressions have arisen among Jews in the South as a result of settling in and adapting to the region and responding to and adopting aspects of the culture of the South.

Although Jews the world over have borrowed, adapted, and transformed the customs of their non-Jewish neighbors, it comes as a surprise

*Most of the data in this article focuses on southern Jewish weddings from 1960 to 1980. During this period, the Jews of the South differed from other American Jews (particularly the statistically larger group of Jews who lived in the northeastern United States), because of their biculturality, relative affluence, smaller population, stronger regional networks, political moderation, and their accelerated conformity to southern culture. Also see my dissertation, " 'Shalom Y'all': The Folklore and Culture of Southern Jews," Indiana University, 1986. I am deeply indebted to the Rockefeller Foundation for its support of this research, which included fieldwork in the South.

to many non-Southerners that persons can be both southern and Jewish. Southern Jews are aware of the outside world's astonishment, particularly the Jewish world's, in hearing a Jew pronounce Yiddish or Hebrew words with a southern drawl or learning of Jews who dine on matzoh-ball gumbo or barbecued matzoh balls or fried chicken, greens, and kugel. This reaction by outsiders to the idea of being both southern and Jewish is just one of the links in the "confederacy" of the Jews in the South. In addition to colorful food hybrids, folklore created from the blending of Jewish and southern traditions includes a body of personal narratives and holiday and life-cycle customs.

Although the emphasis of this study is on the unique traditions of southern Jewish weddings, some details of these weddings resemble those of American weddings anywhere in the United States: bridal gowns and bouquets; wearing something old, new, borrowed, and blue; formal attire for the groom and groomsmen; bridesmaids; ring bearers; flower girls; wedding cakes; the tossing of the bridal bouquet and bride's garter and rice; decoration of the getaway car, etc. All these are familiar throughout American culture, and these common traditions are perpetuated by an active wedding press and retail industry. They also persist for the multiple reasons that folk traditions do during life-cycle events throughout the world. A great many of these and other wedding customs are passed on by attendance and experiences at other weddings.

However, southern Jewish weddings are remarkable for their stylistic and textural variations caused by a synthesis with southern culture. This syncretism arises from the blending of southern culture and Jewish culture and results primarily in innovations in details. These innovations are often inconspicuous to outsiders, but are a powerful expression of southern Jewish identity.

Elaborate southern Jewish weddings differ from other American Jewish weddings in their relative lack of Jewish traditions and in the extra-ceremonial events preceding and following the wedding. In contrast to other American Jewish wedding celebrations, which consist of one-day celebrations, southern Jewish weddings typically include a series of lunch, brunch, dinner, or cocktail parties beginning sometimes as early as Monday or Tuesday, most often at least by Friday, and continuing after the Saturday night or Sunday nuptials. Frequently the southern Jewish wedding escalates to a point where there is a party for every meal until the wedding itself. In this sense, southern Jewish weddings resemble in length European Jewish weddings of the nineteenth century; however, the parties preceding a southern Jewish wedding ceremony have their origin in southern, white, middle-class wedding parties. The friends of white, southern, Protestant brides and grooms also host a variety of parties for the couple including showers, dinners, stag parties, and luncheons, but unlike southern Jewish wedding parties, these are scattered over several weeks or months preceding the wedding. Southern Jewish wedding festivities are generally telescoped into the week or a few days before the wedding in order to accommodate out-of-town friends and family.

The large number of events has led to another southern Jewish wedding custom. Programs listing activities before and after the wedding are printed and often mailed in advance to wedding guests. These programs may contain maps directing guests to their lodgings or to locations for various activities. Sometimes programs are handed out when guests arrive and a form letter is mailed in advance listing the activities, appropriate dress, and directions to events and accommodations. The program design is varied, but generally includes a welcome to visitors, very often in verse ("We are glad you're here for wedding time. We're glad that you could come. And now for days June 8 through 10, this thing should really hum"). This is followed by a listing of times and places for events and information about chartered buses or car caravans to festivities. The hosts are listed with their names and addresses to make later thank-you-note duties easier.

The program can contain practical information—for example, there may be detailed family trees for the bride and groom so guests aren't confused about who's who. The plainest programs are typewritten and photocopied, but the competitive nature of weddings has not only mushroomed the elaborateness of weddings in general, with larger and more expensive flowers and receptions, but changed programs too. Styles range from colored, printed pamphlets to hand-scripted booklets to a printed imitation of *Time* magazine with the bride's and groom's pictures on the front and back covers and a proclamation, "Merger of the Year."

In contrast to other American Jews, southern Jews at their weddings characteristically reserve a block or wing of hotel or motel rooms for guests, provide fruit baskets in their guests' rooms, offer a hospitality suite, and have elaborate rehearsal dinners with skits. At the larger Jewish weddings, the rehearsal dinners, hosted by the groom's parents, may include several hundred guests. While many Jewish weddings in other regions of the country include a rehearsal dinner, it is usually a low-key gathering for the immediate family and wedding party.

The custom at these obligatory southern rehearsal dinners is to have skits, songs, and poems performed by the friends and family of the bride and groom. The intent of this entertainment is usually to describe the courtship of the betrothed couple and to fluster them with descriptions of past flames:

> At the rehearsal dinner all the friends used to get together and gather up all the dirt that they remember about the person who was getting married . . . and then, depending on how creative we were feeling at any particular time, we would either make a song out of it, and usually have to delete part of it because the mothers of the bride or the aunts of the bride or whatever were going to be there, . . . or a poem. And then at the rehearsal dinner we would all get up and perform this and totally wipe the bride out in front of the person that she was marrying, or [wipe out] the groom, and it usually included mentioning all past flames [and] relationships. . . . It's like a roast.[2]

Outside of southern territory, these wedding skits performed by southern branches of family have been received with amusement and amazement. Through the years the wedding skit has become a more frequent and more sophisticated presentation. It seems clear that the full-blown skit, including song parodies and poems, is an outgrowth of a simpler custom of toasts. This tradition, borrowed from the southern Christian culture, has grown in popularity in the last three decades as youths have polished their skills by presenting skits at Jewish camps and conventions. Though some families have never included skits at wedding parties, many families view them as a prerequisite. "You don't dare show up without your skit or your material."[3]

The southern Jewish wedding reception varies a great deal from the typical American Jewish wedding reception. In smaller cities, some southern Jews still make do with a wedding reception that is exactly like an upper-middle-class, southern, Christian wedding reception, except for the food and the serving of champagne. The fare at white, southern, Christian weddings is generally limited to wedding cake, nuts, mints, and non-alcoholic punch. The small-town Jewish reception features a receiving line, a stand-up buffet with finger foods, and the absence of dance music. The cutting of the cake, the tossing of the bouquet, and the throwing of the rice are the major entertainments. In larger cities, southern Jewish receptions are held in country clubs, hotels, or synagogue social halls and almost always feature a sit-down dinner or luncheon, a band, and dancing and thus are almost identical to northern Jewish wedding receptions. However, the southern Jewish reception is never held in a commercial wedding parlor, and, therefore, the emcees generally provided by such establishments at northern Jewish weddings are not present.

In recent years, the high cost of entertaining has limited formal week-day partying and favored weekend celebrations. In order to satisfy the many friends and relatives who wish to host parties, several may join together and host a single party. It is not uncommon, for example, for there to be as many as a dozen hosts and hostesses for one dinner in honor of the bridal couple. The number of occasions during the week-end also continues to grow. A recent innovation prolongs the weekend past the evening nuptials to a concluding brunch the morning after the wedding ceremony.

Although the distinctive features of southern Jewish wedding festivi-ties derive, in part, from a combination of southern and Jewish elements and style and the relative affluence of southern Jews,[4] their unique qual-ities stem chiefly from the necessity of hosting many out-of-town guests and standards that southern Jews perceive as southern hospitality. Whether southern hospitality is mere fancy or reality, it is the lofty aspiration of southern Jewish hosts and hostesses, and every detail of a wedding is directed toward it.

One young unmarried southern Jewish woman, somewhat astonished at the painstaking detail of a southern Jewish wedding, questions, "How many people normally would you know would have a wedding, would reserve the hotel rooms for you, and have fruit baskets in your room when you come in, you know?"[5]

The distinctiveness of social interactions in the South can be partially explained by the strength of fundamentalist Protestantism in the South; southern localism; the importance of the family; distinctive speech accents; regional foods and culinary styles; and the prevalence of an aristocratic ideal. The images of the chivalrous planter and the southern belle have been prominent influences on shaping southern Jewish attitudes toward standards of behavior. The adoption of "surface" southernisms by the Jews of the South reflects the ladylike and gentlemanly ideal of the upper-middle-class, white Southerner:

> The genteel thing is that you don't invite people from out of town and feed them one meal and send them home, you know? Most southern Jew-ish communities are relatively small, so that . . . there are, just naturally would be, . . . relatives coming in from lots of other places. And you know, I mean, most Jews in the South would have relatives in other small Jewish towns. So naturally you have to do something for them, and I think . . . that's part of it.[6]

To be thought less than genteel and hospitable when entertaining guests is considered nothing short of a crime by Southerners and south-ern Jews. For southern Jews, there is the added Jewish duty of overfeeding one's guests. Southern Jews typically scoff at the meager fare of Christian weddings in the South. Those southern Jews who have attended Jewish weddings outside the South are also quick to observe how different they are compared to Jewish weddings in the South. One informant remarked: "They don't pick you up at the airport."[7] Another commented:

> In the South when we have a wedding, when people come from out of town and you have . . . several parties to fill the weekend, [its] because if they're bothering to come several miles you offer some hospitality and have different functions for them to make the trip worthwhile. But the custom as we understand it in the Northeast, in New York and New Jersey, they have the wedding and that's it. That's all you're invited to. And you know they expect people to come from across the country and just attend the wedding ceremony and reception?[8]

Each southern Jewish wedding varies from another. As stated, Jews from smaller towns often opt for less elaborate events—a buffet rather than a sit-down dinner at the wedding reception, a smaller orchestra or no music at all at the reception. A full array of wedding festivities is more likely when the bride and groom are both Jewish or at least when the bride is Jewish and from the South, because the bride's family determines the nature of the wedding arrangements. Some friction may surface regarding protocol when a southern Jewish male becomes engaged to a non-southern Jew. In such a case, southern Jews are often disappointed by the simplicity of the docket of events planned by the new in-laws. Even in the case of a southern Jewish bride who marries a non-Southerner, trouble may arise when the groom's non-southern family is asked to host a large rehearsal dinner.[9]

Before World War II, southern Jewish weddings were quite different in character. A majority of the weddings were performed in the bride's home. Only in the last thirty years has the southern Jewish wedding been transformed from private to public ceremony replete with the features that have branded it in the past two decades. These changes reflected the special circumstances of southern Jewish life and particularly the dispersed community in which southern Jews live.

Southern Jews do not constitute a subgroup of American Jewry by their mere residence in the region of the country called the South. Southern Jews form a group because they interact with one another more than they interact with anyone else. Despite the fact that Jews in the South have been more socially accepted than in other areas of the country, these Jews continue to want, in large part, to voluntarily segregate. Although southern Jews, especially those in small towns, socialize with white, Christian Southerners to a certain extent, the major decisions in life—choice of college, job, and hometown—are based on a desire for more Jewish contact.

Because of the vast area that is the South and the large numbers of people who are southern Jews, these Jews are not a cohesive community in the traditional sense of a small ethnic group. It would be more apt to label them as "a temporary recurring community" within a region.[10]

Because of the difficulties of reinforcing networks of Jewish relationships in the South, a variety of institutions, organizations, publications, and traditions have developed to support this extended folk community.[11] The Jewish wedding is one of the more dramatic and elaborate of these culturally reinforcing institutions and is itself affected, as we have seen, by the widespread community.

Scattered southern Jewish communities maintain close contacts as a matter of survival. The primary motivation for the frenzy of social interplay among southern Jews is the preservation of Judaism. These institutions are perceived as a force to stem the ever-growing possibility of intermarriage. Concerned southern Jewish parents, fearing that their children will marry non-Jews, encourage their adolescent offspring to think of themselves as "regional" Jews through a process that will lead them safely from camp to college to marriage. The tradition of southern Jewish extra-community ties is in complete opposition to the white southern Christian tradition of devout loyalty to one's hometown. Anthropologist Karen Blu writes that southern Jews "have ties through kinship and religious organizations to a wide regional network of Jewish communities and even to Northern communities. Such contacts are considered important, acting to reinforce Jewishness and to provide information and social flexibility."[12]

Southern Jews are linked by being both Jewish and southern, and their sense of unity is forged through many overlapping networks throughout the South. These networks are built on a web of close friendships; kinship ties; extensive travel for religious, social, organizational, and cultural events; group celebrations; and use of the telephone, newspapers, and correspondence. This web of relationships extends across urban, suburban, and small-town settings in the South. Southern Jews who live in small towns with only a handful of other Jewish families especially depend on extra-community events to provide a Jewish cultural, social, and religious environment. To get to the extra-community events, southern Jews have been mobile. No one describes this principal characteristic of southern Jewish life more succinctly than Morris Kertzer in an article entitled "Magnolia Judaism" written in 1967:

Mobility is the word for Jews young and old south of the Mason and Dixon line. A girl from Charlotte, North Carolina, flies down to Montgomery for a picnic; the Jubilee in Birmingham attracts scores of young people from New Orleans, Atlanta, and Memphis. A social gathering in Mobile will have two distinctive qualities: the presence of a number of non-Jews and of friends and kinfolk from Georgia, Louisiana, and Tennessee, and occasionally a stray from Fort Worth or Little Rock.[13]

It is not that other American Jews do not mix, but southern Jewish networks are more intricate, more extensive, and more cherished. Often during my fieldwork I encountered strong opinions concerning the comparative strengths of southern and northern Jewish bonds: "It's sort of like in the South all Jews are *mishpocheh* [family]. You know, I mean everybody's family in the South. It's sort of like wherever you go, there's like a kinship between Jews in the South."[14]

A Jew growing up in Evansville, Indiana, contrasted her own friendships with those of Jews growing up in Alabama during the same period. While she knew only a small number of Jews in Indianapolis, and none elsewhere in Indiana, ". . . the people growing up in Alabama . . . knew everybody in any city anywhere close to Birmingham."[15] One informant, a native of New Jersey now living in Alabama, clearly communicates the lack of a cohesive regional community of Jews in the northeastern United States:

> I grew up in East Paterson [New Jersey] and the next town . . . to me was Fair Lawn and I knew some people in Fair Lawn . . . okay? But I didn't know anybody beyond that. But for y'all (referring to southern Jews), Huntsville is your Fair Lawn. . . . And to me, it's so striking that . . . some place 200 miles away is like two towns over.[16]

Southern Jews are aware of their need for extra-community ties: "I think Jews in the South are very much aware that they are a minority, are aware of the fact that they need to keep, make contacts and preserve contacts with fellow Jews through the region. . . ."[17] One southern Jew describing growing up in the South said that "it was like you didn't just live in your own town. You lived in the entire South."[18]

The result of this mobility is that even though southern Jews are spread through the South, a great number of southern Jews know or know of other southern Jews. Two hours into a visit in Tuscaloosa, Alabama, with Doris Cohen, a schoolteacher who was raised in Memphis, and her law professor husband Harry, a native New Orleanian, my mention of a Jew from south Alabama prompted Doris to say, "See? And that is typically southern Jewish. You haven't mentioned one person now that we don't know." Listening to a recording of our conversation, I noted that prior to Doris's observation, the three of us had talked about Jews living in New Orleans and Shreveport, Louisiana; Memphis, Tennessee; Charleston, South Carolina; Greenville, Mississippi; Tuscaloosa, Birmingham, Selma, Montgomery, and Troy, Alabama; and Little Rock, Arkansas![19]

The mechanisms for regional familiarity and mobility are credited in part to the once-common livelihood in the retail business. One informant comments on the extent of such business practices: "Like my Uncle Punch, for instance, knows Jews in all these little, teeny towns, like every Jewish family in the southeast and every dinky little dot on the map. My Uncle Punch knows or knows of them or something because he calls on all these people."[20]

Familiarity is also reinforced by membership in regional organizations, particularly in youth organizations. These organizations arose informally in the early 1900s out of the many opportunities provided for youth to get together. An annual weekend-long party, known as the Falcon Picnic, took place in Montgomery, Alabama, around 1910 on the occasion of the Fourth of July. As the years progressed, the Falcon Picnic expanded to become an elaborate affair that included tea dances, garden parties, and formal dances at the local Jewish country club and at hotel ballrooms, and in time it came to be known simply as "Falcon." With this expansion of events, participants endeavored to have as many dates in one day as possible, especially late dates and late, late dates, often after official parties were completed. These multiple-date activities frequently resulted in marriages for participants. Other notable gatherings were Ballyhoo in Atlanta and Hollydays in Columbus, Georgia. These, however, were more short-lived than Birmingham's Labor Day gala, referred to as Jubilee, an almost tongue-in-cheek appellation. Jubilee outlasted other well-known weekend gatherings and attracted hundreds of Jewish youth from all over the South.

Out of Jubilee, Ballyhoo, Hollydays, Falcon, and countless unnamed, less regularly scheduled party weekends evolved formal agencies and regional organizations to handle the numerous occasions during which prospective mates could meet. Southern Jewish adolescents meet one another at a string of summer Jewish camps in the South and at regional and sub-regional conventions and weekend conclaves sponsored by any number of organizations—B'nai B'rith Youth Organization, Young Judaea, United Synagogue Youth, and National Federation of Temple Youth. The most important portrayal of southern Jews to date—Eli Evans's *The Provincials*, an autobiographical account of growing up as a Jew in the

South—describes the impact that these youth organizations had on the author:

> From the time I was old enough to drive, or climb in a car with someone who could, my parents had packed me off to B'nai B'rith conventions to be with other Jewish kids—statewide meetings in Raleigh or Charlotte, regional get-togethers in Columbia and Charleston and South-wide weekend conclaves in Atlanta and occasionally Birmingham and even New Orleans. . . . The convention began with a Friday night "mixer" and then Sabbath services, a religious concession that B'nai B'rith insisted on as justification for the event.[21]

Endogamous southern Jewish matches began during courtship weekends, visits to relatives, high school conclaves and conventions, summer camps, college fraternity weekends, college football weekends, and blind dates arranged by friends, as well as during college and while living and working in large southern cities. Robbie from Helena, Arkansas, met David from New Orleans at Louisiana State University. They had been acquainted with each other in high school Jewish youth activities. Carol from Fayetteville, Tennessee, met Steve from Chattanooga as young singles working in Atlanta. Dee from Memphis and Gerald from Clarksdale, Mississippi, met in Atlanta also. Jan from Jasper, Alabama, met her future husband Robert from Mobile during her first week of college at Tulane in New Orleans. Susan from Birmingham, Alabama, met her husband Barry from New Orleans at a regional B'nai B'rith Young Organization convention. They met again during college in Texas. Each one of these relationships was further cemented through mutual acquaintances, friends, and even distant relatives. Each one of these marriages is one of the thousands that create more links in the southern Jewish community.

Although some southern Jewish folklore emerged from a guileless syncretic process, a great deal of the folklore that is unique to these Jews emanated from a more studied, a more forced adaptation to the ways of southern ladies and gentlemen. Most southern Jews in the mid-twentieth century were willing to sacrifice a great deal that was fundamental in Judaism in order to gain acceptance as Southerners. They abandoned many of the basic elements of Judaism. Although they identified themselves as Jews, affiliated with temples, and, more often than not, sought out marriage partners who were Jewish, only a handful of ritual distinctions, primarily displayed during holiday and life-cycle celebrations, differentiated them from middle-class and upper-middle-class, white Christians.

Southern Jews are distinguished from other American Jews by their relative lack of traditions. Although the majority of American Jews long ago gave up strict adherence to the Jewish dietary laws, the South is the only area of the country where one can collect stories of Jewish families celebrating Passover or Yom Kippur with taboo foods such as pork and shellfish.

But regional variation has not only been an attenuating factor. The same motivations have also created a group of Jews who are more apt to be affiliated with temples and Jewish social and philanthropic organizations and to attend religious services. Rather than being Jewish in a cultural and ethnic way, like Jews in other areas of the country, southern Jews chose to be social, and, especially, religious Jews (in a limited way). But it is remarkable in the study of an ethnic group that the lack of retention of customs has been a fundamental characteristic of the group and an ingredient in the unity of the group. Although folklorists have professed to accept everyone as "the folk," the concept of folk group and ethnic folk group is still somewhat circumscribed. Southern folklorists, for example, have not studied southern Jews because of class biases, and folklorists who study Jewish groups have ignored these Jews because they have changed the most due to New World influences and have thus been considered "folkloreless."

For the most part, a typical Jewish wedding ceremony in the South, from the first part of the century until twenty-five to thirty years ago, had more in common with southern Christian weddings than traditional Jewish weddings:

> My wedding was about as Christian as it could be, I suppose. Everything was in English and the rabbi stood in front of you and we drank wine out of a cup and he said a blessing and we maybe said a blessing in Hebrew and that was it. And that's not the way it is today in Southern Jewish Reform communities. . . . I didn't know what a *chupah* (a wedding canopy) was. Most Jewish weddings today [in the South] have a *chupah*.[22]

Cultures are not static and the southern Jewish culture has changed dramatically in recent years. An overall shift in attitude about Jewishness among Jews universally has come in the aftermath of two of the most consequential events in all of Jewish history—the death of six million Jews to Nazi persecution and the birth of Israel as a Jewish state. Particularly in the past twenty years, especially since the Israeli war in 1967 and the Yom Kippur War in 1973, Jewish life in the South has changed radically. Jews in the South are becoming more ethnically Jewish, more knowledgeable about their heritage, and more secure about being out-wardly Jewish.

Southern Jewish weddings provide evidence of this more recent out-ward show of Jewishness. Once the typical southern Jewish wedding ceremony could be distinguished from a Christian wedding ceremony only by the presence of a rabbi and a few Hebrew blessings. It is only in past decades that southern Jews, the majority of whom are Reform Jews, have reincorporated such basic Jewish wedding customs as the *chupah* (the wedding canopy), breaking a glass at the conclusion of the wed-ding, and a *ketubah* (a wedding contract). Some brides and grooms have chosen a traditional procession to the *chupah*, and the groom and bride are escorted by their parents. This more egalitarian approach has been adopted in many Christian weddings as well now. More Jewish music, dancing, and food is evident at southern Jewish weddings in recent years. Southern Jewish weddings are becoming more like American Jew-ish weddings in general.

The small-town southern Jewish population is decreasing rapidly as Jews move to the cities where there have always been more opportunities to be Jewish and to be with other Jews. Jews from other regions of the United States, particularly the Northeast, are moving to the South and bringing their more ethnic ways of being Jewish with them. Jewish cul-ture in the South will always reflect variation based upon a person's length of residence in the South, the size of the person's hometown, Jew-ish denominational affiliation, and personal predilections, but it is clear that the decades when southern Jewish weddings differed from other American Jewish weddings are passing.

Notes to Chapter 11

1. I have excluded the Jews of southern Florida because they have, for the most part, transplanted their northern culture to a warmer climate.

2. Diane Strauss Turner, Birmingham, Alabama, taped interview, April 18, 1980.

3. Natalie Robinson, Knoxville, Tennessee, taped interview, April 28, 1980.

4. Social acceptance and lifestyle, in general, is predicated on the economic success of this group. Virtually no Jews in the South have blue collar jobs. A lower cost of living in the South in past decades, coupled with economic accom-plishments, allowed these Jews to live in large, beautifully furnished homes in the finer neighborhoods of their hometowns, and own luxury cars, fine clothes, and jewelry. The reason that Jews remained in the South was primarily because of their economic successes.

5. Janet Schreibman, Nashville, Tennessee, taped interview, April 21, 1980.

6. Sally Jaffe Friedman, Birmingham, Alabama, taped interview, April 13, 1980.

7. Natalie Robinson, Knoxville, Tennessee, taped interview, April 28, 1980.

8. Phyllis Weinstein, Birmingham, Alabama, taped interview, April 27, 1980. Southern Jews differentiate themselves more often from northern Jews rather than Jews from the Midwest or West. In many narratives, the northern Jew is further particularized as a New York Jew and symbolizes the antithesis of the southern Jew. This North/South dichotomy recurs in scholarship about the South as well as in southern Jewish folklore.

9. There is a high rate of intermarriage in the post-World-War-II South. When a Jew marries a non-Jew, the wedding celebration can vary greatly from the model presented here.

10. Zoltan Fejos, "Hungarians in Chicago," *Journal of Folklore Research* 21 (1984): 243.

11. According to Robert Redfield, *Peasant Society and Culture* (Chicago: University of Chicago Press, 1960), 31, networks of communication begin when a person through kinship, friendship, acquaintance, or a common interest is in touch with a number of people, some of whom are directly in touch with each other and some of whom are not.

12. Karen I. Blu, "Varieties of Ethnic Identity: Anglo-Saxons, Blacks, Indians and Jews in a Southern County," *Ethnicity* 4 (1977): 277.

13. Morris N. Kertzer, "Magnolia Judaism," in *Today's American Jew*, edited by Morris N. Kertzer (New York: McGraw-Hill Book Company, 1967), 266.

14. Sally Jaffe Friedman, Birmingham, Alabama, taped interview, April 13, 1980.

15. Phyllis Weinstein, Birmingham, Alabama, taped interview, April 17, 1980.

16. Richard Friedman, Birmingham, Alabama, taped interview, April 13, 1980.

17. Leon Weinberger, Tuscaloosa, Alabama, taped interview, August 11, 1980.

18. Myra Weinstein, Knoxville, Tennessee, taped interview, April 27, 1980.

19. Doris Cohen, Tuscaloosa, Alabama, taped interview, August 13, 1980.

20. Sally Jaffe Friedman, Birmingham, Alabama, taped interview, April 13, 1980.

21. Eli N. Evans, *The Provincials: A Personal History of Jews in the South* (New York: Atheneum, 1974), 166–68.

22. Anonymous informant, New Orleans, Louisiana, taped interview, May 2, 1980.

V.

Showcasing Ethnicity:
Transformations from Private to Public Arenas

12. St. Lucia in Lindsborg, Kansas

LARRY DANIELSON

Two blocks of shops form the commercial center of Lindsborg, Kansas, and serve as the setting for the public celebration of St. Lucia, the ritual initiation of the Christmas season in Sweden and in many Swedish-American communities. In Lindsborg, the observance takes place the second Saturday of December and entails a variety of activities from midmorning to midafternoon. They include a visit from Santa Claus, a Swedish bake sale, a college students' art sale, Swedish fiddling, and seasonal music, including roving carolers. The festivity concludes with ethnic dances performed by a high school group, the crowning of St. Lucia — chosen from the high-school-age Lindsborg Swedish Folk Dancers — and the distribution of hot cider and ginger cookies by the honoree to observers of the ceremony.

In the past several decades, many American communities have drawn on their ethnic resources to assert their cultural distinctiveness and to develop tourism. Widespread concerns about the economic future of small-town life in the face of the rural exodus to urban centers in the 1960s, identity crises caused by extralocal governmental policies, and the need to distinguish one's home community from its neighbors effected a flowering of ethnic display events and projects.[1] In 1971, I surveyed ethnic celebrations in American villages and towns of populations under 30,000 using questionnaires and magazine accounts.[2] The data indicated that the economies of the communities in question were usually based on agriculture and that official community organizations like the local Chamber of Commerce were interested in developing or expanding a tourist market. The towns had been settled or enlarged by an immigrant group in the nineteenth century and had become less homogeneous in the twentieth century. The ethnic emphasis in public activities had developed no earlier than the 1940s; leadership came from a festival board which was frequently affiliated with the Chamber of Commerce. Program contents varied, but the entertainment almost always included a parade, the coronation of a queen, costumed folk dancers, ethnic cuisine, and arts and crafts displays.

The public St. Lucia festivity in Lindsborg is a colorful example of a community activity that is part of a larger ethnic revivalist movement. It relocates an ethnic tradition from a private to a public context, self-consciously displays several ethnic folk traditions (folk cookery, folk music, folk dance, and folk ritual), encourages the development of tourism, and affirms to local and nonlocal observers the cultural distinctiveness of the community. As an ethnic revivalist activity, it makes creative use of immigrant and old-country traditions and reinterprets these folkloric antecedents as performances for native and nonnative audiences. The history of this festival demonstrates that ethnic traditions are constantly evolving, reacting to internal as well as external pressures. While some purists may decry the commercial element infusing many of the ethnic displays, townspeople view their marketing of ethnic products as a challenge and test of their ability to muster community resources to bolster community pride. As Regina Bendix has shown for folk festivals organized by the residents of Interlaken, Switzerland, tourists are carefully lured in a calculated manner to celebrate local heritage.[3] The control of traditions, their modification and elaboration, are in the hands of the townspeople who benefit as much from these festivals as do the tourists.

In my research, questionnaire respondents and journalists invariably explained the purpose of such ethnic events as the perpetuation of the community's heritage. Some sources explicitly noted other motives, in particular the development of tourism and the assertion of a distinctive cultural identity. Most questionnaire returns cited the publicity value of the festivals and their importance in bringing tourists into the area. The public purpose of such celebrations, then, was to honor the community's ethnic heritage, but the short-term and long-term economic returns and the cultural-identification consequences of the revival efforts were and probably are just as important as the avowed function of the observance.

The ethnic revivalism movement in Lindsborg closely resembles developments in towns like Junction City, Oregon; Frankenmuth, Michigan;

and Kingsburg, California. Junction City, Oregon, a town of 2,400 inhabitants, was bypassed in 1960 by an interstate highway ten miles from the community. A journalist writes that "within the town, morale declined, properties were permitted to deteriorate, many businesses closed, and Main Street began to take on a depression look." A local physician in 1961 organized a Scandinavian festival, based on the Danish, Swedish, Norwegian, and Finnish traditions of the area farmers, in order "to revive the community." That year twenty thousand people observed the ethnic and quasi-ethnic activities. By 1970 the festival attracted between fifty and sixty thousand visitors to the village:

> In a real sense, the festival has revived Junction City. Today, every store on Main Street is occupied and business is thriving. A dozen new buildings have been erected, and a number of stores have remodeled their outside in "rustic Scandinavian manner."[4]

Frankenmuth, Michigan, a small town of some 1,700 inhabitants, has also capitalized on its ethnic background. Its specialty shops, "Bavarian" storefronts, and annual festival—which draws one hundred thousand visitors to the community—are examples of ethnic local color attractive to both townspeople and tourists. An elaborate fifty-page booklet commemorating the town's 125-year history notes the worries of Frankenmuth residents about its future when it was bypassed by a national expressway. The community's reaction to the bypass and the resolution of its fears are familiar:

> When I-75 expressway, which by-passes Frankenmuth by seven miles, was opened in 1958, there was some concern here. Many feared it would jeopardize the tourist trade then already developed. However, the heavier traffic using I-75 plus the popularity of the Bavarian theme, brought in more visitors than ever. People now could reach Frankenmuth in half the time it formerly took on the "old road." A local butcher remarked during an interview: "But you must remember . . . we offer the traveler something which causes him to leave the expressway."[5]

Kingsburg, California, a town of about four thousand residents, developed a "Swedish Village" in the 1960s, even though the population had become quite heterogeneous. At that time, the town's Swedish-Americans numbered only about thirty percent of the local residents. In 1965, a San Francisco speaker addressed the Kingsburg District Chamber of Commerce on "Community Development," "Congress for Community Progress," and "The Tourist Business." He displayed pictures "to show what other communities had done to beautify, improve, and promote

themselves." Shortly thereafter, the Chamber of Commerce began to create a "Swedish Village." A community celebration, based on earlier midsummer festivals in the town, was initiated in 1966. Storefronts were
remodeled and a Swedish cookbook project was undertaken. The city
purchased ninety Swedish flags and constructed eighty-four Dala horses
(figures modeled after a provincial Swedish folk art object) for the 1966
festival. Kingsburg's "Swedish Village" was ready for a lucrative tourist
trade. The Kingsburg Chamber of Commerce pamphlet states: "The creation of a Swedish village has been, and will continue to be, a gradual
process. Because of the progress thus far, and the tremendous interest in
the project, Kingsburg is destined to have a glorious future."[6]

By looking at their own internal resources, ethnic towns have been
able to forestall decline and affirm their ability to be self-sufficient. Ethnic
festivals, and the tourist dollars they bring, demonstrate the resilience of
the townspeople. This function is clearly evident in the Swiss festivals
held by residents of New Glarus, Wisconsin, who attempt to publicize
and promote "America's Little Switzerland." The performance of the
Wilhelm Tell story, for example, embodies this self-sufficiency by laud-
ing the values of pride, boldness, and defiance of authority. Making this
public display interesting and relevant to tourists ensures that the development of community pride remains in the hands of the townspeople.[7]

Although the movement of population from village to city has been
reversed in the past decade, the use of ethnic resources to affirm local
autonomy and to encourage tourism is still important in many American
communities.[8] In the case of Lindsborg, Kansas, the interest in ethnic
revivalism is still strong, even though the movement is almost twenty
years old. The movement continues to stimulate local Swedish-American
events and specialty shop activities. Publicity about the town as "Little
Sweden, U.S.A." in national and international publications has encouraged the maintenance of ethnic attractions in the community.[9] The
Lindsborg Chamber of Commerce sponsors workshops from time to
time in order to motivate merchants to support the movement.[10] In
addition, Lindsborg has successfully participated in a statewide PRIDE
program, "a united effort to draw the entire state together through an
overall resource development emphasis [and] to encourage all Kansas
communities, regardless of size, to compare themselves with others and
compete for state-wide recognition."[11] The community's PRIDE projects
have often made use of Swedish-American traditions. Like the biennial
Svensk Hyllnings Fest (a four-day "Swedish Commemoration Festival")
and the annual Midsummer Festival, the public celebration of St. Lucia
is carefully organized and executed by community organizations and

actively supported by the Lindsborg Chamber of Commerce. It bears all the characteristics of a community effort to distinguish the town from others in the cultural landscape and to augment the local economy through tourism.

These examples of community boosterism suggest the revivalistic purpose of the Lindsborg St. Lucia festival and its role in sustaining a public image of the community as a colorful Swedish-American enclave. But the festival serves other intents and functions which, when examined apart from the private and semipublic ethnic behavior in the community, are less obvious. A single enactment of a folk tradition is multifunctional for its participants and its observers. Consequences may reverberate in community life and in the lives of its members long after the event itself has concluded. To concentrate on the Lindsborg St. Lucia festival solely as a quasi-traditional public display event, as a synthesis of ethnic markers used to boost the local economy and sense of community pride, is to oversimplify its meanings and functions.

I grew up in Lindsborg, spent my first twenty-five years in the area, and have returned to it for extended periods of time since 1965, when I began graduate studies in folklore. On these occasions I have played many roles—active interviewer, participant-observer, and tourist, as well as son, nephew, cousin, and friend.[12] I continue to research Swedish-American life in Lindsborg and to visit my hometown. These diverse and prolonged contacts with community traditions on many levels—institutional, occupational, associational, and familial—have made me cautious in generalizing about Lindsborg traditions. Indeed, I feel less certain about their meanings for townspeople than I did nearly twenty years ago when I defended my doctoral dissertation on the topic. The Lindsborg St. Lucia celebration is more important for some community members than for others, and certain functions and consequences are more significant, at least more obvious, than others. But how does one judge what is important and significant about the event? How does one discern meanings which lie behind so many activities?

Lindsborg, which is located in central Kansas, was founded in the 1860s by a small group of Swedish religious dissenters. The Lutheran church and a small Lutheran college have dominated the town's cultural interests since the late 1800s and in important ways have shaped community mores in the agricultural settlement.[13] The three thousand residents, like other rural Midwesterners, are for the most part committed to the virtues and values of the small community, although they are in daily touch with mainstream urban concerns through the mass media, college students, and Lindsborg visitors. Most of them appear to lead secure, content lives nurtured by extended family associations, religious institutions, active cultural interests, and conservative social values that are indebted to the original Swedish pietist settlement.

However, in some ways Lindsborg differs dramatically from other Kansas towns of the same size. Bethany College musical events and the town's dozen or so local artists have interested the non-Lindsborg world for decades and continue to create a vigorous interaction between Lindsborgians and their urban visitors. Both the regional and national press have described the town as a cultural oasis because of its annual Easter oratorio festival and its resident artists.[14] Since the late 1960s, many community leaders have worked to emphasize the distinctiveness of Lindsborg as "Little Sweden, U.S.A." The majority of its residents, both Swedish-American (about two-thirds of the population) and non-Swedish-American, have supported these efforts in creative ways. The biennial Swedish commemoration festival, the *Svensk Hyllnings Fest*, has become more and more important, attracting thousands of former residents and tourists every other fall. Many merchants have refurbished their shop exteriors on Main Street as colorful "Swedish storefronts," and specialty shops and other stores market Swedish arts, crafts, and foods. The Lindsborg Swedish Folk Dancers participate in community events and regional, national, and international performance tours. The local outdoor museum of historic buildings emphasizes the town's Swedish origins and two public festivities, St. Lucia and Midsummer, are based on calendric holidays important in Swedish life.

The impressive fruits of ethnic revivalism in Lindsborg involve the self-conscious maintenance of immigrant folklife traditions—especially certain foodways and Christmas customs—the revival of other folkways either from the distant immigrant past or from preimmigration life in nineteenth-century Sweden, and the creation of quasi-folk observances and decorative visual motifs. The movement seems to have been motivated by community anxieties expressed in the late 1960s concerning the possible relocation of Bethany College to Colorado, and the by-passing of Lindsborg by the federal interstate highway system about the same time. As a result of these extralocal forces, Lindsborg residents examined the potential for bolstering their native economic resources and alternative means of reaffirming the town's cultural identity. Without the presence of Bethany College and the interstate highway, Lindsborg would "wither on the vine," according to many townspeople, and become indistinguishable from any other midwestern village. Its distinctive reputation would be seriously weakened and its economic future jeopardized at a time when doom and gloom were predicted for rural communities. Fortunately for Lindsborg, the revitalization efforts explored native cultural sources at a time when general American cultural interests were beginning to gravitate toward the ethnic arts and "authentic" cultural displays, however loosely defined.

It is important to view the St. Lucia celebration in Lindsborg within the context of this vigorous community movement, which turned to the ethnic past for inspiration in the development of an integrated sense of cultural distinctiveness and a tourist trade. Like many Lindsborg ethnic traditions, however, the local St. Lucia observance is not merely the product of Chamber of Commerce boosterism. Although it is a self-conscious recreation of an important Swedish seasonal ritual, a slim but strong chain of verbal and behavioral transmission relates it to old-country antecedents.

A century and a half ago the *Sankta Lucia* celebration was observed only in the Lake Vänern region of western Sweden. It consisted of an early morning feast of pork, Christmas breads, and brandy, often served by a young woman of the household. The festivity introduced the month-long Christmas season in the traditional calendar. In the province of Västergötland, a white-gowned Lucia "queen," who wore a crown of lighted candles, served the Lucia breakfast in affluent farm homes, but all classes made special efforts to celebrate the holiday with early-morning feasting and drinking. During the second half of the nineteenth century the tradition spread to the University cities of Lund and Uppsala through the efforts of regional student associations. In the 1890s, the folk museum Skansen in Stockholm included the tradition in its December activities. As a result, the St. Lucia celebration increased in importance as a regional symbol within Sweden, and outside Sweden as a symbol of the Swedish Christmas to the non-Swedish world. When a Stockholm newspaper sponsored a St. Lucia parade and St. Lucia contest in 1927, the folk tradition emerged in public as a significant national observance. Today, public St. Lucia events, church pageants, festivities in business firms, in hospitals, and in schools, and observance of the tradition in the home are commonplace and constitute the first essential act of the Christmas season.[15]

Publicity in the mass media has crystallized the form of the celebration in Sweden over the past several decades. As conventionally practiced, a young woman dressed in a white robe, her head crowned with lighted candles, serves coffee and saffron buns in traditional shapes to her family and others early on the morning of December 13. She is accompanied by other white-robed girls and sometimes "starboys," who wear peaked caps and carry star-tipped wands. As the coffee and food are distributed, the group sings in Swedish the Sicilian song, "Santa Lucia," as well as other songs associated with the season.

In Swedish America, as in Sweden, the ritual is performed in such diverse contexts as ethnic lodge parties, religious programs in Lutheran churches, community pageants, and home celebrations.[16] The development of the tradition in Swedish America is analogous to its evolution in Sweden, albeit highly influenced by media coverage, which has accelerated its distribution in the United States.

The *Lindsborg News-Record*, the town's weekly newspaper, prepares townspeople for the event a week or two in advance and documents its success with appropriate photographs the week following the festival. In the past few years, the newspaper announcements have described the festivity as "A Day of Christmas in Lindsborg" and the community setting as "Lindsborg—Your Christmas Shop: 'Gift Center of the Smoky Valley.'"[17] Chamber of Commerce pamphlets also provide information about the festivity. One recent brochure, entitled "Lindsborg Is Unique," includes a photograph of the candle-crowned Lindsborg St. Lucia and her attendants with the caption, "A haven of Swedish tradition." Another Chamber of Commerce publication provides information about the day's performances, exhibits, and bake sale, and a brief description of the legend of St. Lucia in Sweden.

As a child growing up in Lindsborg in the late 1940s, I was vaguely aware of St. Lucia Day. In the early morning of December 13, coeds on the local college campus served coffee and cookies to women's dormitory residents, and Lutheran high school girls annually made a Lucia pilgrimage to "the old people's home," the Bethany Home. (An anecdote about the old man who cried out at the sight of the candle-bedecked Lucia, "I've died and gone to Heaven!" regularly circulated in mid-December Lindsborg conversations). One local family observed the day by bringing coffee and Christmas cookies to relatives and friends before the sun was up. Few Lindsborgians outside of these groups celebrated Lucia Day, and for me the tradition was picturesque but alien to the familiar round of Swedish-American Christmas customs at home.

The initiation of family celebrations of St. Lucia in Lindsborg in the 1940s can be traced to the peasant ritual practiced in the Lake Vänern area in the early nineteenth century. The late Bernhard Anderson, a second-generation Swedish-American, recalled to me that when he was a small boy in Lindsborg his father served him coffee and cookies early on the morning of December 13 and said to him, "*Det är Lussenatt, Lasse liten*" ("It is Lucy night, little lad"). The elder Anderson was an adult immigrant from Västergötland in the culture area where the St. Lucia tradition was an important calendric custom long before its national distribution.

In 1937, Anderson and his wife decided to visit relatives shortly after midnight on December 13 and bring them coffee and pastries. This family revival of a childhood experience fondly recalled initiated a local tradition of "St. Luciaing" friends and neighbors by several families, mostly Lindholms, relatives of Anderson's wife. As performed by the group in the 1960s, one of the women wore a crown of lighted candles and others carried lanterns as they served coffee and pastries and sang English-language carols to the honored families.

In the 1940s, perhaps inspired by the Anderson-Lindholm observance and most certainly reminded of the tradition through Swedish-American Lutheran periodicals and Swedish publications, various Lindsborg institutions incorporated the custom into their seasonal festivities. Different St. Lucia groups feted Lindsborg Community Hospital patients, Bethany Home residents, and Bethany College coeds. Simultaneously, a few families continued to observe the early-morning ritual as they recalled it from their early-twentieth-century childhoods, although it appears to have played a minor role in early immigrant life in the area.

The official public performance of the St. Lucia custom dates from 1962 when the Chamber of Commerce retail sales committee instituted a yuletide presentation in connection with pre-Christmas shopping nights on Lindsborg's Main Street.[18] The promotion for the night of December 12, 1962, included a "Living Christmas Card" of carolers, a pantomimed "Night Before Christmas," and a brief performance of the St. Lucia ritual organized by Malcolm Esping, a Lindsborg craftsman active in various cultural revivalism projects, and his teenage daughter. Several junior high students were the ritual performers: St. Lucia (Esping's daughter), who wore a white robe, red sash, and a head wreath of evergreen and lighted candles in a brass crown; her female attendants, dressed in Lindsborg versions of Swedish peasant costumes; and two male attendants, also in Swedish costume. The group caroled and served coffee and cookies to shoppers on Main Street. According to the local newspaper, "many" out-of-town visitors and townspeople viewed the event.

In the following two decades the public enactment of the custom varied somewhat from year to year and became more elaborate, although it followed the pattern established in 1962. Malcolm Esping and Elizabeth Jaderborg, another important leader in the ethnic revivalism efforts of the 1960s, directed the presentation at various times, and both acknowledge their use of Swedish and Swedish-American publications in their work. The sponsorship of the pageant shifted occasionally among the

Chamber of Commerce, local Lutheran churches, and the Lindsborg Swedish Folk Dancers, led by Jaderborg. As the presentation became established as a public tradition, other elements were added to it: ethnic accoutrements (in one case a large *julbock*, a gift-giving goat figure fashioned out of straw and displayed during the Christmas season in Sweden), additional personnel in Swedish costume, the crowning of St. Lucia, a pantomime sketch called "Living Christmas Traditions—Little Sweden, U.S.A.," an instrumental group, and the singing of "Sankta Lucia" and other seasonal and religious songs in Swedish. The official crowning of the Lucia Queen and the serving of coffee and baked goods to Main Street shoppers by Lucia and her retinue remained the central focus of the presentation, however. Usually the event took place in the early evening of the Saturday closest to December 13, but in the past few years the time of the performance has shifted to afternoon with a consequent increase in attendance. In 1980, when the festivity was observed on a particularly mild Saturday afternoon, a crowd numbered at two thousand by the *Lindsborg News-Record* circulated in downtown Lindsborg.

Area newspapers and a regional television station have publicized the celebration regularly since its inception in 1962. The *Lindsborg News-Record* has reported extralocal coverage of the event and provided its own descriptions of the activities, including photographs and background information concerning the origins of the tradition and its practice in Sweden. Local news accounts, however, have rarely noted the importance of the presentation as a commercial effort to develop Lindsborg tourism. Instead, they have consistently emphasized the role it has played in characterizing Lindsborg as a unique ethnic community that values its Swedish immigrant heritage.

In 1981, the Lindsborg Arts Council and the Chamber of Commerce, the two organizations that had assumed responsibility for the pageant in the late 1970s, made special efforts to create an appropriate physical, visual setting for St. Lucia Day. At the Main Street intersection stood a large Christmas tree, decorated "not with blinking, multi-colored lights . . . , but with the delicate white lights of Europe" and with *julkärvar* (traditional sheaves of grain customarily put out during the Swedish Christmas season for the birds).[19] Larger *julkärvar* were hung from the West Main Street light poles, as in previous years, and a new decorative element—banners depicting traditional Swedish Christmas symbols— replaced more conventional American Christmas motifs. The banners were a gift to the city from the biennial *Svensk Hyllnings Fest* committee, and the Lindsborg Swedish Dancers provided the oat sheaves. A thank-you letter from the Chamber of Commerce published in the

Lindsborg News-Record aptly summed up the townspeople's satisfaction with the new Christmas look:

> The new Christmas banners are one more reason why Lindsborg is such a special place to live and why others like to come here to visit. Not only are these banners beautiful, it's nice to have Christmas decorations that are in keeping with the Swedish heritage of the community. One can see why the people of Lindsborg have maintained a reputation of doing distinctive things in a tasteful way.[20]

That the community had once again demonstrated its allegiance to its ethnic heritage in a way that was compatible with local aesthetic preferences and with the visitor's quest for old-world charm was clearly apparent in the day's schedule of events for Saturday, December 12. High school and college groups and the Swedish Dance Fiddlers performed special seasonal music throughout the day. A visit from Santa Claus and a storyteller entertained children. A Bethany College student art sale and a community Swedish bake sale to help fund the event represented both local art and ethnic interests. A performance by the Lindsborg Swedish Folk Dancers introduced the central event of the afternoon, the crowning of St. Lucia, followed by the serving of hot cider and ginger cookies to bystanders. It is difficult to estimate accurately the number of people who attended the events. The Chamber of Commerce office reported that about three hundred were present at the crowning of St. Lucia. Out-of-town visitors were obvious, and two bus loads of tourists from Wichita, Kansas, spent the day in Lindsborg.

St. Lucia was celebrated the same weekend at other levels of community life. On Friday, fourth-graders from the Lindsborg elementary school presented a St. Lucia pageant at the Bethany Home for the Aged. On Saturday morning, friends and relatives of the family that revived the tradition gathered for a special breakfast in the local bakery. And before dawn on Sunday, December 13, a college Lucia feted Bethany College dormitory residents. Simultaneously, some Lindsborg families observed the candle-lit ritual privately and informally within the home. Most townspeople, then, experienced, performed, read about, witnessed, or spoke of the St. Lucia tradition in various ways that forcefully illustrated the maintenance of ethnic heritage in Lindsborg and the commencement of the Swedish-American Christmas season. The days to come would involve a number of other traditions—some self-consciously observed as Swedish-American and others conceptualized as ethnic only on occasion—the Christmas Eve feast of Swedish holiday foods and their American variants, the Christmas Eve gift-exchange within extended families, *julotta* (the early-morning church service on Christmas Day), the *annandag jul* ("second day Christmas") religious service in the Swedish language, and the round of socializing among families that continues beyond New Year's Day. In 1981, Lindsborgians observed St. Lucia as an important ethnic-religious celebration in a manner far more elaborate and assertive than past generations had experienced.

Unlike the biennial *Svensk Hyllnings Fest*, the St. Lucia festivity probably has limited short-term economic consequences in Lindsborg life. The celebration, however, attracts visitors to the community and to Main Street, notably to the Swedish specialty shops. Since St. Lucia activities took place both morning and afternoon in 1981, purchases by townspeople may have also increased somewhat. In general, business in specialty shops and grocery stores selling Swedish food items is brisk throughout the Christmas season, making December a peak sales month. Some of this trade is from out of town and is undoubtedly stimulated by area and regional news coverage of the St. Lucia celebration. If tourists cannot visit Lindsborg on the day of the public observance of St. Lucia, they can experience Christmas in "Little Sweden, U.S.A" at other times during December.

Community leaders interested in expanding Lindsborg's tourist economy, sometimes criticized for their commercial motives, have fully supported the seasonal tradition. The celebration in 1981 artfully combined musical events, ethnic decor, and ethnic tradition in a manner calculated to satisfy a variety of audiences and not seem exploitative. "The best way to be commercial is to act like you're non-commercial," commented one Lindsborgian when asked about the development of the town as a tourist center. His insight is applicable to the 1981 St. Lucia Day. Newspapers, magazines, and television stations have long regarded Lindsborg as a rich source for local color stories and have treated its public events both respectfully and enthusiastically.[21] Local and regional media reminded Kansans and other Midwesterners in mid-December, 1981, that Lindsborg deserved its reputation as "Little Sweden, U.S.A." and was a pleasant, interesting place to visit.

Performing ethnic traditions for non-Lindsborgians not only serves to develop Lindsborg's tourism potential, it also affirms the cultural uniqueness of the town, especially during periods of impaired community self-esteem. The ethnic revival that took place in the late 1960s and 1970s affirmed the town's distinctiveness among others in central Kansas and the Midwest. Even if residents do not attend the public ethnic events in large numbers, they may read about them in local and area newspapers, see them depicted on television news shows, and hear visitors endorse the community's ethnic attractiveness. In 1965, the *Lindsborg News-Record* republished a *Wichita Eagle-Beacon* editorial which urged Lindsborg citizens to "do more to carry on the old Swedish customs":

> The Swedish heritage is a rich one. It would be a shame to have it lost. Lindsborg's Swedish old-timers and their descendants can help to preserve it. And in doing so, make their community still more appealing to tourists and a place other Kansans even more will want to visit and point to with pride.
>
> Lindsborg, one might say owes it to the world, if not itself, to play the role of a host.[22]

As the ethnic revival flowered, the old-country distinctiveness of Lindsborg received increased attention in local publications. In an overview of Lindsborg Christmas events in 1981, for instance, a front-page *Lindsborg News-Record* article began:

> With all the charm of the "old world" Christmas surroundings yet with none of the problems of language barriers, Kansans may be treated to a most unique Christmas experience in Lindsborg this year. Nestled in the Smoky Valley region of the state, not far off the interstate highways, lies this village with strong ties to the mother country of her settlers . . . Sweden.[23]

The native perception of Lindsborg as a unique ethnic settlement attractive to the outside world persists, encouraged both by the Chamber of Commerce and by media descriptions of Lindsborg life. It is an important source of community pride. Occasional criticism that derides this self-image as exploitative and parochial usually remains private and is ignored by most townspeople as eccentric and ill-humored. In a season traditionally criticized for its commercialism, when people search for an "authentic" celebration of the holiday, the Lindsborg St. Lucia pageant and its accompanying events offer a purifying antidote.[24] In the opinion of many onlookers, it communicates respect for the past and represents the attractiveness of small-town life uncontaminated by the urban marketplace.

The commemorative purpose of the observance is more difficult to ascertain than that of promoting distinctiveness and tourism. Some community members and many visitors believe that the custom was important to the early community settlers, although it seems that the tradition was not widespread in the settlement period. In the first years of the pageant, its primary personnel interpreted the performance as a tribute to the Swedish immigrants who settled the area. Some of the Lindsborg Swedish Folk Dancers, for example, have described their involvement with the public festivity as "part of [their] Swedish heritage," "a for-real thing to do," according to the organization's founder and first director. The pageant's emphasis on tribute to the local Swedish-American past, however, is much less important than in the biennial *Svensk Hyllnings Fest* in which parade floats, public speeches, and festival publications articulate the commemorative significance of the events.

"Ethnicity is . . . intimately related to the individual need for collective continuity. The individual senses to some degree a threat to his own survival if his group or lineage is threatened with extinction. Ethnicity, therefore, includes a sense of personal survival in the historical continuity of the group."[25] In Lindsborg, as in many other American communities, positive ethnic identification blends with positive local identification to create a sense of heritage. An assessment of the importance of tradition in contemporary society by a fourth-generation Swedish-American Lindsborgian expresses a widely shared sentiment in Lindsborg today:

> I definitely think heritage does mean something. I think the old does mean something. I can't think otherwise. So I think it's good to retain some of the traditions—not to be shown but to give people roots, the sense of belonging to something, which young people desperately need today. I sense this when young people that I know marry and move away from here, especially in recent years. They come back here and seem so proud of where they came from and the things they've grown up with. . . . Of course, there are many ways a community can do it if not done through a Swedish festival. . . . So many times people find themselves in the situation where they are part of nothing and here almost everyone can be part of it if they want to be.[26]

The role of St. Lucia in distinguishing Lindsborg as a unique community in which to live and shop is supported by statements of purpose offered by Chamber of Commerce officials and active participants, by public interpretations of the festivity in the local newspaper and Chamber of Commerce publications, and by the larger context of ethnic revivalism in Lindsborg. Philip Frick McKean, in his analysis of ethnic tourism in Bali, has pointed out that such efforts can intensify local interests in native traditions: " . . . the younger Balinese find their identity as Balinese to be sharply framed by the mirror that tourism holds up to them, [which] has led many of them to celebrate their own traditions with continued vitality."[27] Halfway across the globe among Swedish-Americans in central Kansas, a public festivity performed as much for a nonnative audience as for townspeople is important in the development of the town's tourism potential and in substantiating the town's cultural identity as a distinctive community. But it also helps maintain and invigorate private observances of the holiday ritual and personal notions about their significance in ethnic self-definition. The reality of ethnic identity, then, is born as much out of the need to create a meaningful sense of community as it is out of the legacy left by ethnic forebears.

Notes to Chapter 12

1. In the early 1970s, national news magazines and television shows described the midwestern village as dying, their interpretations based on the 1970 census. See, for example, "Americans on the Move: New Patterns," *U.S. News & World Report*, 16 March 1970, 66–67; Frank Morgan, "Report from the Heartland," *Newsweek*, 11 September 1972, 24, 27; Garrick Utley and Edwin Newman; NBC, "Leaving Home Blues," 27 August 1971, PBS, "Hard Times in the Country," 10 September 1971; "Quiet Falls across the Plains," *Life*, 25 June 1971, 22–31.

2. A full discussion of the survey methods and the data collected appear in Larry William Danielson, "The Ethnic Festival and Cultural Revivalism in a Small Midwestern Town" (Ph.D. diss., Indiana University, 1972), 412–22.

3. Regina Bendix, "Tourism and Cultural Displays: Inventing Traditions for Whom?" *Journal of American Folklore* 102 (1989): 131–46.

4. Ralph Friedman, "Scandinavia in Oregon," *Louisville Courier-Journal*, 28 July 1968.

5. Irene Zeilinger, ed., *Frankenmuth* (N.p.: n.p., 1970), 13.

6. "Swedish Village Concept" (mimeographed item in a packet received from the Kingsburg, California, Chamber of Commerce, 1971).

7. Phillip Zarrilli and Deborah Neff, "Performance in 'America's Little Switzerland': New Glarus, Wisconsin," *The Drama Review* 26 (1982): 111–24.

8. The official United States government census statistics for 1980 indicated this reversal, and several news service releases publicized it. For example, a *Christian Science Monitor* news service article by Peter Grier appeared in central Illinois under the headline, "America's Small Towns Are Growth Spots," *Champaign-Urbana News-Gazette*, 13 July 1983, A-12.

9. Recent examples of such publicity include "The Swedes of Lindsborg, Kansas," *Early American Life*, August 1983, 38–39, 66, 67, 80; Jean Truscott, "Lindsborg: Swedish Traditions Take Root in Kansas," *Check Point* [publication of the United States Auto Club], Fall 1982, 3; and "*Svenskare kan ingen vara*" [No one can be more Swedish], an illustrated article in the major Swedish newspaper *Svenska Dagbladet*, 21 December 1983, 1, 19.

10. In 1982, a marketing consultant and adviser led a series of seminars and provided private consultations to Lindsborg merchants. The *Lindsborg News-Record* enthusiastically described his visit to the community. See "Mouser Sees Tourism as Primary Industry," 21 October 1982, A-3.

11. "PRIDE Task Force Will Establish Goals," *Lindsborg News Record*, 4 September 1980, 1.

12. The ethnographic information upon which this description and interpretation is based was gathered between 1966 and 1983, usually during Christmas and

summer vacations. Participant observation, formal interviews, informal conversations, questionnaires, and the study of photographs and a variety of printed sources have provided the data relevant to this study. I discuss special methodological problems encountered in the analysis of one's native community culture in Chapter 2 of "The Ethnic Festival," 30–60.

13. Community histories of the town include Alfred Bergin, *Lindsborg: Bidrag till Svenskarnas och den Lutherska Kyrkans Historia i Smoky Hill River Dalen* (Rock Island, Ill.: Augustana Book Concern, 1909); *Lindsborg efter Femtio År* (Rock Island, Ill.: Augustana Book Concern, 1919); Emory Kempton Lindquist, *Smoky Valley People* (Lindsborg, Kans.: Bethany College, 1953); *Vision for a Valley: Olof Olsson and the Early History of Lindsborg* (Rock Island, Ill.: Augustana Historical Society, 1970). An insightful sociological study is Wayne Leland Wheeler's "An Analysis of Social Change in a Swedish-Immigrant Community: The Case of Lindsborg, Kansas" (Ph.D. diss., University of Missouri, 1959).

14. To cite but two instances of national media attention to Lindsborg's Messiah Festival: Howard W. Turtle, "Oberammergau of the Plains," *Reader's Digest*, April 1944, 86–87, and William Walter Perry, "Messiah Week," *New York Times*, 2 April 1950. The one hundredth annual community performance of Handel's *Messiah* was televised by Wichita station KPTS in 1981 and transmitted to some 175 Public Broadcasting Service stations throughout the country.

15. For information about the celebration of the holiday in Sweden see Carl-Martin Bergstrand, *Gammalt från Kind: Folkminne från Kinds härad i Västergötland*, Vol. II (Goteborg: Gumpert, 1960), 60–70; Nils-Arvid Bringeus, *Årets festseder* (Stockholm: LTs förlag, 1976), 23–30; Karl Hilding Celander, *Nordisk jul* (Stockholm: Hugo Geber, 1928), 32–48; Tobias Norlind, *Svenska allmogens liv* (Stockholm: Bohlin, 1925), 452–53.

16. Winter issues of *The Vasa Star*, the official publication of the Vasa Order of America, a Swedish-American fraternal organization, regularly describe St. Lucia presentations performed during December lodge meetings. At least three public observances of the custom take place annually in Illinois: in the Chicago Swedish-American neighborhood of Andersonville, in the village of Bishop Hill, and on the University of Illinois campus at Urbana-Champaign, sponsored by the Swedish language faculty.

17. *Lindsborg News-Record*, 9 December 1982, A-4.

18. See Danielson, "The Ethnic Festival," 274–84, for a history of the St. Lucia tradition in Lindsborg to 1971.

19. "An Overview of Christmas to Come: New Decorations for Holidays," *Lindsborg News-Record*, 19 November 1981, 1.

20. *Lindsborg News-Record*, 3 December 1981, 2.

21. For example, a colorfully illustrated article, "Community Cookbooks: The Pleasures of a Heritage Preserved," featured the town's holiday foodways in *Ladies' Home Journal*, December 1975, 26, 29–32, 60. On January 12, 1979, an hour-long documentary, "Little Sweden, Lindsborg, Kansas," was shown on Swedish television as part of a series of nine shows concerning Swedish America. The same year, *Lindsborg — svenskstaden i USA:s mitt* [Lindsborg — Swedish City in the middle of the U.S.A.] by Anders Runewall and Bertil Hagert (Vällingby: Harriers, 1979), was available in Lindsborg specialty shops.

22. "Lindsborg's Role," *Lindsborg News-Record*, 26 August 1965, 2.

23. "An Overview of Christmas to Come," 1.

24. Typical articles in popular print indicative of the search for a more satis-fying Christmas holiday are: Amitai Etzione, "Christmas Blues," *Psychology Today*, December 1976, 23; Andrew M. Greeley, "The Many Meanings of Christmas," *Woman's Day*, 22 December 1981, 75, 151–52; and Jere Daniel, "The Other Side of Christmas," *Family Circle*, 22 December 1981, 30, 32, 148.

25. "Ethnic Pluralism: Conflict and Accommodation," in *Ethnic Identity: Cultural Continuities and Change*, edited by George De Vos and Lola Romanucci-Ross (Palo Alto, Cal.: Mayfield Publishing, 1975), 17.

26. Interview with Esther Johnson (pseudonym), fourth-generation Swedish-American, middle-aged, who has lived in Lindsborg most of her life.

27. "Towards a Theoretical Analysis of Tourism: Economic Dualism and Cultural Involution in Bali," in *Hosts and Guests: The Anthropology of Tourism*, edited by Valene L. Smith (Philadelphia: University of Pennsylvania Press, 1977), 105.

13. Making a Place Home:
The Latino Festival

OLIVIA CADAVAL

Sociopolitical strife and economic crisis in Third World countries, combined with the persistent illusion of an economic paradise in the United States, have precipitated a continuous flow of new immigrants. In Washington, D.C., a Latino community began to form in the 1960s. Cubans came in the greatest number in the late 1950s and early 1960s, during and at the end of the Cuban revolution. In the 1960s and 1970s came a sizable flow of South Americans. The largest number of immigrants in the 1980s have come from Central America. As many as 200,000 Salvadorans are now estimated to live in metropolitan Washington.

Many settled in the neighborhood of Adams Morgan, a mile and ahalf directly north of the White House, an area with a reputation as "the unofficial point of entry of the area's immigrants."[1] Ethnic activities are centered on two commercial streets which join at the intersection of 18th Street and Columbia Road. There can be found Latino restaurants and stores run by people from the Caribbean, Central America, and South America, which share the scene with African restaurants, fast-food shops, and local services. Continuing the neighborhood's long-standing tradition of activism, individuals from the small Spanish-speaking population assumed leadership roles and began organizational efforts in the 1960s.

Out of this growth of activism emerged an annual Latino festival which began in 1970. Starting as a small Latino community affair with a few makeshift booths and floats, by 1980 the festival was attracting ethnically mixed crowds of more than 150,000, and had become the biggest community festival in the city. The fact that the festival took place in the neighborhood recognized the importance of the *barrio* to the Latino community. Through the celebration of the Hispano American Festival, also known as the Latino Festival, the Latino community in Washington, D.C., recorded its nascent history and its growing multiethnic composition, staked its claim in the city and federal government, enacted group dynamics, and culturally marked and defined its living space.

I am interested in the emergence of new cultures among immigrants who use and modify what they have brought with them from their old homes to survive and create new ones. In this essay, I will look at how the food booths in the Latino festival both became a means for asserting and negotiating one's culture and one's right to place and space and for creating the new social patterns needed in Washington, D.C. These booths, called *kioskos* by D.C. Latinos, become the place where contradictions are played out and proclaimed and where a new culture tentatively shows itself and is tested.

The Latino Festival has been instrumental in creating solidarity among the different Latino immigrant groups as well as in laying claim to the neighborhood as the community's symbolic center. The festival transforms physical space into a means to cultural identity. As a temporary center of power, the festival brings together large numbers of Latinos, unifies space, and generates action, during which symbols and traditions are manipulated, cultural forms are given expression, relationships are negotiated, and new social identities are forged. Although traditional animosities exist between several Latino groups, the festival offers a solution of diversity rather than division, with the result that there is pan-Latino support for the alleged purpose of the event—the celebration of a common heritage. What goes on behind the scenes in terms of conflict over how to organize and whom to represent gives way in the festival to solidarity, to *communitas*. Leaders of the festival stroll hand in hand with city officials at the head of the parade. The parade, a mixed procession of nostalgic, allegorical floats and masquerades, confirms the festival's civic purpose.

Ethnicity, immigration, neighborhood, and Third World ideology are topics of discourse which relate to each other both harmoniously and discordantly in the festival. The ethnicity that often tends to divide Latinos from non-Latinos is transformed through various levels of interaction into a unifying agent by welding the concerns of immigrants with those of the neighborhood where they have settled. The immigrant is seeking to restore, if not create, a sense of individual worth and place.

On the one hand, this restoring process consists of establishing differentiating characteristics of the diverse Latino groups in the community to provide a regional or national sense of origin. On the other hand, it highlights these differences not to divide but to build a new pan-Latin American or Latino identity.

In the neighborhood, a sense of community identity and history emerges. Neighborhood becomes the stage for immigrant modes of expression and experimentation. Groups or individuals integrate worlds by drawing from disparate conceptual and material elements, from former experiences as well as from the new environment. New relationships are ordered; older ones are modified. The godparent-based, or *compadre*, ritual kinship system is expanded to cross ethnic and class lines to form new groupings and to develop a Latino power base. The continuous cultural bargaining taking place within and between groups is intensified and highlighted during the festival and particularly in the *kiosko* activity.

The overall *kiosko* style is characterized by its inclusive yet unhomogenized approach utilizing disparate, ready-at-hand cultural elements.[2] The basic *kiosko* frames are constructed by the festival organizing committee. Identical stalls with eight-foot-long counters are built next to each other along the street with two-by-four framing material and plywood. Vendors are required to register and pay a set fee for a stall, but are free to decorate as they choose. A new aesthetic emerges from multiple interacting codes drawn from national and regional identity, tourism, political ideology, language, cultural background, and immigrant status, which interact in the *barrio* under the watchful eye of the spectator.

Erected on either side of the festival streets, 18th Street and Columbia Road, "the two major arteries representative of *hispanidad* in Washington, D.C.,"[3] the *kioskos* provide a frame for celebration and a center for social and cultural interaction within and between groups in the area. Signs beckon and engage the passerby with familiar or exotic artifacts and foods, offering a nostalgic moment or a new experience. For two days the neighborhood of Adams Morgan becomes a "market world" that challenges the compartmentalized order of the everyday as it encompasses a continuum of interactions from the intimacy of the home and family to the competitiveness of the workplace and market. Its smells and its tastes are the heart of the Washington Latino community. It is at once part of the neighborhood and a tourist strip.

The *kioskos* physically define the boundaries of the festival. The different domains — family, ethnic group, community organization, and public agency — contribute to an all-pervasive mood of celebration which bridges the private world of the home and the public life of the neighborhood. The crowds enjoy a time-out-of-time, moving back and forth among the *kioskos* without ever having to leave the immediate surroundings. The crowds equally participate in the spirit of revelry as they are drawn by the marketplace attraction of the *kioskos* that invite interaction from the simple purchase of a dish to participating in a family reunion to encountering a different culture. Both engaging their patrons and discriminating among them, the *kioskos* provide a multiplicity of relationships.

The *kioskos* have been an integral activity of the festival from the beginning, prompted by a combination of social, economic, and advocacy objectives. Ruth Webster, a Black neighborhood activist, recalls that in the early festivals both Black and Latino community groups in the area sponsored the *kioskos* "to raise a little money and to inform people of their activities."[4] In 1987 many of the same motives persist. A local newspaper, *El Pregonero*, quotes a *kiosko* vendor, "I've taken a *kiosko* to try and sell some food because I need *un dinerito*, a little extra money, to pay for my son's registration fee at the university." The article also concurs that "community organizations take advantage of the *kioskos* to acquaint people with their programs."[5] But, unlike earlier years when the *kioskos* were restricted to nonprofit groups, private enterprises, "who are becoming aware of the Hispanic American market potential," are now given space to "promote new products and to deliver their message."[6]

Kioskos offer food, crafts, information, services, or a combination of these. The majority of the food *kioskos* are Latino, but in the last few years there has been an increase of Southeast Asian and West Indian. Crafts have been minimal until recently. Craft vendors are usually non-Latinos. Information and services *kioskos* are usually extensions of existing "outreach programs." The refugee centers distribute pamphlets. The Hispanic Legal Aid Association offers free migration counseling. The Red Cross distributes literature and offers blood pressure tests.

Notwithstanding the growing number of craft and information *kioskos*, foodways are the primary activity in this area of the festival. Complementing the parade, food is one of those "dynamic arenas where sensitivities and meanings are generated, experienced and communicated."[7] Accessible and nonthreatening, and as a *Washington Post* reporter states, "a kind of sentimental ballast" to local and international political tensions,[8] foodways provide a significant way of celebrating ethnicity and group identity.[9] Foodways also reveal the interactions that take place during the festival between the divergent and often conflicting public and private, immigrant and "ethnic," national and Third World perspectives. Identities based on difference rather than commonalities are interactively defined in the *kioskos* in the choice of signage and decoration, in the presentation of the food offered, and in the transactions that take place.[10]

The different worlds of the home, the market, the ethnic festival, *fiesta*, and Carnival are played out through the *kioskos* in this festival market world. I will examine various types of foodways *kioskos* both by internal structure and the distinguishing characteristics which ultimately define the general order of the *kiosko* domain in the festival. I will also analyze how *kiosko* activity reflects and establishes social relationships. I find three major categories and call these the ethnic festival *kiosko*, the market-style *kiosko*, and the family *kiosko*. The ethnic festival *kiosko*, primarily motivated by commercial interests, maximizes ethnic foods and images to attract customers from the general public. This *kiosko* is common to ethnic festivals throughout the United States. The market-style *kiosko* also reflects an entrepreneurial perspective, but it is modeled after food stalls traditionally found in Latin American markets and fairs. This *kiosko* often reflects the vendor's hometown. The family *kiosko* brings the home kitchen into the street (see figure 1).

FESTIVAL MARKET WORLD

FAMILY	MARKET-STYLE	ETHNIC
Reciprocal	- -	Competitive
Familial	Associative	Commercial
	Compadrazgo	
	(kin by ritual association)	
w/in groups	between groups	w/tourists
	INSIDERS OUTSIDERS	
PRIVATE	- -	PUBLIC

FIGURE I

Festival *kiosko* categories and corresponding forms
of organization and relationships.

Each type generates a distinct quality of space that enhances particular social dynamics and sets of identities. Ranging from the most private—the family—to the most public—the ethnic—the *kioskos* establish coordinates for interaction within the community and between the community and the larger society.[11]

Within the range of these *kiosko* types, the degree of decoration and signage increases dramatically in the ethnic festival *kiosko*. The ethnic-style *kiosko* at the festival, much like *kioskos* at other ethnic festivals throughout the United States, consistently relies on a touristic aesthetic which draws heavily on national stereotypes for its decorations and the foods it offers. Whether driven by nationalistic, Third World, or community fervor, and whether the aim is to educate or to make money, these *kioskos* are usually addressed to potential buyers who are not members of the community. The vendor both defines and separates himself from the festival's Latino and non-Latino public by engaging the public as tourist.[12] Symbiotically related, the vendor treats the buyer as tourist at the same time that the buyer characterizes the vendor and his product as ethnic. Each transforms the other through an unconscious complicity.

The use of souvenirs, crafts from tourist markets, and national colors in *kiosko* decoration mirror the aesthetics of the "folkloric" floats in the parade. Stock stereotypes are flaunted by the Mexican *kioskos* which unfailingly decorate their space with conventional national symbols—the national flag, *mariachi* hats, and *piñatas*. In one *kiosko*, the marquee itself is in the shape of a *mariachi* hat.

The association of plants and crafts with a region is common to the national tourist industry of all of Latin America, and is a popular identity strategy of many of the ethnic *kioskos* at the festival. Familiar travel-poster icons like straw hats, palms, and exotic fruits are favorites among Caribbean and Central American *kioskos*. Often jingles written on the sign complement the decor:

PUERTO RICO *"LA ISLE DEL ENCANTO"* (The Island of Enchantment)
PUERTO RICO, LA ISLA DE LA SALSA Y EL SABOR (The Island of Salsa [music or sauce] and Flavor)

Basic crops can also contribute a regional touch. The Salvadoran soccer club *"Liga Salvadoreña LUSCAR"* created a tropical booth framed by corn plants and pineapples.

The homogenizing tendency of tourist arts in *kiosko* aesthetics often underplays or negates regional differences.[13] Two countries strikingly different yet each famous for textiles, Bolivia and Guatemala, have both been represented nearly identically in *kiosko* settings with appropriate regional textiles as a backdrop and decorations of larger-than-life-size carved wooden spoon sets. In the case of the Bolivian *kiosko*, the spoon set was incised with the figures of Inca heroes. The Guatemalan spoon sets were decorated with the Mayan images.

While the ethnic *kiosko* at the festival exploits national iconography, its focus is nonetheless local. Community groups as well as businesses stake their place and assert their presence in the community with their *kioskos*. Statements identifying the group and its relationship to the community or the festival abound in the *kiosko* signage. One of the simplest forms is illustrated by the sign on the *kiosko* sponsored by an herbalist store on Columbia Road which identified itself not with Cuba but with being Cuban:

BOTANICA SAN LAZARO — SOMOS CUBANOS (We are Cuban)

Other signs layer a combination of messages and identities. Typically the *kiosko* uses a sign with formulaic salutary remarks to establish its role as host of the festival:

PARAGUAY ROJHAIJU ("I love you" in *Guarani*)
[map of the country]
BIENVENIDOS (Welcome)
VIVA PARAGUAY
[menu]

This Paraguayan Committee *kiosko* first states the nation's dual Spanish-Indian identity and identifies itself with a map. Framed by national markers, the *kiosko* establishes itself as a welcoming presence in the Latino Festival and further realizes its hosting role by offering an ethnic menu of typical dishes.

One of the local Salvadoran Refugee organizations, *Casa* EL SALVADOR, more openly links its welcome with its political message on its signs:

EL SALVADOR LIBRE (Free El Salvador)
SALUDA A LA GRAN COMUNIDAD (Salutes the Great Community)
STOP BOMBING EL SALVADOR

Other forms of welcome include "Guatemala Salutes You" and "Nicaragua Invites You"; among Third World forms, the "Presente" exclamation predominates. Casa Colombia, Inc., proclaims:

COLOMBIA PRESENTE
XV FESTIVAL HISPANO BIENVENIDOS

"Presente," the conventional roll-call response in Latin American schools as well as in the army, has become an official exclamation of solidarity with Third World struggles.

Food, in particular "ethnic" specialties, is central to the ethnic *kiosko*. The "ethnic" label is usually applied by others, although it may be acknowledged by the group in question. It is further exploited by the commercial market of prepared goods, chain food stores, and restaurants. These foods, basic staples served in the home and sold to strangers at the marketplace, suddenly become representative foods.[14]

The Mexican *taco* heads the list of favorites at the festival in this category. More recently, the Salvadoran *pupusa* or filled corn patty has become a popular item.[15] Selected from common, everyday Mexican and Salvadoran home and market foods, *tacos* and *pupusas* are modified to meet outsiders' expectations. Literally and metaphorically removing the food from the home context protects the "kitchen," while allowing for intercultural play in a public setting. Out of context, the vendor freely separates the traditional from the ethnic concept and more easily accommodates the outside buyer, the tourist, seeking both recognition and approval of the "typical" dish now jointly redefined.[16]

Some vendors feature a variety of what have come to be favorite ethnic festival specialties. Such is the case of a Korean-owned restaurant vending at the festival Mexican *tacos,* Chinese "shrimp-fried rice," and shish kebab. The Korean presence as merchants catering to other ethnic groups is felt not only in the festival but in the larger entrepreneurial world of Washington.[17] Reinforced by successful sales, panethnic specialties such as the skewered charcoal-broiled meat commonly called shish kebab have come to dominate many of the ethnic festival *kioskos.* Because of their popularity, many *kioskos*, regardless of nationality, sell a form of shish kebab. Its popularity suggests that a traditional food may be accepted more easily as an "ethnic specialty" if it has unique but interchangeable qualities, different but like everybody else's. It should be exotic, if only in name, but not too unfamiliar to the palate, like the skewered variants of meat featured above. Furthermore, the shish kebab is conveniently a portable, "walking" entree.

Borderline to and exploiting the power of ethnic festival *kiosko* imagery,[18] some *kioskos* purposely confuse categorical boundaries to impart a message. While ostensibly selling food, a *kiosko* may in fact be offering a very different "product." In 1983, while the *"Kiosko El Mojado"* (the Wetback) sold Salvadoran traditional dishes, its signs advertised:

ALTO A LA	*40,000 MUERTOS*	*65,000*
DEPORTACION	*POR LA JUNTA*	*REFUGIADOS*
(Stop deportation)	*MILITAR*	*SALVADOREÑOS*
	SALVADOREÑA	*EN*
	(40,000 deaths by	*WASHINGTON*
	the Salvadoran	*(65,000 SALVADORAN*
	Military Junta)	*REFUGEES IN*
		WASHINGTON)

In 1979 an ingenious, somewhat carnivalesque, marriage of food and politics was realized by the Nicaraguan "VIVA NICARAGUA LIBRE" (Long Live Free Nicaragua) *kiosko* offering "liberated meat" in celebration of the recent Sandinista victory.

In summary, this type of *kiosko* is defined by an "ethnic" identity constructed and agreed upon jointly by vendor and buyer/tourist. Signage is directed to the outsider and eating is the chief activity. "Ethnic" food cements the relationship between the vendor and his culture and the buyer-become-tourist, who asserts his identity by consuming the cultures of others.[19]

In theory, the different ethnic *kioskos* support a democratic cultural pluralism by offering "equal opportunity eating" for all who come through the use of familiar food. Tasting foods becomes an egalitarian action and allows everyone present to identify ethnically, whether they are Latino or not.[20] Individuals whose heritage may be Latin American but whose regular behavior and cultural patterns are not identifiably ethnic may become Latinos for the day.

Unlike the ethnic *kiosko*, the market-style *kiosko* at the festival reflects a Latin American marketplace system of organization rather than a model evolved within the context of ethnic celebrations in the United States. The Latin American marketplace is an institution reflective of the encounter between cultures in different historical periods, yet it maintains a continuity with its pre-Columbian past. The colonial Spanish amplified the indigenous market system which encouraged interdependence between ethnic and regional groups by encouraging craft, food, and product specialization. In spite of the onslaught of modernization and industrialization, the traditional marketplace has survived and has often provided an economic outlet for cottage industries. Latin American markets are usually controlled by the municipality, but the vendors are, in large part, individual and independent entrepreneurs sustaining the marginal or "invisible economies."[21]

In the towns and villages of Latin America, a variety of market spaces exist within the marketplace itself anywhere between the center and the periphery. Among the vendors offering prepared food, the merchandise most appropriate to the present discussion, the *comedores*—restaurant-like stands providing seating space for their customers—usually offer at least one main meal including a fish or braised meat, potato, rice, or manioc, and bread or tortilla, depending on the region. Individual stands selling snacks or "fast" foods like *tacos, pupusas, tamales, empañadas,* sweet breads, and beverages, tend to be on the outside of the market.

Some of these stands have a permanent place, others not. Some itinerant stands move from market to market, or may be set up in the streets outside the marketplace. During fiestas, it is usually the itinerant vendors who sell food and beverages. Some families create a marketplace outside of the marketplace by setting up vending stands in their own homes. Their food selection may be as varied as that of the *comedores* or may be limited to one or two regional specialties.[22]

The marketplace has been recontextualized in stories treating the beginnings of the Latino community in Washington. The earliest *barrio* markers were the neighborhood markets or grocery stores. Social and commercial centers of the *barrio*, these markets also sold *empanadas* baked by itinerant women vendors supplementing their family incomes.[23] Reminiscent of Latin American markets, Salvadoran *pupusa* vendors set up stands outside the stores. The festival *kioskos* accentuate and exaggerate the everyday patterns, customs, and aesthetics of the local and Latin American markets, transforming the space into a festival place, at once defining and transforming the *barrio*.

Although the market-style *kiosko* decidedly reflects particular customs, aesthetic styles, and ideologies, it is not organized to promote an "ethnic" identity, to compete in decoration with other *kioskos*, or to rally for a cause. Its primary objective is to make a profit by selling what is usually considered by the vendor typical and popular market fare. "Typical" in this sense corresponds to the idea and experience of markets and fiestas in the home country. The food is not raised to the level of an exclusive ethnic or regional symbol, although it is a part of that symbolic system. The nationality of the *kiosko* may be discerned from the menu and decor, but again it is not highlighted in the signage. The primary audience is usually other Latinos who will readily recognize and seek out this market ambience.

Consequently, *tacos* and *pupusas* are presented within the context of the *taquería* or the *pupusería*, typical "fast food" stands found on the margins of marketplaces throughout Mexico and El Salvador, respectively.[24] Glamorized and raised to the status of national symbols in the context of the "ethnic" *kiosko, tacos* and *pupusas* in the market constitute one item of a whole system of "fast foods." A typical *pupusería* sells everything from *pupusas* with *curtido* or pickled cabbage relish to *pan con chumpe* or turkey sandwiches, *tamales* or stuffed steamed corn cakes, *pastelitos* or turnovers, and fried plantains garnished with fresh cream. It may offer coffee, chocolate, bottled drinks, and/or a variety of beverages made from fruits, seeds, rice, or barley. At the festival, as in the markets, the *curtido* and homemade drinks are displayed in large glass jars or vats. *Pupusas* are patted, filled, and "thrown" before the eyes of the customer.

In recent years, the Salvadoran *pupusería*-style *kiosko* has multiplied at the festival. Some are called after their owner, like the "*Pupusería Blanca's*."[25] Others, like the "*Pupusería Cuscatleca*," associate the *kiosko* with a region, in this case the state of Cuscatlán in the eastern part of the country, from which the majority of Salvadoran immigrants to Washington come. "*Pupusería Cojutepecana de la Niña Rita*" conjoins two identities, the town of Cojutepeque and its vendor, who boasts her earned title of respect, "*Niña*." The majority of these stands do not have a name. Their only identification is a handwritten menu. Perhaps a small sign saying El Salvador may appear on a corner.

Often the difference between a *pupusería* and a *comedor* at the festival blurs as *kioskos* expand their menus to include a broader spectrum of "*Comida Salvadoreña*" or "Salvadoran Food." Although the investment is high, *kioskos* respond to the demand of *paisanos* or compatriots from the same region or country looking for a full meal with meat, rice, beans, and salad. A *kiosko* may compromise with a cheap Central American favorite combination of rice and beans variously called "*moros y cristianos*" or Moors and Christians, "*casamiento*" or marriage, or "*gallo pinto*" or speckled rooster, playful names conferring a racially mixed or mestizo cast to simple working-class fare.[26] Salvadoran vendors at the market-style *kioskos* reflect the commercial activity and "invisible economies" of the community. The vendors range from itinerants to restaurant and bakery owners to individuals taking their home cooking to the streets to supplement the family income. *Niña* Rita at the "*Pupusería Cojutepecana de la Niña Rita*" was a vendor in the markets of her hometown of Cojutepeque and often traveled to *fiestas* in the region. In Washington, her customers, mostly Salvadoran, bought her *pupusas* outside *El Gavilan* grocery store on Columbia Road during the week, and on weekends bought *pan con chumpe* from the stoop of her apartment house.[27]

Lacking the same numbers but similar to these Salvadoran *kioskos*, Caribbean and Central and South American market-style *kioskos* also contribute to the make-up of the festival *kiosko* world. Despite the distinctive foods of the different countries, a particular mode of presentation unifies them. In the marketplace as well as in the market-style *kioskos*, the presentation of the final product preserves some link to the food process if not to its source.

The marketplace offers produce and raw meats as well as prepared foods. Often whole butchered animals are in full view. The market-like *kioskos* underline the connection between source, process, and product with personal handling of the food, unusual food wrappings from natural plants, and sometimes the display of whole animals. This market aesthetic is antithetical and challenging to modern urban marketing, which rigorously separates product from process, producer from consumer.

At the festival, the throwing of a *pupusa*, or the *tamales* wrapped in corn husks or banana leaves, both attract and repel the urban non-Latino public at the festival. In an everyday context, these nonindustrial foodways would most likely be avoided by customers, but during festival time social, cultural, and sometimes health prohibitions are suspended. In fact, festival creates a situation for trying things out.

Although the market-style *kioskos* can affect the unaccustomed non-Latino festival visitor strongly, they are intended primarily for a familiar Latino audience. Latinos who come to the festival usually buy from *kioskos* offering foods from their own country and preferably from their own region. Most Latino immigrants in Washington do not go "tasting around," and do not consider everything as food. They mostly crave homemade food from their own regions. The festival sharpens their nostalgia for the familiar and creates a need for the familiar to celebrate properly.

In the market-style *kiosko*, identity is expressed in a different manner from the ethnic *kiosko*. The vendor does not identify as an immigrant ethnic, but continues to affirm his identity with his home country. While solidarity with people from his country and his region is reinforced, familiar customs draw Latinos from other parts of Latin America.

Also, although the market-style *kiosko* does not seek to comply with outsiders' expectations, by the very fact of being part of the festival, it engages everybody, Latino and non-Latino alike. The very presence of the *kiosko* imposes another set of values, behavior, and aesthetics which may conflict with the established everyday order of the neighborhood. Unlike the ethnic *kiosko*, a compromise between different values and aesthetics is not offered. The market-style *kiosko* does not invite engagement through jointly created symbols, but invites the outsider to venture into a different world. It creates an interactive situation which challenges the larger society to experience and accept a different set of values which threatens to go beyond the festival frame and overflow into the everyday. The vendor's interaction with the public from the vendor's own cultural frame of reference transforms the neighborhood. He uses the power of food in the context of festival to make a place. The commercial streets of Adams Morgan become a Latin American town marketplace. Beyond the festival the everyday customs and behaviors in the neighborhood become validated. The space taken by the festival is transformed and could become a permanent place, the Latino *barrio*.

The family *kiosko* is the most pervasive and yet has the lowest profile. Decorations and signage provide a very low level of information with a minimal effort at translation for an unfamiliar public. The most information a *kiosko* will give is limited to "*Comida Salvadoreña*," "*La Pequeña Nica*" (Little Nicaragua), or "*Y se llama Perú*" (And It is called Peru), followed by a listing of typical dishes using regional terminology and phonetic spelling. Quotation marks, commas, periods, hyphens, and capital letters decorate rather than grammatically punctuate signs.

The usual customers to these *kioskos* are *conocidos* (family and acquaintances), and they expect a full meal. At Salvadoran *kioskos*, which make up the largest number in this category, this means grilled meat or *carne asada*, with rice and beans. Peruvians are noted for *caucau, anticuchos*, and *papa a la huancaina* (tripe stew, skewered meat, and potatoes *huancaina* style), Nicaraguans for *carne en baho* and *nacatamales* (stewed beef and corn cakes), and Bolivians for *lechón asado* and *salteñas* (roast pork and turnovers). While rice and salad usually accompany the main dish, a "fast food" item may be included in the meal. "Fast foods" are also for the occasional tourist who is more interested in a portable item.

Understated but overlapping in many ways the market-style *kiosko* and its insider's form of presentation, the family *kiosko* distinguishes itself by the circle of *conocidos* (acquaintances) it draws about it. In contrast to the continuous coming and going of people up and down the streets, from *kiosko* to *kiosko*, the family *kiosko* vendor hosts a private gathering with his clients, who may settle down to enjoy a meal. A form of family reunion confirming and obligating old and new family and the *comadrazgo* ties common among Latino immigrants in the area is reenacted in these *kioskos*.

With many Latinos in the community holding one and even two jobs, leisure time is scarce. Nevertheless, family reunions, in some cases as often as every Sunday, in other cases limited to special days such as Mother's Day and holidays, persist as a major socially consolidating activity in the Latino community.[28] The reunion is usually hosted by the women, who draw from a family network of parents, siblings, affines, children, and grandchildren. This network is further extended to *compadres* who are chosen from friends from the home country as well as from acquaintances who live in the same apartment building or work with the hosts.

The family reunion organizes the women, and perhaps incidentally some of the men, in preparing the food, which in turn brings the guests together and obligates them to the hostesses and their families.[29] Selected from one or several of the interactive domains of national origin, residence, or employment, *compadres* are in turn obliged to assist with employment, housing, and any other social or economic needs of the family. The *kiosko*, like the family reunion, relies on this network to organize the stand. The extended family is expected to patronize the *kiosko*, but in turn, as in the family reunion, the *kiosko* must be a proper host, which means offering a real meal, a main course. As customers, kin will pay like the rest of the public, thereby demonstrating their relationship with the family. Of course, these servings are prepared with extra care, often including a gift, which creates a new level of compromise.[30]

Variants on this *kiosko* form may reflect social changes in family patterns. The *kiosko* "*El Rancho de los Rosales*" is coordinated by Don Conrado Rosales, musician and band director, originally from Santa Ana in the western part of El Salvador. Because Don Conrado is twice divorced, his immediate family network has shrunk to an aging mother, grown children from the first marriage not living with him, and a very young daughter from his second marriage. Assuming the central role of host, he calls on his older children to help him with the *kiosko*. His mother symbolically co-hosts.

The majority of the *kiosko* patrons come from the social *compadre* network Don Conrado has built within his residential and working world, among his apartment building neighbors where the mother plays a central role, and with musicians who play with him. His mother also has a further link with the Hispanic Senior Center where she eats lunch on a regular basis. The home country domain plays a paradoxical role. Although the majority of the neighbors and musicians are Salvadorans, they come from *Oriente*, the eastern region of the country. People from *Oriente* are perceived as backward "hillbillies" by other Salvadorans. Because of the dominance of regional over national identity, Don Conrado's relationships in fact create interethnic links rather than perpetuating a continuity with the country of origin. Of course, the interethnic linkage is also extended to Latino musicians not necessarily Salvadoran.

Through the family *kiosko*, and to some degree the market-style *kiosko*, old loyalties are confirmed and new ones are created within the community. The *kiosko* becomes central to solidifying and sanctioning ties and obligations within the community. Testimony to emerging interethnic relationships, some *kiosko* signs now read "*Nicaragua y El Salvador*," "*Viva Peru y El Salvador*," "*Kiosko Boliviano Argentino*," and "*Auténtica Salteña de Bolivia y Empanadas de Chile*."

In contrast to the ethnic mode, the *kiosko* setting transforms the private domain into an unofficial front region. With this powerful inversion, traditional values and customs centered in the home take control of the event. The "taking *of* the streets" becomes transforming the neighborhood into "home," enforcing reciprocal kinship and hospitality responsibilities most dominant in this domain.[31] This "taking *of*" one domain by another characterizes Carnival. Roger Abrahams argues that during Carnival in St. Vincent, in the West Indies, street values move into the home and displace the order of women.[32] In the case of the Latino Festival the movement is reversed. The values and aesthetics of the domestic Latino world of Washington are taken to the street. Recovering a sense of place and identity with the street, *barrio*, and neighborhood, the Latino community consolidates relationships and publicly asserts common values and responsibilities.

The *kioskos* span a range of social relationship patterns among groups in the Latino community and between the Latino community and the larger society. The range and quality of these relationships are in large part determined by the inclusiveness or exclusiveness of the relationship patterns.[33] In each of the three categories discussed, the vending group balances the inside-outside relationship differently, from defining self as an immigrant accommodating the larger society, to challenging larger society with a different organization of space, to exteriorizing an internal space without regard to the larger society.

The three *kiosko* categories form part of the larger domain of *kioskos* which create a seamless carnivalesque atmosphere of people moving between *kioskos*, around pockets of friends and families visiting, among the ever-growing trash, eating as they go. The social order is suspended; trash, food, Latinos, tourists, everything and everyone is equal; the private becomes public. During the festival weekend, the rows of *kioskos* channel an ocean of people—which briefly separates down the middle on Sunday afternoon for the festival parade—only to resume its promenading, visiting, tasting, and general carousing in the market-like surroundings after the parade passes.

Textured by familiar smells, music, dancing, language, and general crowd activity, the *barrio* is confirmed as a Latino physical and cultural space. Much like home and neighborhoods in the country of origin, the idea of *barrio* functions internally as the area within which neighbors share resources and offer companionship. The *barrio* is also the Latino presence within the larger multiethnic Washington neighborhood of Adams Morgan. As such, Latino residents share neighborhood concerns with the larger community as the neighborhood undergoes changes through immigration and gentrification.[34] The *barrio* is a construct of symbolic political power which temporarily lowers local barriers by encompassing all Latinos living in the metropolitan Washington area and by linking the Washington community with the Chicano movement and with Third World ideology.[35]

In summary, the festival's thematic levels serve many agendas and many voices. On one level they reflect different and sometimes ambivalent attitudes toward being ethnic or civic, belonging to nationalistic and Third World groups, striking out as an individual or operating within a community. On another level, they are complementary strategies for restoring a sense of individual worth and place and affirming a Latino presence. The festival empowers the Latino population of the Washington area to define their values publicly, at the same time allowing for the playing out of differences within a creative process. Cultural identity emerges in the tension between action and self-reflection as they are played out in the multiple arenas of the festival.

Notes to Chapter 13

1. Mary Jordan, "Hispanic Festival Takes Revelers 'Home': Thousands Dance to Salsa Beat in a Whirl of Washington Heat," *Washington Post*, 27 July 1987.

2. There is great resonance between this immigrant aesthetic and what Tomás Ybarra-Frausto describes as "*rasquachismo*" or Chicano sensibility: "A stance rooted in resourcefulness and adaptability yet ever mindful of aesthetics . . . to be *rasquache* is to be unfettered and unrestrained, to favor the elaborate over the simple, the flamboyant over the severe. The *rasquache* inclination piles pattern on pattern filling all available space with bold display. . . . The utilization of available resources makes for syncretism, juxtaposition and integration. *Rasquachismo* is a sensibility attuned to mixtures and confluence. Communion is preferred over purity." Tomás Ybarra-Frausto, "The Chicano Art Movement and the Movement of Chicano Art" (Paper presented at the conference on "The Poetics and Politics of Representation," Smithsonian Institution, Washington, D.C., 26–28 September 1988, photocopy of transcript), 8–9.

3. *El Pregonero*, 23 July 1987, author's translation.

4. Ruth Webster, interview by author, Washington, 7 August 1987. In the early years of the festival the "neighborhood block" organizations were coming into their own.

5. *El Pregonero*, 23 July 1987, author's translation.

6. Ibid.

7. Frank E. Manning, ed., *The Celebration of Society: Perspectives on Contemporary Cultural Performance* (Bowling Green: Bowling Green University Popular Press, 1983), viii. Manning's definition of cultural performance easily accommodates the *kiosko* at the Latino festival.

8. James Conaway, "Pupusas and Politics," *Washington Post Magazine*, 25 September 1983.

9. See Susan Kalčik, "Symbol and Performance of Identity" in *Ethnic and Regional Foodways in the United States: The Performance of Group Identity*, edited by Linda Keller Brown and Kay Mussell (Knoxville: The University of Tennessee Press, 1984), 38.

10. On differential identity see Richard Bauman, "Differential Identity and the Social Base of Folklore," *Journal of American Folklore* 84 (1971): 31–41. Phyllis May-Machunda characterizes this process in the context of migration as "group identities across broad categories in a new environment." She states, "Alliances across national, political, racial, religious, class and educational boundaries arise to preserve a community sense of self in ways that could never occur at home." "Migration to Metropolitan Washington: Making a New Place Home," *1988 Festival of American Folklife Catalog* (Washington, D.C.: Smithsonian Institution and National Park Service, 1988), 36.

11. The patterns of relationships generated by the different types of *kioskos* may be described in terms of esoteric and exoteric, the ethnic festival *kiosko* being the most exoteric and outside-directed, the market-style *kiosko* a balance between inner- and outer-directed, and the family *kiosko* being esoteric or inner-directed. The domain of all three types reflects the multiplicity of relationship patterns in the festival as well as in the community. See William Hugh Jansen, "The Esoteric-Exoteric Factor in Folklore" in *The Study of Folklore*, edited by Alan Dundes (Englewood Cliffs, N.J.: Prentice-Hall, Inc., 1965), 43–51.

12. Dean MacCannell defines the tourist as that post-ethnic middle class "that systematically scavenges the earth for new experiences to be woven into a collective, touristic version of other peoples and other places." See Dean MacCannell, *The Tourist* (New York: Schocken Books, 1976), 13.

13. See Nelson Graburn, *Ethnic and Tourist Arts: Cultural Expressions from the Fourth World* (Berkeley: University of California, 1976), 5. He defines "tourist arts" as "those arts made for an external, dominant world" embracing "those forms that have elsewhere been labelled transitional, commercial, souvenir, or airport arts, but it also includes certain novel noncommercial art forms."

14. Roger Abrahams, "Equal Opportunity Eating: A Structural Excursus on Things of the Mouth," in *Ethnic and Regional Foodways*, 25.

15. The earliest Salvadoran restaurants in the *barrio* in D.C. first attracted customers by offering Mexican specialties, but little by little they began to introduce in the back of the menu regional Salvadoran dishes. At the festival, *pupusas* are usually featured by market-style Salvadoran *kioskos*, but when a *kiosko* offering *pupusas* tends toward the "ethnic festival" model, a commercialized version of *tacos* is also offered.

16. It goes beyond "the willingness of the various ethnic populations to open up their kitchens" by making their in-group foodways more generally available to outsiders; Abrahams, "Equal Opportunity Eating," 25.

17. See Margo Machida, "Seoul on Soul: Asians Take On America," in Washington Project for the Arts Exhibition Catalog, *Cut Across* (Washington, D.C.: Washington Project for the Arts, 1988), 19. She states, "Given the acceleration of current immigration in the Washington area, Asians are becoming a more visible segment within this minority community. This heightened presence has engendered hostility and resentment from many different sectors as Asians compete with other groups for their share of the economic pie." This work was partly in response to the racial confrontations taking place in Washington between Korean store owners and Black Americans. In Mt. Pleasant, many grocery and liquor stores are owned by Koreans, generically called by most Latinos "chinos" or Chinese. Beside marketing familiar Latino products, the Korean clerks are beginning to learn Spanish. See also Joseph McLellan, "Searing 'Seoul House,'" *Washington Post*, 5 March 1988.

18. For a discussion on the manipulation of categorical boundaries and carnival see Barbara Babcock, "The Novel and the Carnival World," *Modern Language Notes* 89 (1974): 911–37.

19. See Abrahams, "Equal Opportunity Eating," and Kalčik, "Symbol and Performance of Identity."

20. Abrahams, "Equal Opportunity Eating," 23.

21. Lucy Cohen, "Latin American Women Lead Migration" in *1988 Festival of American Folklife*, 40.

22. In 1985, Niña Rita Torres, a Salvadoran itinerant market vendor participating in the Smithsonian Institution's Festival of American Folklife, described her experiences in the home country and in the Latino neighborhood of Adams Morgan (interview by author, Washington, D.C., 5 March 1985). Information was also provided by Enma Avilés, interview by author, and Enrique Avilés, tape recording, Washington, D.C., 6 February 1988. Enma Avilés, who also participated in the Festival of American Folklife, had a market stand in her home in El Salvador. On weekdays she served full meals to the schoolteachers from the nearby school. On weekends she sold *pupusas, tamales,* sandwiches, sausage specialties, and bottled and homemade beverages to visitors attending the weekly *fiestas* held at the city hall.

23. See Cadaval, "What's in an Empanada." Unpublished manuscript.

24. On the use of "fast foods" in markets and fairs see Leslie Prosterman, "Food and Alliance at the County Fair," *Western Folklore* 40 (1981): 81–90.

25. Note the attempt at Americanization with the use of hyphen on the name "*Blanca*." The correct Spanish would read "*Pupusería de Blanca*."

26. Awareness of race and class is very strong at the level of what you eat. See Peter Farb and George Armelagos, *Consuming Passions: The Anthropology of Eating* (New York: Washington Square Press, 1980), 133–51.

27. Rita Torres, interview and translation by author. She had a *kiosko* at the festival in 1984 and 1985; in 1986 she went back to her country hoping to return to Washington, but new immigration restrictions made it impossible. *El Gavilán* was originally owned by a Dominican and is now owned by a Salvadoran family. Outside the store is a favorite center of congregation for Salvadoran men. See Joan Nathan, "The Tastes of Many Homelands," *Washington Post Magazine*, 25 May 1986.

28. Some of this data comes from Avilés, interviewed by author; and Adriana and Doris Palacios, interviewed by author, Washington, D.C., 18 February 1988.

29. For a parallel study of the organization of women around food, see Brett Williams, "Why Migrant Women Cook Their Husbands' Tamales," in *Ethnic and Regional Foodways*, 113–26.

30. Even the author, as a fieldworker, has gotten caught up in the system with families she has worked with, and she was reminded of her obligation with the offer of a fried plantain and the sharing of a beer with a *kiosko* hostess. On giving and presentations which appear voluntary, disinterested, and spontaneous but are in fact obligatory and interested, see Marcel Mauss, *The Gift* (New York: Ballantine, 1967).

31. In Washington, D.C., the Latino immigrant is more in control of the world in the domain of the home and can more persistently preserve his or her customs. The reciprocal systems of *compadrazgo* and hospitality are not only preserved but heightened. However tenuous for immigrant communities, the "home" is the most stable center of power. See Williams, "Why Migrant Women Cook Their Husbands' Tamales."

32. See Roger D. Abrahams, *The Man-of-Words in the West Indies: Performance and the Emergence of Creole Culture* (Baltimore: John Hopkins University Press, 1983), 98–108.

33. See Jansen, "The Esoteric-Exoteric Factor."

34. See Williams, *Upscaling Downtown: Stalled Gentrification in Washington, D.C.* (Ithaca: Cornell University, 1988).

35. The meaning of the term *barrio* has been shifted by the Chicano movement from a geographic association to a symbolic group identity. The Chicano movement sees itself as a Third World movement grounded in this concept of *barrio*. See Carlos Cortés, "Mexicans," in *Harvard Encyclopedia of the Social Sciences*, edited by Stephan Thernstrom (Cambridge: Belknap Press of Harvard University, 1980), 697–719.

14. The Brokering of Ethnic Folklore: *Issues of Selection and Presentation at a Multicultural Festival*

SUSAN AUERBACH

Multicultural folk festivals, with their standard offerings of ethnic music, dance, crafts, foods, and other forms of folklore, have become a new arena for ethnic display in America over the last twenty years. Such events are a deliberate staging of cultural-pluralism-in-action, with juxtapositions rarely encountered in the daily course of urban life. Though behind the scenes and seldom seen, festival organizers establish the frame in which these displays of ethnic folklore and pluralism are enacted and understood.

Festival organizers who are folklorists serve as cultural brokers or liaisons between cultures, as well as between participants and audience. In the words of Shalom Staub, "public sector folklorists serve as agents of cultural legitimacy, translating the values and practices of the folk into forms and events understandable to a general population."[1] They do not merely elicit symbolic expressive behavior from ethnic groups for public presentation. In the process of preparing that presentation, organizers select, define, manipulate, and sometimes alter the cultural symbols and strategies of ethnic groups. They thereby create new forms of ethnic interaction and promote a fledgling national folk festival culture, with its own standards of in-group competence and performance.

In the two decades since the first precedent-setting Festival of American Folklife sponsored by the Smithsonian Institution, public sector folklorists have developed their own procedures and traditions for organizing folk festivals.[2] They have also debated the worth of doing folk festivals at all, noting the problems of removing folk artists from their native contexts and of orienting performances to largely white middle-class audiences.[3] Though most continue to organize festivals, there are few discussions in print on the basis for the implications of the choices made by cultural specialists (a title used by funding agencies to refer to those who are academically trained with an orientation to fieldwork) in the festival arena.[4]

This essay explores the process of negotiation between folk culture brokers and ethnic performers to reveal how a folk festival model emerges. A case study of the 1987 Cityroots Festival in Los Angeles, it analyzes the selection and presentation of participants as frames for festival performance and interaction. In how they choose and "stage" participants, festival organizers must confront issues of stereotyping, traditionality, acculturation, and, ultimately, the implications of cultural pluralism as a belief system. Such issues are central to contemporary ethnic folklore. How festival organizers negotiate these issues among various cultures in the public sector can both inform and challenge academic inquiry.

Assumptions and Purposes: Why a Cityroots Festival?

"Cityroots Festival: A Celebration of New Immigrant Traditions," sponsored by the Folk Arts Program of the City of Los Angeles Cultural Affairs Department, was inspired largely by a demographic-cultural phenomenon. The post-1965 "fourth wave" of immigration to the United States from Latin America, Asia, and the Middle East had catapulted Los Angeles to prominence as a major port of entry.[5] Though the newcomers to the city received much media attention, they were rarely represented at existing multicultural festivals. Their cultural traditions were barely known, their needs "underserved" by government arts agencies. With a special festival, it was reasoned, the City could offer these groups a respectful forum as well as a measure of recognition and financial reward. Meanwhile, it could give other Angelenos an educational introduction to their new neighbors in a noncommercial setting.[6] Such assumptions were based on an implicit belief in cultural pluralism—a value touted by numerous city officials in "celebrations of diversity" from political campaigns to running marathons. This objective is explicit in Mayor Tom Bradley's "Message of Welcome" to festival-goers that was published at the beginning of the festival program:

Los Angeles is a city rich in cultural diversity. The Cityroots Festival is a celebration of our wonderful diversity, sponsored by the Los Angeles Cultural Affairs Department. We will have an opportunity to learn about one another and to celebrate the differences which make us unique as a world class city during this two-day festival. This celebration is dedicated to all those who came to our city from around the world and who stayed to enhance the cultural and artistic life of Los Angeles. On behalf of the City of Los Angeles, I welcome all of you to Cityroots Festival—a celebration of new immigrant traditions. Whether you hail from across town or across the globe, I hope you will enjoy and learn.[7]

Multicultural festivals bring together a variety of peoples in a recreational, nonconfrontational atmosphere, and appear to embody a cultural pluralism that is working. For this reason, they are popular with politicians, funding agencies, and the public. Differences between groups which might otherwise be divisive become, in the temporary "time out" frame of festivals, something to be displayed and enjoyed.[8] Items of ethnic folklore, such as distinctive folk dancing or cuisine, are the tools in this illustration of differences. Ironically, as Roger Abrahams notes, "what was once a way to maintain an ethnic boundary becomes a way to momentarily break it down.[9]

At the heart of most multicultural festival planning is the hope or claim that this celebration of differences will enhance multicultural understanding. In the case of Cityroots, face-to-face interaction between newer and more settled Angelenos was meant to counter media portrayals of newcomers as economic threats and political liabilities, and to offer a more rounded view of them as human beings. With its multilingual publicity and its "neutral" setting in a large city park, Cityroots was geared to attract a multicultural audience. Thus, cross-cultural interaction was considered as important between audience members as between audience and participants.

A final set of assumptions and hopes influencing the festival concept derived from the advocacy of traditionality. Festival organizers sought out traditions which had been passed on orally and informally over generations within a community. Such traditions were viewed as part of the cultural baggage new immigrants brought with them, but might be in danger of losing in the press of rapid Los Angeles-style assimilation without the benefit of positive reinforcement.

This working definition of traditionality and its advocacy is the foundation of what this essay terms "festival culture." It may be found in many statements of objectives advertised by public sector folklorists in their brochures, newsletters, and grant guidelines. This is the "folk wisdom" shared by festival folklorists around the country, the *raison d'être* and primary operating principle of the festivals they run. Cityroots planners interpreted and applied these unwritten rules regarding festival membership and appropriate behavior.

In the crucial selection process, organizers had to decide which ethnic groups should be represented; which subgroups or individuals within those groups best reflected traditionality; and which genres or traditional expressive forms would meet festival aims, folklorically and artistically. Decisions on each of these matters involved brokering between festival culture and members of the cultures represented.

The Selection Process: Who Represents a Group?

The Cityroots theme preselected, to some degree, the pool of participants: they would be Asian, Latino, and Middle Eastern immigrants of the past twenty to twenty-five years. A list of target national groups was based initially on data from the Immigration and Naturalization Service.[10] Yet cultural, political, and practical considerations ultimately refined that list.

Culturally, the sponsoring Folk Arts Program was predisposed toward groups which were more likely to be fostering traditional culture and/or groups whose cultures were little known to the general public. Thus, for example, the often-seen Japanese were eliminated but the much smaller Afro-Caribbean Garifuna group was included because its vital traditions seemed deserving of more exposure. Differing adaptation strategies among new immigrant groups also affected the kinds of cultural activity that organizers were likely to find. Some groups with few years of residence in the United States appeared to be strongly preserving traditions close to the source, such as Southeast Asian textile arts, having been encouraged by refugee organizations and market forces. On the other hand, planners had trouble locating possible participants among other groups, such as Central American refugees, where a preoccupation with basic economic and political survival took priority over traditional cultural activities.

Politically, as a program of the municipal government, the festival was obliged to be as fully representative of diversity as possible in a way that was sensitive to local policy and opinion. Hence, Mexicans, the leaders in new as well as older waves of immigration, were heavily and variously represented. And practically, as in any festival with limited resources, staff had to take advantage of preexisting contacts with certain groups and rule out others where contacts proved difficult to establish.

In the end, some twenty new immigrant communities were represented at the Cityroots Festival. There were, for example, Cambodian weavers and singers; Mexican silversmiths and trios; Thai dancers and carvers; Iranian cooks and musicians; Samoan and Armenian choirs; Korean and Cuban instrumentalists; Vietnamese and Chinese opera performers; Asian Indian and Guatemalan Maya musicians; and Salvadoran and Argentine cooks. At Cityroots, as at other multicultural festivals, limitations of time and space allowed only one or two groups to "stand in" for a given community in a given area. Thus, there was little opportunity to represent the range of traditional arts within a given community, except as already noted among Mexican participants.

Finding and selecting those particular performing groups and individuals who could be accommodated was a far more subtle process of decision-making. Planners had to reconcile criteria of traditionality with production values of artistic quality and variety. In other words, academic and agency cultural goals had to be served while pleasing a mixed audience with entertainment. Some fascinating traditional arts and artists could be assembled—but if the product were insufficiently polished, we would lose the audience we wanted to draw and insult the communities represented. At Cityroots, the search for authentic and accomplished tradition-bearers was negotiated through the delicate straits of community self-definition. Among the issues at stake were how to deal with youth groups and revivalists, as well as the spectre of stereotyping.

It is no surprise that many ethnic communities prefer to put their best collective image forward in performances by youth groups. A readily available packaging of ethnicity, such a group is usually formed to promote a positive sense of distinct ethnic identity, chiefly to outsiders. Young people, as the most acculturated generation, embody the future of the ethnic community; at the same time, they display their connection to their cultural inheritance. A youth presentation simultaneously suggests that the culture is alive and reinforces ethnic pride among the youth themselves, who gain recognition. Furthermore, outsider audiences are more likely to be receptive to unfamiliar cultural traits when presented by young people as a perpetuation of their heritage.

Cityroots planners seeking recommendations from community leaders were routinely referred to youth groups, from Vietnamese cooks to Salvadoran performers. Clearly, these young people were hardly as knowledgeable as their parents about cuisine or dance, nor were their skills as well honed, yet for the groups in question, the message of intergenerational transmission of culture was far more important than authenticity or artistic quality per se.

Festival planners, however, gravitated toward the selection of older adults who had grown up with the tradition and who had developed their style according to standards from within, rather than outside, the community. There was a bias against youth groups for perpetuating a frozen, stereotyped mold of a culture already seen at far too many festivals. Yet organizers wanted to encourage those talented young people who were carrying forth an awareness of tradition. Planners also wished to guard against stereotyping immigrant culture as the sole possession of the elderly.

Eventually youth participants were invited when their quality and devotion to the tradition were exceptional and would provide for a more balanced program.[11] It seemed important to show that such demanding arts as Cambodian classical dance, Vietnamese opera, and Armenian instrument building were continuing in good hands with the young. A twenty-three-year-old Lebanese Armenian, for example, was the third generation in his family to craft the pear-shaped *oud* (Middle Eastern lute), enjoying the challenge of "making a better instrument every time" and experimenting with a range of international woods which had been unavailable to his predecessors. A family of Vietnamese youths, ages nine to twenty-four, were impressive exponents of performance genres from each major region of their homeland, thanks to years of study while awaiting resettlement.

Youth folkloric groups are often associated with the post-1970s phenomenon of ethnic cultural revivals in the United States. While festival folklorists tend to be skeptical of revivalists from outside a resident community, such as international folk dancers, they are often interested in revivals from within. Two examples of revivalists—one chosen, one rejected for Cityroots—illustrate the sometimes fluid criteria applied in the selection process.

The group chosen for the festival was a new folkloric singing group of Iranian Armenians in their twenties and thirties. They had learned songs from older relatives and the collections of Soviet Armenian folklorists in a conscious act of cultural retrieval. Spirited and well-rehearsed in purposely unaffected village vocal style, they had impressed local Armenian audiences as well as festival programmers. They were far closer to traditional style than revivalist Armenian youth folk dance groups, westernized choirs, or highly arranged instrumental ensembles. At the same time, their performance was more artful and engaging for a large stage than what the few older, traditional musicians in town might have offered.

Thus, given festival criteria and the options at hand, they were the natural choice for an Armenian performance slot.

The music of another intra-ethnic revival was eventually rejected for the festival after much deliberation. This was the *nueva cancion* (new song) genre that originated in Chile in the 1960s and has since spread throughout the Americas. While incorporating some traditional indigenous instruments and styles of Latin America, this composed music of social protest has the sound, aesthetics, and reliance on the media characteristic of popular rather than traditional music as played by local groups. The most likely local band to represent the genre had production values that were too slick for Cityroots, plus a pan-Latino membership and pop music qualities that were too far removed from the Salvadoran or Nicaraguan grassroots tradition that planners would have liked to present.

Attempting to balance the criteria of traditionality and artistic quality appears to be a concern unique to folk festivals run by cultural specialists and, as such, to festival culture. These selection criteria partake of, but do not wholly subsume, both ethnic community and mainstream artistic standards. They stake out a mediated cultural zone between the two, which seemingly allows local grassroots cultures to communicate with the majority culture. Festival organizers look for participants whom they believe can operate successfully for both their own ethnic group and the mixed audience in this mediated zone. In striving to define the zone's boundaries through their selection of participants, planners must also pick and choose between appropriate genres according to festival goals.

The Selection Process: What Represents a Group?

It is another precept of festival culture that many of the expressive symbols and practices within a folk community can and should be proudly shared and appreciated outside the group, rather than hidden from or slickly packaged for the general public. Cityroots planners wished to validate these insiders' grassroots traditions, particularly those less familiar to a mixed public audience. The point was to get beyond the rather standardized, predictable Korean fan dances, Mexican mariachis and Middle Eastern bellydancing that Angelenos tend to see at ethnic restaurants, "international shows," and commercial festivals.

This was particularly important for the Mexican genres selected, as this culture is at once the most familiar and the least understood by non-Mexicans in the city. Los Angeles media, businesses, and organizers of

Mexican holiday celebrations often equate Mexican tradition with tacos, folkloric dancers, and piñatas. Though plenty of Mexicans undeniably enjoy these things and consider them emblematic of their heritage, Cityroots planners hoped to provide alternatives to such popular ethnic stereotypes. Lesser-known regional or family traditions were selected for presentation at the festival, such as the preparation of cold beet and fruit soup from Guanajuato, norteña music of the Mexican border areas, and saddle making. This, admittedly, was a kind of manipulation-by-selection of the array of traditions practiced in the community. But while norteña music may not be as "typical" as mariachi in the sense of how frequently it is heard, its inclusion suggests the variety of traditions which lie beyond pop culture stereotypes.

Aware that the food area is always the best patronized part of multicultural festivals, planners deliberately chose food vendors who offered to make traditional dishes well known to themselves but little known to the general public. This was a sensitive policy for some groups, for the very stereotypes which festival culture opposes may be those symbols which constitute the most common meeting ground between strangers. Van Esterik notes the tendency to play to mass culture expectations when ethnic festival food vendors choose to sell what the public sees as their "favorite" foods.[12] At Cityroots, Korean cooks who wanted to demonstrate the cooking of barbecue ribs argued: "Wouldn't it be better to show the foods that people associate with us? That they are familiar with? We want them to like our food. If we make something else, they might decide that they don't like Korean food."[13] Organizers maintained that given exposure and introduction, Americans might not only like more exotic Korean food but learn something more about the culture. In the end, it was decided to demonstrate another meat dish, *bulgogi*, which had a similar taste but was largely unknown to non-Koreans.

Programming other forms of expression for the festival sometimes produced a felicitous coinciding of the genre a group preferred and the criteria of festival organizers. The most successful such instance was the Filipino Santacruzan (May Festival of Flowers) procession, a restaging of an event which annually brings together local Filipinos in a positive reflection of community self-image. Cityroots organizers were pleased to incorporate this "festival within a festival," which brought an entire indigenous celebration to the audience rather than a decontextualized art form. A dozen young elected queens in elaborate, modern formal wear paraded through the festival site under floral arches held by male attendants to the tune of a Santacruzan hymn played by a *rondalla* string band. Suggested, coordinated, and narrated by two Filipino folklorists, the pageant exemplified that community's highly elaborated organizational structure and urbanized, acculturated identity.[14] It was a beautiful spectacle of ethnic self-presentation which ultimately enhanced the authenticity of Cityroots by its inclusion.

In the final juggling of participants and genres, planners looked for a balance of types and styles of ethnic folklore. The more familiar followed the more exotic; the more popular alternated with the more strictly traditional, as in two Cuban groups who represented, respectively, the old-style *salsa* favored by 1960s immigrants and the Afro-Cuban folkloric style associated with a more recent wave. The final mix reflected various stages of acculturation and sophistication among new immigrants, from a professional Veracruz harpist, accustomed to the festival circuit, to Garifuna singers, who had never before sung onstage, to the self-conscious folklore of ethnicity in the Filipino procession.

Selection, of course, was only the first step in brokering the ethnic folklore that would be seen at the festival. Perhaps even more important than the participants and forms chosen was presentation: how the available materials within the tradition were to be conveyed by the participants and staged and interpreted by the festival staff. Through the means of presentation, the staff tried to communicate the values of mediated festival culture in order to bring audiences and participants closer together.

The Presentation Process: Appropriate Frames and Behavior

Presentation, even more than selection, puts the assumptions of culture brokering and festival culture to the test. Having brought folk artists out of their natural surroundings to perform at the festival, folklorists strive to recontextualize those arts within the mediated cultural zone they have created. In other words, they offer background information to the audience to reconnect the genres presented with their broader role and function in the community. Such information was available to interested Cityroots visitors in program booklet essays, photodocumentary exhibits, and interpretive signage. But its most immediate manifestation at the festival was through masters of ceremonies, known in festival culture parlance as "presenters."

A key feature of multicultural folk festivals is that informed presenters be onstage and in other areas, serving as interpretive bridges between the audience and the participants. These presenters become the translators of ethnic culture as well as the ambassadors of festival culture.

Their style and message frames the performance, but participants also challenge and bely that frame, communicating their ethnic self-concept directly to the public, as will be seen.

Presenters are considered necessary because the ethnic cultures presented—and festival culture itself—are unfamiliar to many of the people present. Ethnic performers are more accustomed to commercial events or smaller gatherings in their own communities; audiences, meanwhile, are confronted with unfamiliar sights and sounds or with familiar ones in an unfamiliar context. The presenter's task, as the Cityroots guidelines explain, is "first and foremost to help make both the audience and performer comfortable with the festival experience. This means conveying your understanding and enthusiasm for this type of performance, giving the artists a sense of dignity and respect and helping the audience appreciate what is special about the performance."[15] Though these sound like noble goals, festival presentation underscores the insider/outsider distinction and is understandably resented by some groups. Performers accustomed to presenting themselves through their own announcers believe they know their culture best, and may see outside academic presenters as an imposition of cultural imperialism.

While these concerns are valid, festival organizers are likewise concerned that there be continuity of approach in a respectful, informative style of presentation. The folk wisdom of festival production posits that performers should generally be left to concentrate on performing, while the right outsider as presenter can actually make the performance more accessible by serving as an advocate for the curious audience member. Wherever possible at Cityroots, knowledgeable presenters from within the culture were employed, though they were rarely members of the actual performing group. Ideally, festival folklorists should be recruiting and training many more such presenters.

Another aspect of festival presentation standards which disturbed and confused some participants was the casual, educational format. Cityroots presenters were encouraged to promote communication in an informal, participatory, conversational, and informative style. For instance, they sprinkled their ad-lib introductions and explanations with direct questions to the performers onstage. The intention throughout was to make performers more human and accessible while contextualizing and enhancing their performance.

While presenters tried to break down the barrier between performers and audience, some performers seemed to prefer being elevated and separated from the audience with greater formality. Clearly, the distinctively American festival culture was alien, particularly to the more recent newcomers. These groups often wished to be presented in a far more formal and ceremonial way, reflecting what was appropriate and dignified in their culture. For example, the Vietnamese performers were used to making long speeches of praise and appreciation before playing, and wanted the festival presenter to do likewise. Such an introduction, however, would likely have been tedious, unspontaneous, and inappropriate for the mixed audience at this casual, outdoor event.

The contrasts between participants' own inclinations toward self-presentation and the presentation standards of festival culture are revealing. Two examples illustrate how Cityroots participants expressed their own rules of appropriate behavior through presentation decisions — the first at variance with, the second complementary to, planners' hopes and guidelines.

The first case, a Samoan church choir, was the most extreme example of a style of ethnic self-presentation markedly different from that of festival culture. The group had insisted on having its own announcer, a lawyer and member of the choir, to supplement the introduction of an outside presenter. The announcer seemed almost embarrassed by the informality of the introduction which preceded him. In a booming circus-barker's voice, he announced, "Ladies and gentlemen, we are bringing you to Samoa. We are going to entertain you with one of our authentic dances. . . . " He billed each piece as an "item" and explained customs in the continuous historical present, as in "the *kava* is always prepared by the daughters of one of the highest chiefs of the village." When asked by the folklorist presenter to comment on the styles of Samoan dress in evidence or explain the role of the church in local Samoan culture, his answers were perfunctory, as if he felt the information would bore the audience.

Clearly, the Samoan MC had announced "cultural shows" for non-Samoans before; he considered the same narration appropriate at Cityroots, in spite of the planners' avowed educational approach. His model was likely derived from tourist shows in his homeland, or from American and international show business. It is this popular culture model of packaging and entertainment which has permeated both commercial and community multicultural festivals, and which many ethnic performers assume the public expects and enjoys.

In the second case, by contrast, a Peking opera group had no "cultural show" agenda, being used to performing mainly in intimate settings for themselves and their fellow Mandarin speakers. Members spent considerable effort trying to work out the best way to present themselves in the unusual situation of the outdoor multicultural festival. As presenter, they wanted an Anglo student filmmaker whom they had worked with, feeling that this would show that non-Chinese were interested in Chinese culture. When she proved unavailable, the group opted for a sixteen-year-old girl, the daughter of an influential member of the troupe, ostensibly to give the girl valuable announcing experience; festival organizers rejected this option as undependable. In the end, the group designated its adult singer most fluent in English as presenter, to be oriented to presenter guidelines by festival staff. This woman proved a charming and informative guide to the complex, initially inaccessible opera scenes mounted by the group. She kept the audience rapt with simultaneous translations of songs and ready explanations of operatic practice, along with Chinese jokes to break the ice.

Of course, regardless of the identity or style of the presenters, the performance itself is the main presentation. Performers gain control through choices they make about what repertoire and personnel to include, or what degree of traditionality to express. While some organizers work closely with performers to decide these matters before the festival, this was not possible given the time and staff constraints of Cityroots. Nor did it seem desirable, given the impression many performers gave that they would find such negotiations intrusive: what they would perform and how they would do so was, they felt, their business.

Their business was necessarily conducted according to their own values rather than those of festival culture. For example, a Guatemalan marimba group's choice of pieces and featured players was influenced by egalitarian group dynamics among its membership of both Maya and Ladino (non-indigenous) Guatemalans of varying levels of musical experience. Thus, in an effort to be fair to all, traditional Maya village repertoire and popular pan-Guatemalan pieces were played, and all took turns on the lead part. Festival planners, on the other hand, would have preferred more village repertoire and solos by the most experienced player.

Generally, participants kept within the traditional framework festival organizers requested. Where they departed from it, and why, was significant. For instance, the Vietnamese performers featured the theme from "The Godfather" soundtrack, played on the eerie, one-stringed monochord. Their reasoning was that audiences liked it and that it dramatically brought home their effort at cross-cultural communication; indeed, it brought down the house. Similarly, during the Filipino Santacruzan presentation, the old-style string band gave way to three trendily dressed teenagers crooning pop songs in English to a synthesized beat in a "new version" of the custom of serenading. And Guatemalan fiber craftsmen made Bugs Bunny figures along with traditional *quetzal* birds. These and other participants clearly felt the need to express the part of themselves that was acculturated and "just like everybody else," rather than distinctly different. One should not underestimate the need of ethnic traditional artists to show their awareness and mastery of mainstream American styles.

While some instances of acculturation and crossover fit well into the Cityroots format, the case of the Samoan choir was more dubious. The group had been asked to perform a variety of rousing hymns, folksongs, and locally composed songs in traditional style, as they did at their local church dedications, with singers of a variety of ages. Instead, due partly to the unexpected absence of the choir leader, they chose to dramatize "ancient" Samoan ceremonial customs and stressed music and dance that capitalized on the "primitive," exotic aspects of their historical culture, using almost entirely young performers. This was clearly what they were prepared to do for outside audiences, and what they thought those audiences would like; it was not, however, a glimpse into their community traditions in Los Angeles.

Careful selection and presentation criteria at festivals like Cityroots are, as we have seen, festival culture's attempt at insurance against the perpetuation of stereotypes. Of course, too narrow a focus on traditionality in selection and presentation may create alternative stereotypes. For instance, a number of traditional artists regularly play the national folk festival circuit, having adapted their presentation to festival culture criteria. While they are models of high quality by any standard, theirs is not the only acceptable presentation style; festival organizers continue to experiment with a range of appropriate styles. Indeed, festival culture's concern with informed selection and presentation distinguishes events like Cityroots, making them more conducive to substantive multicultural exchange than commercial or community festivals which do not involve cultural specialists.

Conclusion: A Model of Cultural Pluralism

The mediated culture of multicultural festivals draws from and alludes to both ethnic differences and similarities. In programming such festivals, culture brokers are by definition stressing the differences between groups. Yet, paradoxically, the result is that a sense of commonality and relatedness is reinforced. At Cityroots, for instance, an interviewer recorded numerous audience comments reflecting this dual nature of festivals:

> It's nice to see all the different ethnics coming together and enjoying each other's cultures.
> This is one of the few things that makes L.A. feel like one place instead of a whole lot of different places jammed together.
> Something like this breaks down barriers; you know, the opposite of wars is to have parties and get to know your neighbors.

Not surprisingly, these comments were collected near the food booths, as the sharing of food is easily the most accessible part of multicultural festivals.[16] In these responses and in the collective effervescence observable at times at Cityroots is a genuine longing for a common denominator, for cultural sharing rather than confrontation. This longing may itself be a reaction to continuing interethnic tensions at a time when the demographic and power balance of majority and minority cultures is shifting, at least in California.

Multicultural festivals like Cityroots are a small-scale, partial model of what cultural diversity looks like, sounds like, and tastes like. Festival time is special because of the abundance and juxtaposition of cultures represented, because of the easy access and proximity participants and audiences of various backgrounds have, because the differences highlighted are innocuously cultural rather than political or socioeconomic. If Los Angeles' identity is in its diversity, as politicians would have us believe, then the image of that diversity at festivals is richly impressive.

For audiences, then, multicultural festivals are an enjoyable and informative exercise in face-to-face encounters with diversity. They guide the public through a sort of harmless, microcosmic tour of how cultural pluralism should work. The implicit message is that the prospect of diverse peoples cooperating and sharing, side by side, is not only possible but desirable. Creating such opportunities for exchange is as important as any specific knowledge transmitted about an ethnic community and its folklore.

A successful multicultural festival promotes meaningful opportunities for cross-cultural exchange, rather than multicultural understanding per se. Careful choices made in selection and presentation may facilitate this communicative process, negotiating a middle ground of festival culture between ethnic enclaves and the civic arena in which all participate. Though the public is generally oblivious to the distinctions festival staff make about traditionality or to their efforts to contextualize traditions, these behind-the-scenes processes lend multicultural festivals their special quality. Festival culture also introduces participants, especially new immigrants, to an alternative "American way" of showcasing aspects of their culture, one built on knowledge of ethnic folklore and sensitivity to community self-definition and internal diversity.

Notes to Chapter 14

1. Shalom Staub, "Folklore and Authenticity: A Myopic Marriage in Public Sector Programs," in *The Conservation of Culture: Folklorists and the Public Sector,* edited by Burt Feintuch (Lexington: The University of Kentucky Press, 1988), 166.

2. See Joe Wilson and Lee Udall, *Folk Festivals: A Handbook for Organization and Management* (Knoxville: University of Tennessee Press, 1982).

3. See Charles Camp and Timothy Lloyd, "Six Reasons Not to Produce Folklife Festivals," *Kentucky Folklore Record* 26 (1980): 67–74, for one of the early critiques of folk festivals.

4. A notable exception is the recent publication of papers from a 1985 conference at Western Kentucky University on "Folklife and the Public Sector" under the title *The Conservation of Culture: Folklorists and the Public Sector,* in which folklorists reflect on their experiences in festival work and other aspects of this emerging profession.

5. See Thomas Muller and Thomas J. Espenshade, *The Fourth Wave: California's Newest Immigrants* (Washington, D.C.: Urban Institute Press, 1985) and Elliot Barkan, "Los Angeles and the New Immigration: Gateway to the American West," in *Cityroots Festival: Seven Essays on New Immigrant Cultures in Los Angeles,* edited by Susan Auerbach (Los Angeles: City of Los Angeles Cultural Affairs Department, 1987).

6. See Auerbach, editor, *Cityroots Festival.*

7. Ibid., 2.

8. See Penny Van Esterik, "Celebrating Ethnicity: Ethnic Flavor in an Urban Festival," *Ethnic Groups* 4 (1982): 207–28.

9. Roger Abrahams, "Folklore," in *Harvard Encyclopedia of American Ethnic Groups,* edited by Stephan Thernstrom (Cambridge, Mass.: Harvard University Press, 1980), 378.

10. INS data on legal immigration to Los Angeles from 1982 to 1985, for example, noted the top ten groups to be Vietnamese, Koreans, Chinese, Filipinos, Mexicans, Iranians, Kampucheans, Salvadorans, Soviets, and Asian Indians (Barkan, "Los Angeles and the New Immigration," in *Cityroots Festival,* edited by Susan Auerbach, 6). Each of these groups, except Soviets, were represented at Cityroots, as well as Argentinians, Armenians, Belizeans, Cubans, Egyptians, Ethiopians, Guatemalans, Laotians, Lebanese, Thai, and Samoans. Though the latter are officially migrants from a United States territory, their migration coincides with fourth-wave immigration.

11. A separate, nonimmigrant portion of the festival, called Kidlore, featured what may be considered part of the indigenous folklore of children of all backgrounds: handclapping and singing games, passed on within children's own culture.

12. Van Esterik, "Celebrating Ethnicity," 219.

13. The author is indebted to folklore student Sandra Weatherby, coordinator of cooking demonstrations at Cityroots, for reporting this observation in her unpublished paper, "Preparations of the Food Demonstrations for the Cityroots Festival."

14. See Herminia Meñez and Susan Montepio, "The *Santacruzan* Festival in the Filipino Community of Los Angeles," in *Cityroots Festival*, 12–15.

15. Susan Auerbach, "Guidelines for Presenters: Cityroots Festival," 1987.

16. See also Van Esterik, "Celebrating Ethnicity."

Notes on the Contributors

SUSAN AUERBACH is a Freelance Arts Consultant with a Master of Arts degree in Music (Ethnomusicology) from the University of Washington. Formerly Folk Arts Coordinator for the City of Los Angeles Cultural Affairs Department, she is the author of the forthcoming handbook, *How to Grow a Multicultural Community Festival* (L.A. Cultural Affairs Department).

BETTY A. BLAIR is a doctoral student in the Folklore and Mythology Program at the University of California, Los Angeles. Her current major research projects focus on folklore and modern health attitudes and treatments, particularly in relationship to AIDS. Forthcoming articles will appear in the *Encyclopedia of American Beliefs and Superstitions*, *Health Education Quarterly*, and *Knowledge from the West: Health Education* (English and Chinese).

OLIVIA CADAVAL is a Folklore Specialist with the Smithsonian Institution Office of Folklife Programs and has been curator and consultant for several projects, most recently the "U.S. Virgin Islands" festival in 1990. Her articles have been published widely, and she is a contributor to the volumes *Urban Odyssey* (forthcoming from Smithsonian Press) and *Washington at Home*.

JOHN ALLAN CICALA is a doctoral candidate at the Folklore Institute at Indiana University completing a dissertation on Sicilian family foodways. He has published articles on Italian food culture and conducts urban folklife research on ethnic communities in the Midwest. He is former City Folklorist of, and current consultant to, the City of Detroit.

LARRY DANIELSON is Associate Professor in the English Department, University of Illinois, Urbana-Champaign, where he teaches folklore, film, and literature courses. His publications include articles on ethnic folklore, oral history, and paranormal experience narrative. His research interests focus at present on the interaction between folk tradition and the mass media in American vernacular culture.

MARIA HERRERA-SOBEK is currently working on a book-length study of Mexican immigrant songs, "Northward Bound: The Mexican Immigrant Experience in *Corridos* and *Canciones*." She is also professor of Spanish at the University of California, Irvine. She has published *The Mexican Corrido: A Feminist Analysis*, *The Bracero Experience: Elitelore Versus Folklore*, and *Beyond Stereotypes*. She is a former Stanford Visiting Professor and recipient of the Orange County Book of the Year Award.

JAMES P. LEARY is Staff Folklorist with the Wisconsin Folk Museum at Mount Horeb and Faculty Associate in the Folklore Program at the University of Wisconsin, Madison. He is the author of *Folk Humor of the Upper Midwest* and, with Robert T. Teske, *In Tune with Tradition: Wisconsin Folk Musical Instruments*. He has been a Folk Arts Panelist with the National Endowment for the Arts from 1987 to 1990 and researched and produced four recordings chosen for the American Folklife Center's Select List of American Folk Music.

CAROLYN LIPSON-WALKER is Administrator of Congregation Beth Shalom in Bloomington, Indiana. She received her Ph.D. in Folklore and American Studies from Indiana University and was a Rockefeller Foundation Fellow from 1977 to 1981.

WILLIAM G. LOCKWOOD is Associate Professor of Anthropology at the University of Michigan in Ann Arbor. In addition to many journal articles and other publications, he is the author of *European Moslems: Ethnicity and Economy in Western Bosnia* and editor of *Beyond Ethnic Boundaries: New Approaches in the Anthropology of Ethnicity*.

YVONNE R. LOCKWOOD is Michigan Folklife Specialist at the Michigan State University Museum in East Lansing, Michigan. She is coeditor, with her husband, William G. Lockwood, of *The Digest*, a review for the interdisciplinary study of food. She is the author of many journal articles and books, most recently *Michigan Folklife Reader* (edited with C. Kurt Dewhurst) and Finnish American Folklore (special edition of *Finnish Americana*).

RICHARD MARCH holds a Ph.D. in Folklore from Indiana University. Since 1983 he has been the Traditional and Ethnic Arts Coordinator for the Wisconsin Arts Board. In that capacity he manages folk arts grant programs and coproduces the "Downhome Dairyland" radio series for Wisconsin Public Radio. He is also an active polka musician, playing button accordion in the Madison, Wisconsin, area.

CAROL SILVERMAN is Associate Professor of Anthropology at the University of Oregon in Eugene. She has done research in Eastern Europe on ethnicity and the politics of culture supported by an IREX Fellowship, 1990, and has received an ACLS Fellowship, 1988–89, and an NEH Fellowship for Independent Research, 1986–87.

MADELINE SLOVENZ-LOW is a doctoral candidate in Performance Studies at New York University. She has been an Adjunct Professor in American Folklore at Drew University and Adjunct Professor in Asian Performance Theory at New York University. She is coauthor (with Kate Waters) of *Lion Dancer*, and has had articles published in *New York Folklore* and *The Drama Review*.

DAVID P. SHULDINER is currently Humanist in Residence with the Connecticut State Department of Aging in Hartford and Adjunct Faculty member in Human Development at St. Joseph College in West Hartford. He is the author of articles that have appeared in *Folklore and Mythology Studies*, *Western Folklore*, and *California Anthropologist*, a contributor to several volumes, including the *Encyclopedia of American Popular Beliefs and Superstitions*, and the author of *Humanities for Older Adults: A Guide to Resources and Program Development*.

STEPHEN STERN is Vice Chair of the Folklore and Mythology Program at the University of California, Los Angeles. He is the author of numerous articles on American, ethnic, and Jewish folklore, and the coauthor of

American and Canadian Immigrant and Ethnic Folklore: An Annotated Bibiliography, with Robert A. Georges.

JANET THEOPHANO is Assistant Director and Assistant Dean of the College of General Studies and Adjunct Assistant Professor in the Department of Folklore and Folklife at the University of Pennsylvania. She has been a researcher, writer, editor, advisor, and consultant. She is a coauthor of the forthcoming *Diet and Domestic Life in Society*, with Anne Sharman, Karen Curtis, and Ellen Messer. She has also written articles published in *Practicing Anthropology*, *American Foodways*, *Food and the Social Order*, and *Pennsylvania Folklife*.

BARRE TOELKEN is a professor of English and History, Director of the Folklore Program, and Director of the Graduate Program in American Studies at Utah State University. He has been Chair of the Board of Trustees of the American Folklife Center in the Library of Congress, President of the American Folklore Society, and is currently Chair of the Board of Directors of the Western Folklife Center in Salt Lake City. He has written *Dynamics of Folklore*, and, with D. K. Wilgus, *The Ballad and the Scholars: Approaches to Ballad Study*, as well as many articles in a wide variety of journals.

PATRICIA A. TURNER is Assistant Professor in the Afro-American and Black Studies Program at the University of California at Davis. She is the author of "Safety in Stereotypes," *International Folklore Review* (1987), and "Church's Chicken and Klan," *Western Folklore* (1987). The latter, along with "The Atlanta Child Murders" article in this volume, are chapters in her book in progress on the nature of rumor and urban legend in the African-American community.